Accumulation Cris

Dedicated
to the memory of
Paul A. Baran (1910–64)
and
Stephen H. Hymer (1934–74)

Accumulation Crisis

JAMES O'CONNOR

Basil Blackwell

OESTERLE LIBRARY, NCC
NAPERVILLE IL 60540

© James O'Connor 1984

First published 1984
First published in paperback 1986
Reprinted 1986

Basil Blackwell Ltd
108 Cowley Road, Oxford OX4 1JF, UK

Basil Blackwell Inc.
432 Park Avenue South, Suite 1505,
New York, NY 10016, USA

All rights reserved. Except for the quotation of short passages
for the purposes of criticism and review, no part of this
publication may be reproduced, stored in a retrieval system, or
transmitted, in any form or by any means, electronic,
mechanical, photocopying, recording or otherwise, without
the prior permission of the publisher.

Except in the United States of America this book is sold subject
to the condition that it shall not, by way of trade or otherwise,
be lent, re-sold, hired out, or otherwise circulated without the
publisher's prior consent in any form of binding or cover other
than that in which it is published and without a similar
condition including this condition being imposed on the
subsequent purchaser.

British Library Cataloguing in Publication Data

O'Connor, James
    Accumulation crisis.
    1. Capitalism I. Title
    330.12′2   HB501
    ISBN 0-631-13552-9
    ISBN 0-631-14947-2 Pbk

Library of Congress Cataloging in Publication Data
O'Connor, James.
    Accumulation crisis.

    Includes index.
    1. Capitalism. 2. Marxian economics. 3. Individual-
ism. 4. Depressions. I. Title.
HB501.026 1984   330.12′2   84-16781
ISBN 0-631-13552-9
ISBN 0-631-14947-2 pbk.

Typeset by Oxford Verbatim Limited
Printed in Great Britain by The Bath Press, Avon

330.122
Oc5a

Contents

Acknowledgements

This work is a synthesis of economic, sociological, and political theories and their applications to the contemporary crisis of American capitalism. In this age of intellectual and political specialization, few, if any, social theorists and political analysts have been foolhardy or ambitious enough to embark on the search for a "totalizing" theory of the modern crisis. Yet such a journey is indispensable today. One reason is that as social theory becomes more specialized, the economy, society, and polity become more unified. Another is that as bourgeois thought dispenses with the concept of class struggle, the world today appears to be erupting with class struggle. Finally, never before has ideology become so embedded in material life or so inscribed in the division of labor. Hence, never before has it become so essential to invent, however crudely and provisionally, a method which combines historical interpretation, ideology critique, political economy, economic sociology, and political sociology.

The friend and coworker most responsible for helping to see me through this seemingly endless task is Robert Marotto. I doubt whether I could have completed this book in its present form without his loving encouragement, patience, sharp eye for unclear theoretical points, and faith in the project. Next in line for thanks is Dale Tomich, an unfailing friend in every respect, whose conversations over a span of ten years convinced me that I was on the right track and also helped me find and stay on that track. Next come Anatole Anton, Roz Baxandall, Douglas Dowd, Saul Landau, Richard Lichtman, Pat Morgan, Deborah Smith, and Dwayne Ward – all dear friends and coworkers laboring in critical philosophical, social psychological, sociological, economic, historical, and/or political traditions, whose faith in this undertaking and moral support as well as keen insights and help at various stages of the development of the present work were invaluable.

Over the last six or seven years, the following friends and acquaintances read one or more chapter drafts, and I wish to thank them for their sympathies with this project as well as their critical yet supportive comments and suggestions: Robert Alford, Rod Aya, Dudley Burton, Wally Goldfrank, Suzie Helburn, John Keane, Michael Lebowitz, Claus Offe, Enrico Pugliese, Marianne Rodenstein, and Eric Wolf. Members of informal seminars organized by the University of California (Santa Cruz), Berkeley *Kapitalistate*, Max-Planck Institute (Starnberg), and the Institute for Policy Studies, in which I presented some of the theses developed here, were unfailingly helpful. So was J. C. A. Davey, my editor at Basil Blackwell, who gave me nothing but encouragement, and allowed me to exceed deadlines more than once. I am most grateful to Steve Cox, whose fine editing job I greatly appreciate.

Last, but not least, I wish to thank the people who so accurately and courteously typed and retyped the manuscript of this book: Beverly Stevens, Melessa Hemler, Pat Sanders, Carole Degen, and Judy Burton.

The irony of an individual social scientist writing a critique of individualism in an age when social cooperative labor has largely replaced individual craft labor in most spheres of production will be obvious to most readers. Not so obvious are the theoretical and political influences most operant in these pages. Sources of ideas and direct and indirect influences are, I hope, adequately acknowledged in the footnotes. In a way, this book is a gift to those people working in the Marxist and neo-Marxist and critical theory traditions – one made with full understanding that there is nothing as disconcerting as a gift which one does not want or need.

I take full responsibility for the interpretation of the social science works used in this book, as well as for the theses it presents. In particular, the thesis that the current crisis of American capitalism may be regarded as an underproduction crisis of capital is mine alone, not because of "possessive individualism," but because no one else, even those closest to this work, should have to be stuck with this idea if it turns out to be wrong.

Preface

It is well established that the effects of the present world crisis of capitalism are particularly debilitating in the traditional industrial sectors of the developed countries. During the 1960s and 1970s, average profit rates and the profit share of national income in the developed countries declined and average unemployment and/or inflation rates increased.[1] However, if we take the USA as an example, both profit deficits and stagflation were confined to manufacturing, transportation, and other old line industries, and agriculture. Profit growth rates in energy, service, and high technology industries were good or adequate.[2] Some observers have interpreted these facts to mean that the present "crisis" is the result of a massive restructuring of capital and the international division of labor.[3] Others have theorized that world capitalism has entered a new downswing of a "long wave" which is exacerbated by increased international competition.[4] Still others have warned of a global financial collapse and/or depression which threatens even the strong (albeit small) industrializing economies of the Pacific Basin and elsewhere.[5] Some who have thought or written about the subject believe that a resolution of the crisis favoring international capitalist interests will require further restructuring of the division of labor and the

[1] S. H. Heap, "World Profitablity Crisis in the 1970s: Some Empirical Evidence," *Capital and Class*, 11, 1980/81; Samuel Bowles and Herbert Gintis, "The Crisis of Liberal Democratic Capitalism: The Case of the United States," *Politics and Society*, 11, 1, 1982, 54, Table 1.

[2] "America's Restructured Economy," *Business Week*, June 1, 1981.

[3] For example, Folker Frobel, Jurgen Heinrichs, and Otto Kreye, *The New International Division of Labour* (Cambridge, 1980).

[4] For example, Ernest Mandel, *Long Waves of Capitalist Development* (Cambridge, 1980); David Gordon, "Stages of Accumulation and Long Cycles," in T. Hopkins and I. Wallerstein, eds, *Processes of the World System* (Beverly Hills, 1980).

[5] Daniel R. Fusfeld, "The Next Great Depression II: The Impending Financial Collapse," *Journal of Economic Ideas*, 4, 2, 1980.

international economy generally in ways which will permit capital to re-establish social and political control over global labor and key petty bourgeois nation-states (e.g. resolution of the class and national struggles in the Middle East, Southern Africa, and Central America in favor of multinational capitalist interests).

The crisis of American capitalism is indisputably part and parcel of global patterns of capitalist accumulation and crisis. It is both a cause and consequence of the new international division of labor and international economy.[6] It is a cause in the sense that problems of labor discipline, high wages, welfarism, profit deficits, and so on have "pushed" US capital into the cheap labor havens and "new industrializing countries" of the world. It is a consequence in the sense that new developments in communications, manufacturing, and other technologies, the tremendous increase in the supply of cheap labor in the Third World, and the rise of fascist and authoritarian states since the early 1960s have "pulled" American capital into these "newly industrializing countries" and other profit havens. Furthermore, the increase in international economic competition between the established industrial powers has dethroned the dollar as the world reserve currency and weakened or destroyed the competitive edge enjoyed by many American industries during the 1950s and early 1960s. In addition, the internationalization of production and circulation has reinforced the internationalization of the capitalist cycle. The growing synchronization of the economies of the old industrial powers has meant that traditional attempts to control the cycle in one country by expanding exports are no longer possible without worsening the balance of payments of other countries. By 1980, the "synchronous economic slump at home and overseas" in which "ailing foreign economies offer no help"[7] forced multinational capital to try to find new forms of international economic and political cooperation (although nationalist policies of various kinds, especially exceptionally high interest rates in the USA, have largely undermined such efforts). It follows from these lines of reasoning that a full analysis of crisis trends in the USA requires study of the new internationalization and interregionalization of production and labor migration and changes in the composition of capital in favor of high technology industries and services, among other developments. These crucial issues, however, are by and large beyond the scope of this work.

The focus of this study is the conditions of economic and social repro-

[6] This is recognized in Barry Bluestone and Bennett Harrison's *The Deindustrialization of America: Plant Closings, Community Abandonment, and the Dismantling of Basic Industry* (New York, 1982). The authors also stress the diversion of US capital from productive to unproductive investments.

[7] "International Forecast," *Business Week*, Dec. 29, 1980, 76.

duction (and their relation to economic and social crisis tendencies) which are specific to American capitalism and/or which appear in exaggerated forms in the USA. Two empirical and one theoretical justifications may be cited. First, the USA remains the most important capitalist country and the main engine of world capitalist economy because of its sheer economic weight and technological and military capabilities. Second, certain features of the crisis are more or less peculiar to the USA (although some may be found in some European countries as well). These include capital's obsession in recent years with protecting rather than expanding profits; its refusal to lay out large sums for expansion investments (confining itself to modernization investments); its heavy reliance on military expansion as a "growth industry" of the 1980s; declines in productivity associated with shifts from industrial/commercial construction to residential construction in the 1970s, Environmental Protection Agency (EPA) and Occupational Health and Safety Administration (OSHA) regulations, top-heavy corporate management, and economic and social inflexibilities and immobilities of various kinds, among other factors; the role of consumption spending as the dynamic force in recent "economic recoveries"; unusually high real interest rates which have attracted foreign currencies in floods, meanwhile weakening important domestic industries; and, last but not least, the systematic use of neo-liberalism and neo-conservatism as ideologies of crisis management (only Great Britain compares in this respect).

However, the main reason why the focus of this work is American society is theoretical in nature. The premise of this study is that conditions of economic and social reproduction (hence economic and social crisis tendencies) in particular countries are inexplicable outside of the context of the dominant national ideologies in those countries.[8] Put another way, material life in capitalist societies is infused with and oriented by dominant cultural features, especially capitalist ideologies of domination of labor, which are inscribed in the division and mode of imposition of labor, and the mode of production, extraction, and utilization of surplus labor.

In the USA, the dominant national ideology is individualism in all its forms. While we can identify certain convergent ideological and cultural trends which the USA shares with some European countries – social fragmentation, populism, struggles for sectional advantages, interest-

[8] Consider, for example, the crucial role of Confucianism in Pacific Basin economic development; the ideology of revolutionary nationalism in Mexico; various forms of corporatism in continental Europe; the peculiar collectivism of Japan; and so on. Any study of conditions of social and economic reproduction in these countries and regions (and the links between reproduction conditions and capitalist accumulation and crisis) which neglects the ways in which these ideologies and cultural attributes stamp the division of labor, class composition, and economic life generally would be not so much inadequate as wrong.

group competition for state benefits[9] – the modern hegemonic ideology in the USA is natural rights individualism combined with the Romantic obsession with the expressive "self" and modified by New Deal-Democratic Party utilitarianism (Chapter 1). The argument developed in this study is that American individualism became self-contradictory and outlived its usefulness as a source of economic and social integration. In the regime of consumer capitalism, individualist ideologies became very expensive economically. In the "culture of narcissism" individualism became costly socially and psychologically.[10] In the interest-group liberal state, individualism became a political extravagance. These theses were, in fact, indirectly acknowledged by many commentators on contemporary American society, e.g. those who call for lower living standards;[11] new forms of labor-management partnership or an America-style corporatism; new "corporate cultures" in which individuals are taught to accept corporate values and goals and in this way find meaning in an otherwise meaningless life; and revitalized plans to socialize social and economic reproduction processes with the aim of cheapening the costs of wages, salaries, and welfare (Chapter 8).[12]

In Western thought, individualism has long been associated with crisis tendencies of various kinds. The historical connection between Western individualism generally and what some call the "moral crisis" of the sixteenth century was drawn in the last century by Jacob Burckhardt: "The fundamental vice of [the Italian upper-class] character was at the same time a condition of its greatness, namely, excessive individualism" – "excessive" because what the great historian considered to be modern standards of morality based on individual conscience remained undeveloped.[13] The theoretical connection between bourgeois individualism and social and political crisis tendencies appeared three centuries later in various French texts (and, to much lesser degree, English and German

---

[9] These trends are documented in Great Britain by Samuel Beer (*Britain Against Itself: The Political Contradiction of Collectivism*, New York, 1982) and in Nordic Europe by Barry Turner (with Gunilla Nordquist) (*The Other European Community: Integration and Co-operation in Nordic Europe*, New York, 1982). Writings on the Italian state as a "spoils allotment system" are relevant in this connection. So are books such as Lester Thurow's *The Zero-Sum Society* (New York, 1980) and Theodore Lowi's *The End of Liberalism* (New York, 1969) in relation to the USA.

[10] Jason Epstein calls the "American ideology of personal success and the belief that whatever inhibits one's eventual happiness can be overcome" a "religious sentiment" ("Going for Broke," *New York Review of Books*, Sept. 23, 1982, 17) – one which, it may be added, has created more tortured souls than saved them.

[11] For example, Paul Volcker and Charles Schultze.

[12] For example, Hubert Humphrey.

[13] Jacob Burckhardt, *The Civilization of the Renaissance in Italy*, vol. II (New York, 1958), 427, 442–3.

writings). The fear that individualism would cause social atomization and disorder was expressed in the first decades of the last century by both conservatives and utopian socialists. An (at least implicit) connection between individualism and economic crisis also first appeared in France. At the end of the last century, Emile Durkheim argued that economic rationality and well-being presupposed forms of social solidarity or social integration rather than unmitigated self-interest and "possessive individualism," as English liberalism held. While later in his life Durkheim reasoned that ideas and practices of individualism might be sources of social solidarity to the degree that they were widely accepted as such, in *The Division of Labor in Society* he made a theoretical connection (however tenuous and indirect) between individualism and economic crisis. Neither French socialism nor conservatism relinquished the general idea that individualism and "crisis" were inseparable (e.g. in the mid-twentieth century Leo Moulin attributed "the crisis of the 20th century to the explosion of individualism which took place at the time of the Renaissance and the Reformation").[14]

The development of these themes was possible only in a country such as France, with strong traditions of "solidarity" in the crafts and trades and the towns and villages, small-scale production and trade, and organic conceptions of society. The French critique of individualism was in this sense backward-looking – a judgment confirmed by the fact that conservatives and socialists shared many of the same views. Little did it occur to either that "individualism" posed dangers not only for petty capitalism, small commodity production, and traditional values and authority, but also for modern capitalism based on the more or less full development of the wage form of labor and the commodity form of need satisfaction.

At least, this is the leading idea of the present work. The attempt is to show that during the stage of Western industrial capitalist development (from roughly the mid-eighteenth to the mid-twentieth century) French thought was deadly accurate in the sense that capitalist development in fact destroyed the traditional individuality (or indivisibility) of the small producers as well as remnants and traces of Absolutism and the old order (Chapter 2). At the same time, however, capitalist accumulation created the basis for the development of modern *ideologies* of individualism, especially in the USA, where (as we have suggested) individualism was and remains the defining national ethic and also (as we will see) the form in which the modern class struggle appears and an important source of modern economic and social crisis.

This novel and hopefully provocative thesis sharply contrasts with

[14] Leo Moulin, "On the Evolution of the Meaning of the Word 'Individualism,'" *International Social Science Bulletin*, 7, 1955, 84.

traditional Marxist crisis theory, especially its application to nineteenth-
and early twentieth-century capitalism and its crisis tendencies. These
tendencies in the form of "internal barriers" to capitalist accumulation
(i.e. the fall in the rate of profit) were thoroughly analyzed by Marx and his
orthodox successors. The orthodox Marxist theory developed as a kind of
"systems theory" based on economic deterministic premises. These were
more or less plausible in an epoch in which the economic system was
relatively unmanaged (although the same cannot be said of Marx's social
and political crisis theory, which fails to distinguish adequately between
economic system integration/disintegration and social integration/
disintegration). However, economic systems theory became less and less
plausible with the development of modern wage labor, large-scale capital,
and the state – and the class struggles therein. It is not only that "cultural
control and administration are much more important than economic
operations . . . [and] that economic operations cannot effectively function
unless they are preceded by cultural efforts."[15] More important, the distinction between cultural/ideological, economic, and political processes
tended to collapse with the development of "full capitalism." The interpenetration between economic efficiency and legal-rational and moral-
normative values in effect abolished autonomous "economic laws" defined
in traditional Marxist terms. Capitalism rather became "mixed" in the
sense of combining in ambiguous ways diverse features of capital logic,
ideological culture, and political-administrative technique. Modern social
struggles in the context of developed ideologies and practices of individualism themselves became implicated in the production of economic
and social crisis tendencies (Part Two). Put another way, Marx and his
orthodox followers left few clues regarding possible "external barriers" to
capitalist accumulation in the form of either "limits to growth" determined
by the availability of natural resources or (what is the focus of this work)
limits to accumulation determined by cultural-ideological conditions of
economic and social reproduction.

More specifically, Marx may be regarded as the premier theorist of the
historical process whereby the modern working class (and large-scale
capital) was created. The question arises, however, which Marx himself
did not and could not ask: what did the modern working class in fact do
once it appeared on center stage of Western history in the mid-twentieth
century? Many answers to this question have been proposed during the
past half century or so. The Frankfurt School theorists argued that the
working class did little or nothing because it was locked up in new

[15] Tetsuo Kogama, "Adorno's 'Strategy of Hibernation,'" *Telos*, 46, Winter 1980–81,
147.

political, cultural, and ideological "iron cages." Many Marxists claimed that the working class was fatally weakened when its leadership and morale were destroyed by fascism and war or (in some versions) because of the fatal influence of Soviet Marxism. Marxist economists theoretically articulated what they construed as modern capitalism's maximum security prison – commodity fetishism and the hard rule of the law of value. Political sociologists (Marxist and non-Marxist alike) agreed that the working class in effect had become powerless because modern political parties, productivity bargains, and the triumph of symbolic politics and technocratic/administrative democracy succeeded in their task of integrating the working class into "one-dimensional" capitalist society.

Other theorists claimed that the rise of the modern working class made social democracy and the modern welfare state both necessary and possible – necessary because of the dangers of modern depression and mass unemployment and possible because of the organized power of the unions and labor parties. Meanwhile, Marxist writers in the "workerist" tradition argued that the rise of large-scale production and its diffusion through the economy created potentials for working-class structural power within the factory. In the 1960s, this thesis was widened by Italian Marxists and others to include the concept of the "social factory." They stressed that the emergence of the "mass worker" and the institutionalization of capital required the development of socialized mechanisms for extracting surplus value. But they added that the autonomous working-class struggle was the key to the iron cages of both the traditional factory and the new social factory. Increasingly, "worker autonomy" theorists not only in Italy but also in the USA and elsewhere drew attention to the relationship between workers' struggles in all spheres of life and capital valorization and economic crisis tendencies.[16] These theoretical approaches which state frankly

[16] For example: "the struggle of both the waged and the unwaged parts of the [working] class thwarted the fundamental tool of accumulation – the division between the waged and the wageless. Those struggles against capital show a unity of demand – more money, less work – and not an organizational unity . . . it is the political recomposition of the waged and the unwaged that imposes the crisis on capital . . . the working class struggle *against* work is the source of the crisis and the starting point of organization" ("Introduction," *Zerowork*, Political Materials, 1, 1975, 4–5). Again: "Non-work, the refusal to work, becomes the worker's point of view, the basis from which the law of value can be inverted and the law of surplus value reinterpreted" (Toni Negri, *Marx Beyond Marx*, unpublished MS, ch. 7, 29.). See also, Harry Cleaver and Peter Bell, "Marx's Crisis Theory as a Theory of Class Relations" (forthcoming in *Research in Political Economy*, 5, 1982).

Other writers drew connections between historical social struggles and economic crises. Upper turning points of "long waves" have been correlated with "social and political disturbances" which are said to "shatter [capital's] state of confidence and discourage investment activity" (Ernesto Screpanti, "Long Economic Cycles and Recurring Proletarian Insurgencies" (forthcoming in *Review*, 11, 13).

that workers' struggles were sources of economic crisis were a great advance over "capital logic" economic systems theories of crisis (although they paid little or no attention to the multiple determinations underlying modern legitimate worker struggles, nor to the whole problem of the relationship between hegemonic ideologies and class struggle).

In this work, it is also argued that the working class moved itself into the center of Western capitalist history. The claim is that the recomposition of capital, the working class (and salariat), and the state through historical economic crises and traditional class struggles revolutionized the conditions of social and economic reproduction not only within the production process but also within society and the state generally. The thesis is that these new conditions of reproduction and conditions of capitalist accumulation became increasingly incompatible. The basic reason, which we have made the focus of this work, was the development of ideologies of individualism and their practices, which flourished in the USA in proportion that the expansion of the division of social and industrial labor abolished traditional "individuality." It is argued that although these ideologies appeared to be indispensable for economic and social domination and integration, they increasingly subverted both. To the extent that individualism ideologies divided the working class, they legitimated class struggle in the form of the struggle for "more" and for the "self". Class struggle in the "individual" and "pluralist" forms was possible precisely because these forms made it appear that class struggle did not even exist. While traditional worker struggles during the stage of capitalist development used individual means to defend local collective ends, the modern class struggle used more universal collective means to advance individual ends. The result was an increase in the costs of reproducing the working class and salariat and increased inflexibilities in utilizing labor-power from the standpoint of capital. More specifically, the average consumption basket became too big, and its value content too high; the social consumption basket became too great, and its "value content" likewise; class struggles in the individual form within and against the law of value interfered with capitalist processes whereby labor-power was produced and reproduced as variable capital. In these ways, inflation-free surplus value and profits became increasingly difficult to realize. Individualist ideologies and their practices also led to a reduction in the mass of surplus value which capital was able to utilize in directly productive, and the state in indirectly productive ways. The result was high interest rates, inflation, increased fiscal crisis trends, upward spirals of credit, and/or growing unemployment – the manifestations of the modern underproduction crisis of capital – that is, a crisis in which capitalist accumulation became constrained by conditions of direct and indirect exploitation of labor and resource availability[17] rather than by conditions of effective demand. Put another way, individualist ideologies and their practices – the legitimating cement which held together the economic and social order – weakened in proportion that individual workers and the salariat demanded that material contents be poured into capital's ideological molds. The structural gaps between conditions of social domination/integration and economic system domination/integration in this way became so many limits on capitalist accumulation. So also did social struggle *against* individualism ideologies and their practice, i.e. against a reified social existence, and for a new "social individuality."

---

[17] "Natural limits" posed obstacles to capitalist accumulation in the form of resource shortages, declining soil fertility and agricultural productivity, pollution, and so on, on the one hand, and environmental struggles against the exploitation of nature, which raised capital costs and increased circulation time of capital, on the other.

Part One

Introduction

1

Individualism

Introduction

"American individualism" is capital's most powerful weapon of ideological domination of labor in the USA. Ideologies of individualism are stronger than racist and sexist ideologies because they are more deeply embedded in English, hence Anglo-American, economic, social, and political life.[1] Unarguably, bonds of ethnicity, race, and sex mediate the dominance of ideologies of individualism in subtle and profound ways. However, these hegemonic ideologies and their myths of the "self," private property, and natural rights "mediate back" ethnicity, race, and sex with a fateful and unconscious power which subverts or reifies "traditional" community, ethnic, and sexual identities.

This is so because individualism is associated with the foundations and purposes of the American nation itself.[2] While individualism was firmly rooted in English soil, it flowered only when it was fertilized by New World material and social conditions. In the "old country," individualism was tempered by the values of the landed aristrocracy, strong class identifications, the psychological effects of the absence of a domestic transcontinental frontier, and the insular and traditionalist character of the ordinary Englishman. In America, Lockean individualism and liberalism were considered to be the "final stage of human progress," a "new order based on the spontaneous relationship of free and authentic personalities," a "living faith," and the basic source of social solidarity.[3] In economic life, laissez-

---

[1] The origins of English individualism lie in the Germanic system of "absolute private property," i.e., the absence of any idea "that the family and the resources were inextricably linked" (Alan Macfarlane, *The Origins of English Individualism*, Oxford, 1978, 170).

[2] Yehoshua Arieli, *Individualism and Nationalism in American Ideology* (Cambridge, 1964); Louis Hartz, *The Liberal Tradition in America* (New York, 1955).

[3] Arieli, *Individualism and Nationalism*, 200, 328, 195–7.

faire and the individual wage and commodity forms of production and
consumption fetishize social existence to a degree unknown in England
(and any other capitalist country), which helps to explain the readiness to
equate individualism and the American nation with capitalism in the
popular consciousness. National individualism is considered to be the
"ideological antithesis of [international] socialism" and in this sense also
Anglo-American individualism runs deeper than its English forebear. The
same is true in political life, where anti-statism and the "atomization of the
body-politic into what are called 'individuals' "[4] fetishizes the public
sphere to a degree unknown elsewhere, in this way reinforcing the two
great pillars of social domination, "blame the victim" and "scapegoating,"
which nowhere else function so smoothly and insidiously. In social life, the
modernist obsession with immediate and intense individual experience,
"authenticity," constant physical movement, and experiment and explo-
ration is also nowhere else so apparent.[5] The same may be said about the
doctrine of individual privacy (withdrawal from public life into the private
existence of the imperial "self") as a moral category. Philosophically, the
idea that the source of all knowledge lies within individual minds and the
sensations they receive, while imported from England, flourished under
the rule of American deism. The same is true of the doctrine that individuals
were or should be the ultimate moral judges and arbiters of their fate. In
short, no other nation has more religiously suppressed Marx's concept of
social individuality, the premise of which is that "the individual *is* the
social being . . . is equally the *whole*, the ideal *whole*, the subjective
existence of society as thought and experience . . . the representation and
real mind of social existence . . . "[6] Nowhere else is it assumed so
uncritically that "the physical, intellectual and social crippling and
enslavement which afflict an individual owing to existing conditions [is
due to] the individuality and peculiarity of that individual."[7] Yet, as
Arthur Brittan states: "privatization is about the bureaucratization of
consciousness or . . . 'the industrialization of the mind.' There is no way in
which human beings in the late twentieth century can really claim that they
alone are responsible for the integrity of the self or the uniqueness of their
biography."[8]

[4] Nicos Poulantzas, *State, Power, Socialism* (London, 1980), 63.
[5] Robert Jay Lifton, "Protean Man," *Partisan Review*, 35, 1968.
[6] *Karl Marx: Early Writing*, trans. and ed. T. B. Bottomore (New York, 1963), 158.
[7] Karl Marx, *The German Ideology* (London, 1965), 476. Of course, Marx is aware that
every individual is "unique," but argues that for the concept of "uniqueness" to rise above
biological meanings it should refer to particular skills, abilities, and so on, which are in his
mind social values, expressed within the community.
[8] Arthur Brittan, *The Privatised World* (London, 1977), 148.

Individuality as Indivisibility

Prior to the development of the European idea of the intrinsic and supreme value of the individual, or the "self," during the rise of independent commodity production/merchant capitalism and early agricultural capitalism, "individual" meant "not divisible." The connection between "individual" and "indivisible" was made in twelfth-century England, where there developed strong principles of both individual ownership of land and also indivisibility of land (e.g., primogeniture).[9] In Continental feudalism, there existed more specifically social connections between "individual" and "indivisible." "Many arguments about the 'individual'," Raymond Williams writes, "now confuse the distinct senses to which *individualism* and *individuality* point. *Individuality* has the longer history . . . stressing both a unique person and his (indivisible) membership of a group." By contrast, "*Individualism* is a 19th century coinage . . . a theory not only of abstract individuals but of the primacy of individual states and interests."[10] Despite the early development of individual rights in property and law in England, there and on the Continent the word "individual" was rarely used without explicit reference to a group.[11] "Individual" did come to mean "singular," but "in this form of thought, the ground of human nature is common; the individual is often a vain or eccentric departure from this."[12]

"Individual," in the traditional sense of "indivisible," in the most general terms involved the notion that "the *polis* is prior to the individual" (Aristotle). In medieval Europe, "individual" as "indivisibility" referred to the unity of human labor-power and means of production, mind and manual labor, "employer" and "worker" functions, labor and culture. Especially on the Continent, this concept meant that an account of any particular person began with an account of kinship, community, and social hierarchy. "As was natural, perhaps, in a society in which kinship was, above all, regarded as a basis of mutual help," Marc Bloch wrote, "the group counted for much more than its members taken individually."[13]

[9] Macfarlane, *The Origins of English Individualism*, 187–8.
[10] Raymond Williams, *Keywords: A Vocabulary of Culture and Society* (New York, 1976), 136.
[11] In Macfarlane's account of English individualism there is a strange absence of discussion of the *social* as compared with the *legal* use of the word.
[12] Williams, *Keywords*, 134.
[13] Marc Bloch, *Feudal Society*, vol. I (Chicago, 1964), 135. Given the historical practice of the exchange of women between men of different groups, it must be added that "men counted more than women." See also, Walter Ullmann, *The Individual and Society in the Middle Ages* (Baltimore, 1966).

Although private property was legally sanctioned in feudal Europe, "in practice the solidarity of the kindred was frequently extended to community of goods."[14] The meaning of "individual" thus may be construed as assuming that a person was the ensemble of social relationships, the uneven and combined development of untamed social and ideological forces which, using the medium of unique biological structures, created unique persons. Labor and culture hence assumed self-consciously social forms (especially in that these social forms were grasped as an organic collectivism dominated by the feudal ruling classes). Social nature – especially the class character of society – was yet to become opaque, as it did with the development of the capitalist mode of production.

The Development of Modern Ideologies of Individualism in the United States

The breakdown of feudalism, the rise of the absolutist state, primitive accumulation, and the development of wage labor created the material, cultural, and political conditions for separating the individual from the group in Western history. Individual property in the forces of production, defined in terms of individual rights to exclude others from use of property, and impersonal market relations began to atomize society. While the small producers defended regulation of material life and attacked market competition, the ascendent capitalist class defended the new regime of competition and attacked regulation. Subsequently, individuals, crafts, trades, and communities more or less rapidly lost control over processes of material and social reproduction (Chapter 2). "Economic individualism" and "liberalism" finally resulted in the operation of the law of value on a world scale, the triumph of commodity fetishism, or the growing sense that the "economic world" was an objective, natural force acting independently of individual will and volition.[15]

As we have noted, in America "individualism" (called "self-reliance" and "self-help" until the late nineteenth century) became the defining concept of the nation-state in the economic, social, political, and moral senses of the word. The uniqueness of American individualism lay in the fact that the hegemonic themes of anti-statism, privatization, autonomy, self-development, and laissez-faire were regarded as sources not of economic and social dissolution (as, for example, in French conservative and

[14] Ibid., 130.
[15] This is not the place to review the different meanings and usages of "individualism" and "liberalism" in the main European countries (see Steven Lukes, *Individualism*, New York, 1973, and Maurice Cranston, *Freedom*, New York, 1967).

socialist thought), but rather of economic strength and social and national bonding. On the one hand, independent property was seen as the basis of economic wealth. Inequalities of wealth and rewards were required to insure that the most productive people were given incentives and the unproductive spurred to action. Social or collective property was "inferior" because it could not inspire hard and productive work. Individualism in this sense underwrote the idea of what may be called "economic system integration." On the other hand, independent property in the forces of production was also seen as the basis of social order, hence political stability. It was thought that widespread private property anchored the passions of society, or moderated them with calculating "interests."[16] A large "middle class" of property owners was regarded as the best insurance against social conflict. Individualism in this sense underwrote the idea of what may be called "social integration."

These concepts of economic well-being and social solidarity were originally grounded in widespread ownership of independent productive forces by white males. The context of the idea and experience of the frontier and strong illusions of social mobility provided abundant opportunities, motives, and weapons for white males to develop strong and autonomous egos based on independent property and skills. This was perhaps as true during the early stages of industrial capitalist development as in the period of independent "commodity" production and merchant capitalism. In sum, in America, where free land, cheap resources, favorable climates, and independent property inhibited the hegemony of large-scale capital until the 1880s, individualism in the sense of both economic and social integration found greater material expression than in any other country (including most if not all of the other "white settler capitalist countries").

During the nineteenth century, the small producers increasingly resolved ambiguities between commodity economy and moral economy in favor of "I" and against "Thou." The impetus which an increasingly capitalist mentality gave to the development of large-scale industrial capitalism in the latter part of the nineteenth century is obvious. By the 1880s, American individualist doctrines became fused with ideologies of big business. The rise of industrial and finance capital and the modern division of social and industrial labor increasingly emptied concepts such as the " self-reliant individual" and "traditional community" of social meaning. America as a "new order based on spontaneous relationships of free and authentic personalities"[17] was receding into the past. Instead, "individualism tied together the American nation, democracy, and industrial enterprise into

[16] Albert Hirschman, *The Passions and the Interests* (New Jersey, 1977).
[17] Arieli, *Individualism and Nationalism*, 200.

one identity *in which the newly elected* [capitalist class] *hoped to stabilize its position.*"[18] Individualism henceforth became an increasingly illusory basis of both economic well-being and social bonding.

More specifically, privacy, autonomy, and self-development at one time constituted the basis of respect for person, equality, and freedom in liberal thought.[19] These values were once rooted in self-earned property in the forces of production, which were both the means and objects of privacy, autonomy, and self-development. The development of capital and wage labor, however, destroyed the social basis of these values. In place of privacy or freedom from interference, there developed centralized state and large-scale capitalist intrusion into private life; in place of autonomy and self-direction grew dependence, passivity, and individual wills colonized by capital and the state; instead of self-development grew standardization, apathy, and self-stultification. In place of political individualism and a society based on voluntary groups established to defend the interests of free individuals, there developed a kind of "corporatism" in which individuals exist to legitimate the interests of "intermediary associations." In place of economic individualism, there developed the forced collectivization of the capitalist division of industrial labor. In these senses, modern ideologies of individualism become mere shadows of that traditional American individuality which flowered in the old subsistence economy, small-town life, the frontier, and, later, small-scale capitalism.

Even more specifically, first, the classical liberal idea of individuality as freedom from external constraint perversely describes the relation between capital and labor in the process of capitalist production where "individualization" in the quantitative sense of the lowest common denominator is a "terribly real phenomenon" (Chapter 5).[20] In the USA more than anywhere else, "individual" in the sense of the logical and abstract category of the "irreducible" is made into the real category of wage labor, or social, abstract labor. Individualization is thus homogenization which "not only serves to mask and obscure class relations . . . but also plays an active part in the division and isolation of the popular masses."[21]

However, second, workers are not merely "factors of production" but irreducibly human beings who are not only the objects but also the subjects of the wage relation and the labor process, i.e., individuals who possess their own labor-power which consists not merely of technical capacities but also of moral attributes and cultural and ideological skills. The individual worker is not *merely* the "whole" but also the irreducibly singular,

[18] Ibid., 341. Italics added.
[19] Lukes, *Individualism*, 125.
[20] Poulantzas, *State, Power, Socialism*, 64.
[21] Ibid., 67.

sensuous human being.[22] Modern capital thus consists in part of ideological practices which *appear* to recognize the worker's individual particularity and humanity. Within the labor process, the individual worker both *is* and *appears* as a "person," i.e., a sociological construct defined to mean "a self-conscious being capable of choosing between alternative modes of behavior on the basis of reflection."[23] The individual thus appears as a "job," "occupation," "position," "status," or "role," while also in fact remaining a unique being.

In this second sense in which the classical liberal idea of individuality obscures and is obscured by the modern capital-labor relationship, there develops a deep rationalization of social relationships because of increasing "functional interdependence" among economic, social, and political activities and institutions. "Modern property" assumes the form of roles, positions, and statuses, which the real individual adapts to, and/or comes to personify and/or negate. Normative structures of action are predetermined by role structures to which not only the salariat but also the working class are expected to conform. Jobs, positions, and roles are "irreducible," and individuals filling roles become differentiated and heterogeneous only to the degree that they fill and/or negate differentiated and heterogeneous roles. Real individuality based on autonomous property in the forces of production is replaced by mirages organized by managerial ideological practices. Yet the definition of the individual in terms of position, job, and so on manifests reality (albeit, a reified one) as "authentically" as the real social process of labor.

Third, the classical liberal doctrine of individuality based on ownership of autonomous property in the forces of production is perverted in modern capitalism to mean ownership of means of consumption (Chapter 6). Individual freedom is defined in terms of choices, not only in the supermarket of job roles, but also of consumer goods and services and their "meanings." The individual consumer is "deconstructed" and defined in terms of status acquired through consumer roles, which also manifest a (reified) reality as "truly" as the real processes of material and social production of labor-power, working class, and salariat. Classical liberalism held that needs were formed in the context of the individual's social relationship to the means of production. In modern capitalism, needs – construed as applying to consumer commodities which are individually acquired and used – are hence interpreted as individual needs in

[22] "The unity of man with man ... is based on the real differences between men ..." (letter to Ludwig Feuerbach, Aug. 11, 1844, in Marx/Engels, *Collected Works* (New York, 1975), vol. III, 354).

[23] George A. Theodorson and Achilles G. Theodorson, *A Modern Dictionary of Sociology* (New York, 1969).

terms of both their origin and fulfillment. However, "consumers" remain irreducibly human beings who constitute themselves historical subjects as well as objects of the consumption process. In short, the commodity form of need satisfaction, together with the wage form of labor, means that to the degree that needs are satisifed in the "individual" form, they are frustrated in the social form.

Fourth, the classical liberal doctrine obscures the real relationship between capital and labor in public sphere and political life (Chapter 7). Capital opened up a public sphere in its struggle against Absolutism, which it subsequently tried to close off to protect itself against the working class. The form of this closure is the transformation of the "individual" in the sense of the logical category of "irreducible" into a political category which expresses a (reified) reality corresponding to that of role, position, consumer status, etc., and which is as "authentic" as the real processes of political organization and struggle. The individual is homogenized into the "voter," who exists as an object of pollsters, as a statistic, which replaces the "citizen," a concept once rich in social and political meaning.[24] In the relationship between individuals and the state bureaucracy, real people are reduced to "files" and "cases" and anonymous "taxpayers" who inhabit the administrative jungle of modern bureaucracies. The individual is thus defined as an abstraction who acts politically in the medium of abstractions without, however, totally becoming them and/or being totally incapacitated in the struggle to negate them.

In sum, the modern wage and role forms of labor, commodity form of need satisfaction, and "voter" form of political life figuratively "suppress individuality."[25] The sensuous individual has not one, but at least four, "second natures" which exist at one and the same time in "real reified" and "reified real" forms. These are the roles of individual owner of the commodity "labor-power," holders of positions or jobs in work, bearers of individual needs, and voters with claims to rights and abstract entitlements. Each of these roles is subdivided and splintered into a thousand smaller abstractions which reify existence in ways which create growing economic costs as well as mass confusion and social dissonance, and social and political struggle. Individuals become so many personifications not merely of categories of capital, but also of social and political categories which function primarily as ideologies of individualism and their respective social practices. Consciousness is thus fragmented and the self "disinte-

[24] "The specialization of centralization of the capitalist State, its hierarchical-bureaucratic functioning, and its elective institutions, all involve the atomization of the body-politic into what are called 'individuals' – that is, juridical-political persons who are subjects of certain freedoms" (Poulantzas, *State, Power, Socialism*, 63).

[25] Herbert Marcuse, *One Dimensional Man* (Boston, 1966), 1.

grated" and individuals are isolated from one another in specialized roles; meanwhile, "individualism" becomes a luxury from the standpoint of the costs and expenses of capital and also working-class needs.

Conclusion

Individualist ideologies and practices diffused throughout capitalist production, distribution, exchange, and consumption, as well as culture and politics, are the social cement of US late capitalism. However, the social psychological fits between individuals and the effective internalization of work roles, the establishment of consumer statuses, and forms of voter participation, are not and cannot be airtight. The basic reason is that the divisions of labor, including the division of labor between home, school, and private and public workplaces, are in fact *class* (as well as sex and race) divisions. Reified social existence and social change in class society based on capital's appropriation of nature to exploit labor, and its scientific utilization of labor to exploit nature, is in reality a world out of control. Individuals are interdependent in ways which they cannot know or regulate. They are systematically dominated and exploited in ways which are not apparent or obvious. Individual self-consciousness and immediate experience produced within the totality of material life and role structures which remain unmediated by discursive reason and practical struggle are thus inherently untrustworthy.

Individual escapism becomes a kind of safety valve, which, however, is inadequate and frustrating precisely because the individual remains materially and socially dependent.[26] The search for individual "autonomy," which seeks to compensate for material and social interdependence over which no real person has any control, expresses itself in many ways, all of which presuppose forms of ideologies of individualism. "Individuality" is something you get by beating the system; or by ideologies of proud and militant Americanism; or, at the other extreme, by joining a cult and finding a vacant corner of society remote from the law of value and imperialism and its tragedies, and discovering the illusion of community and/or individual "freedom" there. Or "individuality" is something you get by various forms of naturalism: environmental mysticism with its obsession with individual redemption through "ecological good manners," or bodily narcissism which promises redemption through yoga, running, bodybuilding. Or, finally, "individuality" is acquired by more sophisti-

[26] Richard Lichtman, *The Production of Desire* (New York, 1982), chs. 7–8; "Notes on Accumulation, Time, and Aging," *Psychological and Society Theory*, 1, Spring/Summer 1981.

cated forms of naturalism in which one discovers oneself by adaptation to one's sociobiological or evolutionary niche. All these ideologies are merely so many ways of making capital's domination of labor more opaque, as well as covering up the failure of other ideologies of individualism in work, consumption, and political life. All of them negate possibilities of "taking care with" the other, of discursive collective will formation, of growing up through struggle. The tensions between the two poles of helplessness and omnipotence grows in direct proportion that individualism ideologies and ideological practices flourish. Manic-depression and the cycle of obsessive compulsions in this event become more frequent and intense. Social disintegration increasingly threatens system integration. A reified existence results in the disorganization of labor as a productive force from the standpoint of labor defined as both a factor of production and the traditional trade union movement. Real bonds and "caring with" become impossible outside of social and political struggles which in class society define maturity and which, in effect, replace classical liberal definitions of respect, equality, and freedom with more social, copperative meanings.

Such is the fruit yielded by the American "liberty tree." In modern capitalism, a terrible and painful ambiguity exists between individual labor and social labor, individual needs and social needs, and individual and social political life. In this reified context, no unambiguous definition of self is possible. Self instead becomes the battleground on which psychologically bloody conflicts are fought.

Yet there exists a key to human emancipation. As Adorno discovered, it is the nonidentity of the individual's first and "second nature," sensuous object and reified object, concrete individual and abstract individual. The dissonance between these two worlds points the way to human freedom – not the attempt to exploit the discrepancy between the bourgeois promise of liberty, fraternity, and equality, and the reality of tyranny, conflict, and inequality. The struggle to bring social reality in line with bourgeois ideology can only produce in fact what the bourgeoisie promises in theory, which, however, developed precisely to conceal the fact. It is, therefore, an impractical struggle. More, its fulfillment would be an egoistic bourgeois paradise, not a cooperative world based on mastering the relationships between human beings and history and nature.

The destruction of bourgeois truths is a necessary but not sufficient condition for emancipatory socialism. The sufficient condition is the struggle within and against the framework of capitalist constructions of reality, that is, the struggle with and against real sensuous persons who, at one and the same time, do and do not constitute the "whole." This implies a rejection of the Marxist structuralist discussion of the illusion of "self" in terms of the absence of meaning. It also implies a rejection of the phenomenologist total interiorization of meaning and its discussion of the illusion of "structure" in terms of the presence of meaning alone. It implies an acceptance of social struggles when these struggles demystify capitalist ideological reality theoretically, and when they dereify life practically through praxis which unites *real people*, rather than roles, positions, "class fractions," and other categories.[27] In fact, it may be that only the determined, practical dereification of labor and needs and culture and politics oriented by practical reason, discursive truth, and collective will formation can prevent the present economic, social, and political crises from being dissolved by nuclear barbarism. The mastery of the relationship between human history and nature, the reorganization of labor as a productive force and production relationship which requires political means and political objectives, collective goals as well as collective means to goals, social needs defined in terms of the need for definite social relationships – these remain the social property of those for whom individualism has become a luxury which they can no longer afford economically, politically, and psychologically: those struggling within feminist socialism, environmental socialism, democratic socialism, international socialism. In practical terms, these struggles against material and social reification and for "social individuality" are the most useful weapons at hand to combat the attempt by capital and the state to ideologically construct and politically use the current crisis to restructure economic, political, and social life with the sole purpose of renewed capitalist accumulation, including a new "long wave" of ideological innovation.

[27] "A reified everyday praxis can be cured only by creating unconstrained interaction of the cognitive with the moral-practical and the aesthetic-expressive elements [and] cannot be overcome by forcing just one of those highly stylized cultural spheres to open up and become more accessible" (Jürgen Habermas, "Modernity and Post Modernity," *New German Critique*, 22, Winter 1981, 11).

2

Historical Crises, Class Struggles, and the Origins of Modern Capitalism

Introduction

Marx's general theory of capitalist accumulation and proletarianization is that capitalist development consists of the accumulation of capitalist wealth, on the one side, and capitalist wage labor, on the other. "Accumulation reproduces the capital-labor relation on a progressive scale," Marx writes, "more capitalists or larger capitalists at this pole, more wage-workers at that . . . this reproduction of labour-power forms, in fact, an essential of the reproduction of capital itself."[1]

In the present chapter, "more wage workers" is interpreted historically to mean "fewer independent commodity producers" as well as "fewer feudal dependents." In England, independent property and small commodity production appeared no later than the thirteenth century. In continental Europe, the rise of the guilds and trades beginning in the eleventh and twelfth centuries developed independently or semi-independently from feudal relations in the countryside. The peasantry also passed through a long period of development which combined the "moral economy" of feudalism with the new "money economy." Small-scale manufacture, trade, transport, and so on were also, for a long time, infused with moral elements. The sharp distinction between economic and social activity which characterizes capitalist society remained undeveloped until the eighteenth century.[2] Until then, the "individuality" of the small commodity producer was defined in terms of the "indivisibility" of the household, guild, trade, village, and/or commune. Economic and social life constituted a kind of unity.[3]

[1] *Capital* I (Kerr edn., New York, The Modern Library, 1906), 673.
[2] England seems to be the only major exception to the rule of *pater familias*.
[3] Naturally, there were exceptions, e.g., the woolen industry, in which wage labor appeared at an early date.

"More wage workers" in Europe also meant "fewer rural and urban poor," i.e., fewer landless and land-poor families who were forced to contract their labor services to the ruling classes and well-to-do and who were in effect raised to proletarian status with the rise of capitalism. The struggles for survival of the landless and land-poor classes do not have immediate relevance to the argument advanced in this chapter. The reason is that it was not the poor, but the small commodity producers on the tightrope between moral and money economy, who led the battles against the development of capitalist material and social relationships. In brief, the defensive struggles of the small producers against the "modernization" of capital and the state during economic crises were "engines of capitalist accumulation" and, at the same time, the beginnings of the Great Tradition of the labor movement.

The vital conception that "accumulation of capital is increase in proletariat" is the grand bridge between economic and social history. It spans the historical development of capital and wage labor and the hundreds of seemingly unrelated cultures and struggles organized by the pre-capitalist and semi-capitalist producing classes. It permits us to examine the ways in which small commodity production declined because capitalism developed and vice versa.[4] It also allows us to identify the motor force governing the relationship between the decline of older modes of production and the rise of modern capitalism – namely, the class struggles between two distinct kinds of culture and ways of life and work.

The method used in the present chapter is to examine the historical "defensive" movements of the traditional producing classes (and, later on, the semi-capitalist producers) in isolation from modern working-class "offensive" struggles. This method was devised not only to organize historical facts about worker movements and their relation to capitalist accumulation and crisis, but also to interpret these facts in a way which clarifies the difference between the two "proletarian movements." Bluntly put, it is a mistake to identify the real origins of the modern working-class movement with the struggles of the direct producers in the eighteenth and nineteenth centuries; the workers' movement strictly defined in Marxist terms began only yesterday.

Marx grounded the theory that the accumulation of capital is "increase in proletariat" on the historical evidence available to him. More than a century later, we know that he was right in the sense that Western capitalism combined the processes of capital concentration/centralization and proletarianization. The reason is that these processes have been

---

[4] The traditional producing classes, in effect, "supplied" markets, labor-power, and means of production to early, developing capital in Europe.

mapped by three or four generations of historians and sociologists.[5] We also know that Western capitalist development "reproduced the capital-labor relation" in the qualitative sense of the growth of more capitalistic social relationships (e.g., the commodification of needs), because these also have been charted by social historians and others. For example, the growth of a specifically capitalist culture has been elaborated by critical theory, "Western Marxism," and modern neo-Marxism.

Historical study has also made it abundantly clear that capitalist development in the West was a crisis-ridden process. Historical evidence, however, cannot prove one way or the other that capitalism was inherently either crisis-ridden or crisis-dependent. The only way to know that capitalism required periodic and structural "crisis fixes" is within the framework of Marxist crisis theory.

Economic crisis theory thus has a different epistemological status within Marxist thought than the theory that capital accumulation is "increase in proletariat." The different foundations of crisis theory and the theory of the proletariat perhaps explain why the connections between the two remain implicit in Marxist theory, i.e., why the historical connection between worker struggles and capitalist accumulation and crisis has not been worked out in any systematic way. Whatever the case, economists have largely ignored the process whereby economic crises historically created new "social class conditions" and "conditions of social reproduction" which the resolution of crises and renewed accumulation historically depended upon. Moreover, sociologists have neglected the process whereby social class composition and relationships were forged in the crucibles of historical economic crises. Finally, political scientists have played down the ways in which modern state structures developed within processes of crisis, class struggles, social class recomposition, and capital restructuring. In this sense, not only economic sociology but also political economy and political sociology remain in a rudimentary state.[6]

[5] See Charles Tilly, "Sociology, History and the Origins of the European Proletariat," Paper given to the American Historical Association, Washington, DC, Dec. 1976, 19; "Demographic Origins of the European Proletariat," University of Michigan Center for Research on Social Organization, Working Paper No. 207, Dec. 1979, 76. Capitalist accumulation on a world scale created, of course, a different class structure in the Third World.

[6] This is the project that theorists such as Michel Aglietta have taken up today in response to hiatuses such as those Mike Davis describes as "the underdevelopment of economic history [which] resonates in labor history as the absence of a theoretical level linking class struggles to their structural (partial) determinations in the accumulation process (as well as, conversely, the absence of a theory of the role of class struggle in U.S. economic development)" (Mike Davis, " 'Fordism' in Crisis: A Review of Michel Aglietta's *Régulation et crises: L'expérience des Etats-Unis*," *Review*, 2 , 2, Fall 1978, 209).

These thoughts suggest that interpretations of the development of capitalist concentration/centralization, class struggles, working class (and
salariat), economic crises, and the capitalist state which rise above historical
description require that the theory of proletarianization (and capitalist
concentration/centralization, etc.) and the theory of crisis be combined or
"brought into line" with one another. Crisis theory needs to be historicized,
and the historical development of worker struggles and the proletariat
needs to be theorized.[7] The theory of capital, proletariat, and the state
needs to be studied within the problematic of the theory of crisis. The
theory of crisis needs to be understood within the problematic of the
development of capital and wage labor, class struggles, etc.[8] The structural
connections between the development of the working class and worker
struggles, the form and nature of capitalist crisis, and the forms and
functions of the state, which are obscured by the process of uneven and
combined development, need to be made explicit and elaborated. In
particular, it needs to be shown that Western capital, proletariat, and state
were forged in the crucible of economic crisis, whose features were themselves transformed by the flowering of "full capitalist" production forces
and relations. In sum, our approach raises the questions, first: what were
the effects of crises and worker struggles on capital composition and
working-class composition?;[9] and, second: what were the effects of
changes in capital composition and working-class composition on capitalist
accumulation and crisis?[10]

Economic Crisis and Proletariat in Western Capitalism

The development of abstract social labor and the Western working class/
salariat since the late eighteenth century is inexplicable outside of the
context of economic crisis.[11] Theoretically, Marx drew the connection
between economic crises and the development of human labor-power as
variable capital when he wrote that capital's need to vary labor "imposes

---

[7] This task, Marx himself began with the thesis that capitalist accumulation is a double
process of accumulation of proletariat and also of labor movement and labor struggle.

[8] See Chapters 3–7.

[9] Some merely suggestive comments will be made on the historical relation between
economic crisis, class composition and struggle, and the development of the modern state.

[10] See Chapters 3–7.

[11] Even in Braverman's classic study of proletarianization, "there is little indication of the
manner in which scientific management and related initiatives arose out of any crisis in the
process of accumulation of capital, of the manner in which capital was compelled to increase
its scale and intensify its control over the labour process" (Tony Elger, "Valorization and
Deskilling: A Critique of Braverman," *Capital and Class*, 7, Spring 1979, 78–9).

itself after the manner of an overpowering natural law . . . that meets with resistance, at all points [but] Modern Industry . . . imposes the necessity of variation of work [into] a question of life and death."[12] Empirically, major technical innovations, which were invariably associated with "variation of labor," reached their peak in the middle of depressions, e.g., 1764, 1825, 1886, 1935.[13]

These clues to the relationship between economic crisis and the development of abstract social labor are very suggestive. When Marx's theory of "accumulation through crisis" is combined with the theory that "accumulation of capital is increase in proletariat" (and also "increase in capital concentration/centralization"), the result is "proletarianization and capital concentration/centralization through crisis." This clumsy expression means that systemic economic crises were cauldrons not only of capital restructuring (e.g., elimination of inefficient capitals, acquisitions and mergers, development of new production processes, etc.)[14] but also of the socially and politically explosive process of proletarianization. Crises were major threats to the way of life of the direct producing classes, especially to their individuality defined in terms of their traditional indivisibility. Crises

[12] *Capital* I, 534. In *Capital* II (Moscow, 1957), Marx writes that large-scale technological reorganizations are "mainly enforced through catastrophes or crises" (170).

[13] Gerhard Mensch, *Stalemate in Technology: Innovations Overcome the Depression* (New York, 1979).

[14] Crises and their aftermaths, whatever their effects on the size distribution of capitals, relations between big capital and the petty bourgeoisie, etc., invariably resulted in the growth of the largest capitals through internal expansion and acquisition and merger. The growth in the absolute and relative size of the larger capitals and the development of abstract social labor and the modern working class/salariat are, of course, two sides of the same historical process. While the latter is the main concern of the present work, a few words need to be said about capitalist concentration/centralization, in general, and the development of product competition, in particular. First, while economic crises and credit expansion typically resulted in the concentration/centralization of not only money capital but also productive capital, there seems to have been a trend for the latter to decentralize its *operating* units in crisis periods (e.g., General Motors' decentralization of its internal operations in the crisis of 1921–2). Second, at a certain critical stage in the development of large-scale capital, the traditional entrepreneur became an increasingly socialized "abstract capitalist"; i.e., there was a disassociation between individual capitalists and particular capital units producing particular use values, the former being transformed into a species of *rentier*. Third, while technological change (e.g., coal power, electricity, etc.) created the material basis for the growth of the large-scale, integrated enterprise, the key social change in terms of the thesis of the present work was the growth of a generalized capitalist class interest in developing and marketing new commodities for consumption. This was associated with shifts in social and political power in favor of wage good capitals, retailing, service industries, and bank capitals specializing in mortgages, consumer loans, credit to wage good and merchant capitals, etc. This general trend was exemplified by the shift in political power from investment good capitals (e.g., steel, railroads, heavy industry) to wage good capitals, wholesalers and retailers, etc. during the early New Deal period. By the 1950s, the famous slogan "what's good for General

forced larger numbers of direct producers into the wage laboring class. They also transformed more semi-capitalist craft and other wage labor into capitalist wage labor strictly defined, i.e., variable capital. Economic hard times thus may be regarded as crises of the relationship between the direct producers and capital in that they were the vehicles of the former's loss of control of markets, means of production, skills, work processes, the products of labor, and cultural autonomy. Crises were in this sense means of economic, social, and political alienation and reification. Economic recoveries and expansions occurred when capital successfully restored its domination of labor by restructuring the direct producing class itself. Crises and recoveries were in this way processes not only of economic restructuring in the technical sense but also social restructuring in the political sense. In sum, the cumulative result of periodic, structural, and related sectoral crises throughout the nineteenth century and first three decades of the present century was that the labor process and working class were reshaped and made to resemble more closely Marx's model of abstract social labor.[15]

Motors is good for the country" exemplified the shift in the center of political economic gravity from traditional heavy industry to consumer durables, mass retailing, and so on. At this stage in the development of US capitalism, new product development became systematically integrated into managerial strategies. Individual capitals no longer rose and declined with the development of new commodity lines. Rather, individual capitals organized as branches of conglomerate corporations expanded or contracted. Large-scale capital assumed the task of producing commodities which were, by and large, standardized but which were made and/or described as bigger, better, or different. Further refinements came about with the stratification and segmentation of markets. By the 1960s, "product extension mergers" brought together more and more capital units producing commodities sold through the same marketing outlets. The "mass market" was developed using increasingly refined demographic data to orient sales strategies. Finally, capital forged the concept of markets segmented by "life style" (see Chapter 3).

With the more or less full development of abstract social labor and abstract social capital, the "capitalist enterprise" became a huge block of money capital controlled by one or more fraction of the capitalist class with the participation of more or less the entire class. The separation of ownership and management corresponded to the change from the formal to the real subsumption of labor. The enterprise became permanent, devoted to abstract "progress." It internalized competition and/or organized its decentralized accumulating units or branches in accordance with profitability and monopoly power in the market. Ultimately, capital became totally impersonal. In the same proportion that particular commodities lost their individual specificity and became as "impersonal" as the needs they satisfied, individual capitalists "detached" themselves from particular commodities and became as impersonal as the money capital *they* personified. From the standpoint of capital, every owner was merely a stockholder, every use value merely a "product," every worker merely a factor of production.

[15] Sectoral crises are by definition "place specific." As Harvey shows, crisis-induced changes in class composition (and class struggle) were regionally differentiated and often pitted one region against other regions (David Harvey, *The Limits to Capital*, Oxford, 1982, 420).

No systematic historical study exists of the connections between historical economic crises and the development of capital concentration/centralization and wage labor. Many historians, however, have described the general relation between economic hard times and proletarianization. In England, "it was safer, if less efficient, to stick to the old ways unless pressure on profit margins, increased competition, the demands of labour or other inescapable facts forced a change . . . The periods of major economic adjustment . . . subjected employers to just this kind of pressure, and hence led to major modifications in the methods of labor utilization."[16] In France, there was a "long-term structural crisis that skilled workers encountered in the course of industrialization."[17] In the USA, the social crisis of artisans, tenant farmers, semi-capitalist craft and skilled workers, among others during major economic crises is well documented.

Historians and demographers have also pointed to the close association between proletarianization and urbanization, especially after 1800, when the industrial cycle and capitalist structural crisis tendencies first appeared. As Western Europe and the USA became increasingly urbanized, the importance of the city proletariat in national life was enhanced. Crises resulted in the progressive impoverishment of the growing urban working class in the sense of losing control of means, processes, and products of labor (and, at the same time, the decline of more or less self-contained and semi-autonomous rural workplaces and communities). In sum, crisis-induced introduction and diffusion of technology and mass production, an increasingly refined division of social and industrial labor, and rapid urbanization expanded both working class and also salariat in both the quantitative and qualitative senses of the word.

At first glance, the formula "crisis created proletariat" appears to invert the real historical connection between capitalist accumulation and crisis and social class composition. The employed working class and salariat, in fact, increased during economic recoveries and expansion and declined during crises and depressions. Also, the growth of fixed capital, specialized tools, and the development of specifically capitalist labor processes presupposed expectations and the experience of market expansion. However, the pace of proletarianization, in the sense of life and labor becoming more the "object" of the law of value, as well as of material impoverishment in the forces of production (especially in relation to skills and the control of work), was more rapid during cyclical, structural, and sectoral crises. Also, market expansion presupposed crisis-induced increases in wage

---

[16] Eric Hobsbawm, *Labouring Men* (London, 1964), 356.
[17] Bernard H. Moss, *The Origins of the French Labor Movement, 1830–1914: The Socialism of Skilled Workers* (Berkeley, Cal., 1976), 158.

labor, which expanded the commodification of needs on the one hand, and available labor supplies on the other.

More specifically, *cyclical* crises in the West destroyed the crafts and trades, bypassed established skills, and/or incorporated these skills "in a modified form in a radically transformed organization of the labour process."[18] In all three situations, the effect was loss of control over the workplace and the subjugation of labor-power and labor to the forces of international competition and the law of value. Cyclical crises also resulted in the mechanization of traditional manual work, which, however routine, required the "craft" of strength and durability, downward mobility from higher- to lower-paid work, bankruptcy of small capital, and weakening of small-scale agricultural production.[19] *Structural* crises associated with the completion of long periods of technological change (connected, in turn, with changes in the cycle of renewal of fixed capital in different branches of the economy) and new patterns of regional specialization also resulted in loss of worker control of labor, rural impoverishment, regional declines, and the decay of older urban centers. Changes in international power relations within the nation-state system and world market conditions arising from major political and economic crises of various kinds had similar effects. *Sectoral* crises associated with the senescence of particular industries, and the decay of diversified labor processes characteristic of traditional subsistence and small commodity sectors and regions, had comparable results.[20]

In sum, latent labor reserves composed of rural populations, women, oppressed minorities, deskilled craftsmen, and others who were recruited into the active labor army during expansions were "economically available" precisely because of the destructive effects of antecedent crises, which undermined peasant communities, independent farmers, artisans, male heads of household, and precapitalist and semi-capitalist ways of life and labor.[21] Historically, only in the Third World did capital systematically

[18] Elger, "Valorization and Deskilling," 73.

[19] By comparison, what Marx called "minor trade crises" (e.g., 1851–2) caused few, if any, significant material or social changes.

[20] A stunning example is described in Raphael Samuel, "Quarry Roughs: Life and Labour in Headington Quarry, 1860–1920: An Essay in Oral History," Raphael Samuel, ed., *Village Life and Labour*, History Workshop Series (London, 1975).

[21] For example, in Toronto, between 1896 and 1914, while "the traditional artisanal character of the building trades was profoundly altered . . . by a building boom . . . this upsurge . . . fed on an expanded pool of unqualified but agile handymen" who migrated from Europe and the Ontario countryside (Wayne Roberts, "Artisans, Aristocrats, and Handymen: Politics and Trade Unionism Among Toronto Skilled Building Trades Workers, 1896–1914," *Labour/Le Travailleur*, 1, 1976, 92, 94). This unqualified group probably was proletarianized during previous periods of economic hard times.

maintain the reproduction of unwaged male labor with the dual purpose of minimizing the costs of reproducing labor-power and preventing proletarian class struggle. While contemporary historians have not established this as unarguable fact, it is a powerful hypothesis that historical capitalist crises and depressions transformed precapitalist and semi-capitalist labor (as well as capitalist wage labor strictly defined) into unemployed and underemployed labor reserves, which, in turn, fueled subsequent economic expansions.

Economic Crises and Worker Struggles

It is an unarguable fact that crisis-induced (or crisis-accentuated)[22] rationalization of labor markets, work processes, product markets, and general conditions of social reproduction normally met with more or less fierce worker resistance. Crises momentarily helped to strengthen social bonds and "indivisibility" within groups of direct producers under economic and/or political attack. Also, capitalists themselves united and organized ideological and political forces with the purpose of reinforcing their economic offensives against the direct producers. "Proletarianization through crisis" thus was not an "objective" historical development but rather a process whereby the resistance of the direct producers became a "moment" in the proletarianization process itself. In this sense, "crisis created the labor movement," which powered not only the development of labor organization and labor politics but also the process of capitalist accumulation. Crisis-induced worker struggles were engines of accumulation, as well as of labor unions and parties and working-class cultural practices.

It is not an established fact, but another good hypothesis, that economic recovery and expansion occurred when capital re-established its domination over labor by changing the work force in ways which destroyed not only particular cultural foundations of unity and resistance (e.g., ethnicity), but also particular social bases of indivisibility and power (e.g., the strength of the craft). On one front, crises and their aftermath deprived workers of particular cultural practices, including the social and political weaponry which particular cultures afforded. On a second front, capitalist crises destroyed particular configurations of crafts and skills which developed more or less independently of particular cultural and/or ethnic practices. It needs to be stressed, however, that the working class was not only passively made and remade through crises, but also actively made and remade itself.

[22] Wally Goldfrank suggested the expression "crisis-accentuated" rationalization of labor and associated worker struggles.

Thus, not only did "crises create proletariat," but also "worker struggle created proletariat," albeit in indirect ways in which the results of social actions were the opposite of individual wills and intentions.

Marx himself first put forth the general thesis that worker struggle functioned in a contradictory way; on the one hand, as the development of the labor movement; on the other, as an engine of capitalist accumulation. *Capital*'s famous chapter on the struggle to reduce hours of work highlighted the linkage between struggles over worktime and the development of modern industry and relative surplus value. In this sense, Marx's focus was not only on "worker resistance as a force for changing the mode of production [but also as] a force which also causes accommodating changes within the mode of production."[23] These two "forces" were in fact not historically incompatible. Worker struggles took place through changing forms of the capital relation. They developed these relations to their fullest and simultaneously created seeds of new forms of the capital relationship. Specifically, the successful defense of the normal worktime in most trades and industries, and the workers' offensive against absolute surplus value in textiles, mining, and other sectors of the economy in which capital had increased worktime beyond "normal" limits,[24] compelled many if not most capitalist enterprises to place themselves on a more advanced technical basis, which, in turn, effectively recomposed the work force.

The Marxist literature contains many examples of the connection between modern worker struggles in particular regions and industrial geographic relocation, and also between worker struggles within particular industries and the reorganization of production processes, e.g. the introduction of automation and the substitution of plastics for metal-working processes.[25] Historians have also shown the historical connection between traditional worker practices and "modernization." For example, in the earliest days of "outwork," technology was developed primarily to seize control of raw materials, prices and markets from the outworkers. In the USA, "both workers' submerged resistance and their articulate programs have turned out to be causes, as much as effects, of the rapid evolution and

[23] Andy Friedman, "Responsible Autonomy Versus Direct Control Over the Labour Process," *Capital and Class*, 1, Spring 1977, 44.

[24] M. A. Bienefield, *Working Hours in British Industry: An Economic History* (London, 1972), 6–7, 223. Bienefield shows that the struggle to make the customary worktime the normal worktime was more or less accomplished in Britain by 1850. By 1843, "the only major industries to have lost this customary limit on their normal day were textiles and mining." The author stresses that the attack on the normal workday (long, but leisurely hours, many holidays, etc.) began not with the Industrial Revolution, but in the mid-seventeenth century, i.e., during the "puritan revolution."

[25] For example, "Workers' Struggles and the Development of Ford in Britain," *Red Notes*, Pamphlet No. 1, London, June 1976.

diffusion of managerial practices."[26] The general connection between worker struggles and capital restructuring is therefore fairly well understood. Capitalist efficiency drives and "modernization" often inspired various kinds of worker resistance, which in turn engendered new capitalist "thrusts for efficiency."[27]

In this general sense, Western capitalist development has always been subject to the ebb and flow of militant labor struggles. Faced with worker solidarity on one front, capital opened new fronts where new forms of exploitation could be imposed. Capital shifted back and forth between absolute and relative surplus value with surprising facility. The capitalist system as a whole has moved from "technological rents" to merchant monopoly profits and/or absolute ground rent and bank profits with considerable flexibility. As we recalled, when workers fought to reduce long hours of work, capital expanded labor productivity. When workers demanded minimum wages, work conditions were often left to deteriorate. When unions exercised some control over wages, hours, and/or working conditions, capital used its monopoly power in commodity markets to raise prices and reduce real wages. In sum in the historical flux of everyday life, surplus labor rose or fell in accordance with many seemingly unrelated conditions, including the forms and aims of worker struggles.

More immediately relevant for the present argument are the connections between *economic crises*, worker struggles, and capital restructuring; i.e. the hypothesis that crisis moments were seized by the direct producers to organize or reorganize defensive positions in and out of the workplace with the aim of resisting capital restructuring, in this way constituting themselves as "barriers" to capital restructuring and potentials for renewed capitalist accumulation.[28]

[26] David Montgomery, *Workers' Control in America* (Cambridge, 1979), 5. Also, see Dan Clawson, *Bureaucracy and the Labor Process: The Transformation of U.S. Industry, 1860–1920* (New York, 1980).

[27] The *reaction* of workers to the "thrust for efficiency" in the USA in the first two decades of the twentieth century is described in Bryan Palmer, "Class Conception and Conflict: The Thrust for Efficiency, Managerial Views of Labor and the Working Class Rebellion, 1903–1922," *Review of Radical Political Economics*, 7, 2, Summer 1975.

[28] For example, David Brody, *Steelworkers in America: The Nonunion Years* (Cambridge, Mass., 1960); Robert Ozanne, *A Century of Labor-Management Relations at McCormick and International Harvester*, (Madison, Wisc., 1967). J. Foster's *Class Struggle and the Industrial Revolution* (London, 1974, Ch. 7) shows how profits crises and working-class militancy forced the reorganization of engineering and cotton spinning, whereby skilled workers were more subordinated to capital and skilled workers were increasingly remade into foremen supervising the unskilled.

"In crises capitalists will try to solve their problems in the context of class struggle as well as the competitive struggle among themselves" (Andy Friedman, "Worker Resistance and Marxian Analysis of the Capitalist Labor Process," Conference on Socialist Economists, unpublished paper given at Leeds, England, 1979, 270).

Capitalist history in fact reveals that there has been a certain historical and structural logic to worker struggles. The crucial struggles over control of labor-power, work processes, the product of labor, and life conditions typically occurred in the crucible of material and social hardship. In periods of bad times, small producers, craft laborers, "unskilled" hands whose strength and durability capital depended upon, workers with specifically capitalist skills rendered obsolete by capital restructuring, and older trades organized across industry lines were subject to economic, political, military, and ideological attacks by individual capitals, capital blocks, and local and national states.[29] These capitalist offensives against direct labor and the community were often countered with forcible resistance. The reason was that capital alone was free from the deep ambiguity between moral economy and commodity economy, use value and exchange value, individuality and "individualism," process and product of labor, and "nonrational" and "rational forms" of culture[30] which made up the world of the direct producers. The historical capitalist struggle was to establish clear-cut individual property rights, money and labor markets, and other changes which the law of value both presupposed and created. The workers' struggle was more ambiguous. They sought to maintain individual ownership and/or control of the forces of production with the aim of producing and selling commodities (including labor-power) and, at the same time, to keep individual property rights (including rights to dispose of labor-power) under some kind of social control, i.e. to preserve at least traces of "indivisibility" in order to prevent the reckless development of the law of value.

In England (and much of Europe), the crafts, "having achieved a degree of control over their own trades 'distrusted innovation,' and had a liking for 'distinct social classes' [and] favoured a sort of feudal stability 'based on each man being secured and contented in his station of life.' "[31] This can be explained by the fact that while craft work was highly skilled, it was normally relatively uncreative and inflexible. Economic crises threatened the stability of craft work because in hard times capital needed new creative and flexible forms of social labor. Declining demand for the products of the direct producers also provided incentives to reorganize in the defense of established conditions. Similarly, reduction in demand for particular crafts and trades limited labor mobility by drying up chances for

[29] For an example of capital's ideological practices, see David Montgomery, "Workers' Control of Machine Production in the Nineteenth Century," *Labor History*, 17, 4, Fall 1976, 508.

[30] Francis Hearn, *Domination, Legitimation, and Resistance: The Incorporation of the Nineteenth-Century English Working Class* (Westport, Conn., 1978).

[31] Irving Richter, *Political Purposes in Trade Unions* (London, 1973), 20, quoting the Webbs.

alternative employments, and so inspired various economic and political reorganizations by workers. Particularly in depression conditions, workers were forced to reorganize to fight to retain employment, control of work, work conditions, skill levels, pay scales, and the diverse forms of independent and semi-independent ways of life and labor which could be found in Western capitalism before the modern epoch.

This appeared to be especially the case in relation to craft and other workers organized into unions reinforced by solid ethnic communities, whose work was a way of life as well as a means of obtaining income. While some craft organizations at times "chose strategically to accept machinery with little disruption on the condition that they retain other craft privileges,"[32] others tried to meet the law of value head-on, e.g., to persist in trying to fix the supply price of labor and work quantity and quality by non-economic criteria.[33] Historically, craft and skilled workers sometimes claimed special expertise which they alone possessed when they were threatened by competition from "incompetent" or less skilled workers. In hard times, older craft ideologies were often strengthened to show strong self-images "to help meet and adapt to pressure from the outside."[34] Craft workers almost invariably developed a "cohesive aggressive group spirit to keep opposing power seekers on the defensive"[35] as well as forging diverse strategies to tighten up control of apprenticeship and labor recruitment.[36] In the skilled trades with craft traditions, occupational morale in fact depended to one degree or another on various myths and fictions.[37]

The scope of worker struggles which were inspired or "accentuated" by crisis was much wider than craft worker resistance to lost control of the workplace and traditional pay scales. In bad times, it extended to the struggles of small farmers, peasants, artisans, tradesmen, teamsters, and others who were forced to resist the devaluation of their services and products, the destruction of organized and protected local markets,

[32] Friedman, "Worker Resistance," 272.

[33] Hobsbawm, "Custom, Wages and Work-Load in Nineteenth-Century Industry," in *Labouring Men*.

[34] Andrew Pettigrew, "Occupational Specialization as an Emergent Process," *The Sociological Review*, New Series, May 1973, 275. Pettigrew's subject is computer programmers. In the building trades there has been a similar situation (R. C. Meyers, "Inter-Personal Relations in the Building Industry," *Applied Anthropology*, Spring 1946).

[35] Michael Crozier, *The Bureaucratic Phenomenon* (London, 1964), 153. Crozier's subject in this passage is maintenance workers.

[36] For example, W. F. Cottrell, "Social Groupings of Railroad Employees," in S. Nowsow and W. H. Form, eds, *Man, Work, and Society* (New York, 1962).

[37] "In those trades which are struggling most vigorously to protect their identity, the recourse to myth was most pronounced": Richard C. Myers, "Myth and Status Systems in Industry," in Robert K. Merton et al., *Reader in Bureaucracy* (Glencoe, Ill., 1952), 273.

and the consolidation of commodity culture and the law of value generally. In particular, there was considerable popular resistance to the subversion of local power and community by national states, which, although relatively well-developed in the epoch of Absolutism and merchant capitalism, became more "intervention-minded" during nineteenth- and twentieth-century economic and war crisis periods.[38] Workers' motives were nearly always crisis conditions and new economic and political attacks by re-structured capital and state on strongholds of precapitalist and semi-capitalist workers and communities. Opportunities were the pre-existing forms of culture and class composition, including communal, familial, ethnic, and craft, social networks and associations. Weapons were also the workers' own work rituals, cultural symbols, ideas and attitudes, and organizations.[39] In other words, the direct producers *used* their ways of life and class to defend these ways of life and class positions. Tactics included food riots, refusal to pay taxes, attacks on census-takers, machine breaking, strikes, political struggles, cooperation, Socialism, craft associations and unions, labor parties, and anarcho-syndicalist organizations, each of which followed its own complex development trajectory governed by political and ideological factors and the periodic capitalist cycle, structural crises, and sectoral or regional crises resulting from uneven capitalist development and the worker struggles associated therein.

Worker struggles during the nineteenth and twentieth centuries were thus typically outside of and *against* the law of value, the subsumption of use value under exchange value, the internationalization of the circuits of capital and the centralization of the state – all closely associated historically with economic crises and their aftermaths.[40] These struggles unquestion-ably contributed in complex ways to theory and practices which remain valuable today. However, they typically were based on "tradition," in-cluding idealized versions of the past, real social and economic possibilities,

[38] The long history of state interventionism in periods of crisis is documented in H. Miskimin, *The Economy of Early Renaissance Europe, 1300–1460* (Englewood Cliffs, 1969), 105–12; 164–70; E. Miller, "Government Economic Policies and Public Finances, 1000–1500," in C. Cipolla, ed., *The Middle Ages*, vol. I (London, 1972). Also, C. B. Macpherson ("Do We Need a Theory of the State?" *European Journal of Sociology*, XVIII, 18, 1977) describes the growth of state intervention inspired by crisis conditions. See also Franz Schurmann, *The Logic of World Power* (New York, 1974), 22.

[39] The view that culture is *used* by people in their daily life and struggles has been developed in various works. A stunning application of this idea to the life and labor of craft workers is Bryan D. Palmer, "Most Uncommon Common Men: Craft and Culture in Historical Perspective," *Labour/Le Travailleur*, 1, 1976, passim.

[40] George Rudé's classic study, *The Crowd in History, A Study of Popular Disturbances in France and England, 1730–1848* (New York, 1964), documents the small producers' struggles against middlemen using the weapon of the food riot and motivated by unfavorable movements between the prices of commodities the producers sold and bread prices.

and future millenarianism. In England, according to Perry Anderson, worker struggles occurred in the context of ruling-class ideological hege- mony, i.e. empiricism and "insufferable" traditionalism, which the working class more or less absorbed, and which combined with the conservative pre-industrialist capitalist values of the direct producers. At best, these struggles were "an organized and concerted effort to realize the ethical ideals of the pre-Capitalist past through a radical change in the structure of industrial society."[41] In the late nineteenth-century USA, the workers' norm was "the vision of a past society (perhaps one that existed only in their minds) where the independent artisan combined in his person both employer and employee functions,"[42] i.e., where individuality was defined as indivisibility between direct producers and forces of produc- tion. However militant and well organized, worker struggles in Europe and the New World were primarily defensive and often conservative reactions to the general historical process of "proletarianization through crisis"; a "mass revulsion against the exacting disciplines of industrial urban civilization,"[43] including competitive individualism. "The *sine qua non* of violent protest activity was the material deprivation, broadly defined to include political and social as well as economic 'goods,' of groups of people sharing and united by a common experience."[44] These struggles typically were "reactive" conflicts[45] around economic, social, political, and cultural threats which exemplified one general issue – the "reassertion of established claims when someone else challenges or violates them," i.e. maintaining traditional control of social reproduction in the spheres of work, consumption, exchange, state control, and politics.[46]

It is important to stress that these conflicts were fragmented and local- ized, based on individuals with strong wills and egos forged in the "indi-

[41] John Alt, Review of Francis Hearn, *Domination, Legitimation, and Resistance*, in *Telos*, 37, Fall 1978, 209.

[42] Gerald Grob, *Workers and Utopia: A Study of Ideological Conflict and the American Labor Movement, 1865–1900* (Chicago, 1969), 7–8.

[43] David Thomson, *Europe Since Napoleon* (New York, 1962), 505.

[44] Richard Tilly, "Popular Disorders in Nineteenth-Century Germany: A Preliminary Survey," *Journal of Social History* 4, 1, Fall 1970, 33 (italics added). Gwyn A. Williams (*Artisans and Sans-Culottes*, New York, 1969) refers to the "fierce *collective* independence" of the English artisans.

[45] Charles Tilly, "Major Forms of Collective Action in Western Europe, 1500–1975," Center for Research on Social Organization Working Paper 123, University of Michigan, 1975; "Town and Country in Revolution," CRSO Working Paper 84, University of Michigan, July 1973.

[46] It is thus not adequate merely to say that nineteenth-century worker struggles were conflicts produced by a lack of incorporation of workers within the institutions of capitalist society (cf. Anthony Giddens, *The Class Structure of the Advanced Societies*, New York, 1975).

visibility" of the household, culture, craft, and community. Confined to particular trades, localities, provinces, and regions, they expressed different kinds of responses by different kinds of people to different crisis tendencies.[47] For example, in some places and times, tailors, shoemakers, iron molders and other crafts established industrial cooperatives during hard times.[48] In other situations, the small producers and skilled crafts made themselves the social basis for popular revolutionary upheavals against the "old regime" and its political traces through the nineteenth century. Sometimes the peasantry and direct producers who were threatened by capitalist restructuring found their way into "revolutionary" coalitions; at other times, the same or similar groups were strongholds of political moderation or even reaction. Putting aside the myriad of local differences, a reasonable interpretation of the findings of modern social, economic, and political history is that until the third decade of the twentieth century the most militant conflicts were organized by pre-modern worker fractions and groups and that these conflicts were directly or indirectly related to crisis-induced threats to the popular control of the institutions and processes of economic and social reproduction.[49]

Uneven and Combined Development of the Working Class

In the capitalist West, capital restructuring and technical change, working-class recomposition, and political and state reorganization, which economic crises imposed on capital, labor, and government, were not "linear" economic and social processes. Still less were worker struggles – which, in effect, mediated economic crises, class recomposition, and economic recovery – governed by any obvious "cause and effect" relationship. Historicist readings of Western history based on the idea of the progressive development of the productive forces have been discredited within and

Paul Faley, "Cultural Aspects of the Industrial Revolution: Lynn, Massachusetts, Shoemakers, and Industrial Morality, 1826–1860," *Labor History*, 15, 3, Summer 1974.

[48] Arie Sharon, "The Industrial Relations System of Industrial Cooperatives in the U.S., 1880–1935," *Labor History*, 13, 4, Fall 1972.

[49] A sample of this literature is: E.P. Thompson, *The Making of the English Working Class* (New York, 1966), especially the passages where the author shows the sources of political radicalism to be the "debased trades" (244). For examples from France, Italy, and Russia, respectively, see Joan Wallach Scott, *The Glassmakers of Carmaux: French Craftsmen and Political Action in a Nineteenth Century City* (Cambridge, Mass., 1974); Gwyn A. Williams, *Proletarian Order: Antonio Gramsci, Factory Councils and the Origins of Communism in Italy, 1911–1921* (London, 1975); Peter Arshinov, *History of the Makhnovist Movement (1918–21)* (Detroit, 1974). For the USA, the works of David Montgomery and Herbert Gutman are central.

outside of Marxism, if only because worker struggles possessed an irreducible autonomy, hence unpredictability. Moreover, the structural
dynamics which regulated the process of capital accumulation and crisis,
worker struggle, and proletarianization were subject to the principles of
"continuity through change." Most important in the present context,
capitalist accumulation and crisis were characterized by uneven and combined development, hence by contingencies of many kinds.

One meaning of "proletarianization" is the different forms of the
capital-labor relationship which historically coexisted in different branches
of capitalist economy, and which developed more rapidly in some
branches of the economy than in others. There appear to be three general
sources of the uneven development of the Western proletariat. In the first
place, Western capitalism was characterized by the uneven development of
wage and capital goods sectors as a whole, and also of particular industries
and firms within each sector, arising from the uneven growth of social
demand, development of new industries based on new technologies, and
the uneven growth of older industries owing to differences in the cycle of
renewal of fixed capital, among other factors. In the precapitalist industries
and capitalist industries where the composition of capital was relatively
low, crisis-induced capital restructuring *produced* separation of conception and execution of work, new recruits for the latent reserve army of
labor, and often deskilling of work and workers. By contrast, in relatively
capitalized industries and firms, crisis-induced capital restructuring *reproduced* new forms of capitalist labor processes and reserve labor forces. In
the former branches, direct producers were stripped of their means of life,
skills, control of work, etc.; in the latter, workers were subject to new
forms of established capitalist imposition of labor and fresh rounds of
unemployment. We should distinguish between crisis-induced production
and reproduction of proletariat.

In the second place, in some industries and enterprises, and in branches
of small-scale capital which large-scale capitalist accumulation constantly
reproduced, the development of the mass production workers and salariat
remained permanently retarded.[50] One reason pertained to the process of
combined development whereby the more backward branches of production and circulation assimilated techniques developed in advanced sectors
and adapted them to more primitive forms of exploitation. Especially in
spheres of the economy in which the direct producers retained nominal
independence, self-exploitation in the form of unpaid family labor and
long hours of work permitted the survival of marginal capitals eking out
meager profits.[51] Another reason was the reproduction of small sub-

[50] See James O'Connor, *The Fiscal Crisis of the State* (New York, 1973), chs. 1–2.
[51] Marx, *Capital* III, 708, 806.

contracting firms "structurally created out of the larger and more central monopolistic firm's need to maintain both a competitive business sector and a reserve army of workers . . . at a clear distance from their own exchange transactions and labor relations."[52]

Thirdly, crisis-induced capital restructuring and working-class recomposition were uneven processes because national economic development occurred more or less independently of particular changes in the structure of capital, and hence followed more or less different paths. In France, for example, because of the political strength of the "old middle class" and the direct producers, traditional small-scale capital has persisted until the present day, and mechanization and the destruction of job autonomy in most trades were delayed until the twentieth century.[53] Changes in the cultural composition of the working class arising from autonomous changes in the ethnic and sex composition of the proletariat via immigration and internal migration patterns also affected the rates and forms of proletarianization and worker resistance and struggles. In the USA, "the serviceablity of divisions based on certain ascriptive traits – notably race, sex, and styles of personal self-representation – has meant that the capitalist class, assisted by sexist and racist mass ideology, has been able to integrate many divisions based on ascription into the American political economy."[54] The same is true of the process of "salariatization," or the development of the typically European-American male salariat. In the USA, immigrant workers moved into manual jobs and "native Americans" (English workers, etc.) moved up into salariat employments. In this way, "native" workers assumed control of immigrants, and ideologies of racism and national chauvinism fostered not only the division of the working class but also the control of the mass worker by the salariat.

Uneven and Combined Development of Worker Struggle

As we have seen, the development of the working class and salariat was an uneven and combined historical process. This means that capitalist crises had uneven and combined effects on the scope and kinds of resistance of

[52] Alexander Lockhart, Review of Andrew L. Friedman, *Industry and Labour: Class Struggle at Work and Monopoly Capitalism* (Atlantic Highlands, NJ, 1978), in *Contemporary Sociology*, 8, 5, Sept. 1979, 773; Robert Averitt, *The Dual Economy: Dynamics of American Industry* (New York, 1968).

[53] Edward Shorter and Charles Tilly, *Strikes in France, 1830–1968* (London, 1974), 67, 149–55, 202–27.

[54] Daniel D. Luria, "Trends in the Determinants Underlying the Process of Social Stratification: Boston, 1880–1920," *Review of Radical Political Economics (RRPE)*, 6, 2, Summer 1974, 174.

workers to capital restructuring and capitalist political consolidation,[55] i.e., the social and political significance of successive capitalist crises varied in accordance with changes in the composition of the working class. Historians have studied the importance of changes in population growth within the working class and different kinds of migration patterns for social control, working-class culture, and class conflict.[56] In the present crisis model, the basic "determinant" of the meaning of crisis for capital restructuring and the renewal of accumulation was the size and social weight of the artisanry, peasantry, and craft worker in relation to that of the modern working class and salariat. Another determinant was the organizational and ideological relationship between the artisanry, craft worker, and so on, and modern industrial workers. A third determinant was the relationship between the work force as a whole, independent of its specific composition, and capital and its various organizational forms.

As has been suggested, class composition and organizational and ideological relationships between and within capital and the working class depended on and, at the same time, determined the uneven and combined development of mass production and large-scale capital. Specifically, until wage good industries were heavily capitalized, the market for capital goods remained small and localized. In turn, slow capitalization of capital goods industries, in effect, permitted craft and skilled workers in wage goods industries to retain some semblance of control of work and life chances. At the same time, the control of labor-power, labor, and/or the product of labor exercised by workers in wage good industries was a barrier to the capitalization of the capital goods sector. In fact, in crisis periods it was precisely this bottleneck which probably inspired the rapid capitalization of the wage goods sector.

Uneven development in this way strengthened the position of the work force in the wage goods sector, which hurried along the development of the capital goods sector, which, in turn, foreshadowed the ultimate downfall of traditional work groups in both sectors. Over time, in more branches of the economy, crises undermined the "old" working classes in increasingly systematic ways. Defensive worker struggles increased in number, circu-

[55] In David Montgomery's words, industrial conflict assumed many forms and "may be treated as successive stages in a pattern of historical evolution, though one must always remember that the stages overlapped each other chronologically in different industries, or even at different localities within the same industry, and that each successive stage incorporated the previous one, rather than replaced it" (*Workers' Control in America*).

[56] Charles Tilly, "Sociology, History . . .": "To the extent that natural increase was the main source of growth in the proletariat, we would find it easy to understand autonomous, persistent proletarian culture . . . To the extent that net migration was the primary source, we might expect the proletariat to be the locus not only of alienation, but of aliens, and to be correspondingly resistant to unification" (9).

lated more rapidly between the wage and capital goods sectors, and assumed a more militant character. The climax occurred during the period culminating in World War One and its sequel of skilled worker rebellions centered in the European metals industries.

In rough proportion as the position of independent producers, the crafts and trades, and the semi-autonomous skilled workers was undermined, successive crises created fresh recruits for the reserve army of labor. Drawn from newly proletarianized rural populations, the expanded latent reserve armies of labor fueled successive booms in the new mass production industries. Meanwhile, hard times also increased unemployment among workers already established in the mass production industries. Crisis itself and crisis-induced mechanization and capital restructuring thus had a twofold effect; in Marx's words, it created a "surplus working population . . . partly by opening out to the capitalist new strata of the working class previously inaccessible to him, partly by setting free the laborers it supplants."[57]

The result was that during each crisis there appeared a combined development of three kinds of struggle. First, the traditional resistance of the "old" work force to loss of markets, subversion of community, and deskilling, which expressed itself in many ways, including the organization of the first trade unions; second, early forms of the struggle for employment and against wage cuts by wage workers in established mass production industries;[58] third, the struggle against industrial work by newcomers to the latent reserve army, exemplified by the refusal to enter the factory, the growth of a "hobo" population, prostitution, and criminal activity by a new proletarian stratum sharing "preindustrial" values.[59] Another result was the changing ideological composition of the expanding working class. For many displaced farmers and artisans, deskilled craft workers, and newcomers to wage labor, "working class ideology [was] an attempt to find new forms to safeguard or realize 'traditional' values assaulted by capitalist industrialization. It is the 'spectre' not the reality of full proletarianization which seems to unite the working classes of the 19th century."[60]

In early capitalist crises, the leading role of skilled artisans in worker

[57] *Capital* I, 445.
[58] David Montgomery has stressed the combined nature of labor struggles in the USA between 1900 and 1922, and the particular character of simultaneous fights by skilled workers against Taylorism alongside unskilled worker struggles for higher wages.
[59] For example, see Herbert Gutman, "Work, Culture, and Society in Industrializing America, 1915–1919," *American Historical Review*, 78, 3, June 1973.
[60] Leon Fink, "Class Conflict in the Gilded Age: The Figure and the Phantom," *Radical History Review*, 3, Fall–Winter 1975, 58.

struggles has been documented by a generation of social historians;[61] workers in early mass production industries played relatively passive roles in crisis-induced periods of social conflicts, even though potential factory workers created by the "decomposing processes of small commodity producers and peasants" often resisted capitalist wage labor per se. Most experienced factory hands in capitalized wage goods industries were women and children who faced enormous obstacles in their fight to establish equal footings in the labor market, and also in the struggle to assume a leading role in the workers' movement (e.g., early strikes in the textile and garment industries), which finally transpired because women suffered fewer illusions about the importance of their individual skills in capitalist production, and because they did not enjoy the same range of political rights and power as men.[62] Also, in capitalism's early and middle stages of development, most workers were recruited from village and farm, where social and economic conditions were absolutely impoverished and alternatives to mass production factory work were marginal farm labor, domestic service, or outwork.

In the course of successive crises, workers in large-scale industry became a growing fraction of the work force as a whole and more active in worker struggles. The relationship between new industrial workers and the "traditional" work force shifted gradually, albeit unevenly, in favor of the former. In the raw material production, miners, lumber workers, farm laborers, and dock workers nearly everywhere organized unions without regard to status or skill.[63]

However, most industrial workers looked to craft and skilled workers for leadership, organization, and ideology. For their part, the older trade unions were increasingly unable to ignore the growing industrial work force, which was perceived as a competitive threat or rival and/or potential ally.

As the nineteenth century wore on, a complex relationship evolved between new recruits to the latent reserve army and experienced workers thrown into the active reserve army during crises. The growing division between oppressed minorities who were confined to small-scale, marginal capitalist firms and/or dead-end jobs and national or "nativist" working-class fractions further complicated this relationship. The new, rootless, mobile populations produced by crisis conditions generally and sectoral crises in agriculture in particular lived and worked "without ready access

[61] For example, William H. Sewell Jr, *Work and Revolution in France: The Language of Labor From the Old Regime to 1848* (Cambridge, 1980), 1, 285 (n. 1).

[62] Hannah Creighton called my attention to the latter point.

[63] Mario Tronti, "Workers and Capital," *Telos*, 14, Winter 1972, 29.

to more traditional forms of working class life and organization."[64] In many places, these workers turned to anarchism and syndicalism in various forms. In the industrial sector, estabished craft and skilled workers at times turned a deaf ear to the "unskilled" factory hands. More typically, however, the craft unions ideologically influenced the industrial workers in deep and lasting ways; the growing industrial work force developed a kind of craft worker consciousness. Moreover, the industrial workers were often politically manipulated by the craft workers. In Europe and the USA, some industrial unions were not only influenced but formally controlled by craft worker unionists.[65] Nearly everywhere industrial union politics were infiltrated by craft labor, national chauvinist, and traditional individualist ideologies. In Europe, some unions in mass production industries remain to this day dominated by "native" skilled workers. In the USA, there has been a long tradition of skilled worker "conservatization" of industrial unions (e.g., the adoption of the old AF of L skilled worker policy of tying wages to productivity, officially established at the AF of L convention in 1925, by the industrial CIO unions in the post-World War Two period).

The great turning point in the mixed character of the workers' struggle occurred in the Depression of the 1930s. In the USA, worker demands were increasingly based on the needs and life conditions of the industrial proletariat. Traditional resistance to "industrial values" had weakened. The established industrial working class was larger, more experienced, and contained increasingly more male workers. Perhaps most important ideologically and organizationally, the recomposed craft and skilled workers transformed themselves from at times a militant and "revolutionary" force into conservative corporatist groupings within the mainstream of the industrial work force.

First, they enjoyed more political rights (needed to defend themselves socially and economically) within the capitalist state and society generally. Second, they were increasingly threatened with the possibility of being replaced by less skilled workers during successive economic crises. "Skilled laborers under pressure of mechanization were closing ranks against threats from above and below."[66] Finally, most craft and skilled workers remained wedded to the status distinctions which characterized earlier stages of capitalism. They were therefore wary of the egalitarian demands

[64] Kevin D. Weir, Review of Gerhard Botz et al., *Im Schatten der Arbeiterbewegung* (Vienna, 1977), in *Labor History*, 20, 1, Winter 1979, 153; Moss, *French Labor Movement*.

[65] Moss, *French Labor Movement*; Scott, *Glassmakers of Carmaux*.

[66] John A. Garraty, *Unemployment in History: Economic Thought and Public Policy* (New York, 1978), 95.

raised by the modern proletariat in both the economic and social fields.[67] In the USA, skilled workers played a conservative role in the crisis of the 1930s, although they were finally bypassed or overwhelmed by the needs and demands of the industrial working class and the politics of the New Deal.

The conservative turn of the traditional workers occurred because underlying the early "violence and rebellion which are the political weapons of those whose role in ordinary politics is curtailed or even nonexistent"[68] were conservative needs. This was especially true in relation to the patriarchal family and also in relationships with oppressed minorities and "foreigners." In fact, it was the conservative nature of the "old" worker struggles which helped to make it possible for the crafts and trades to win demands for democratic rights, which, in the last analysis, turned out to be more or less useless in the struggle to protect traditional individuality and to prevent their labors and lives from being ruled by the law of value.

In the USA, by World War Two, the foundations of industrial unionism and the political base for the "interest-group liberal" American form of social democracy were established. With the development of the industrial working class after World War Two, traditional struggles around wages, hours, and working conditions were broadened and supplemented by what Charles Tilly has called "proactive claims" ("support of claims not previously established"), i.e., demands to narrow wage differentials, modify status distinctions within production, unify the wage demand under the banner of industrial unionism, expand wages independently of productivity changes, and modify the division of industrial labor through "job rotation," among others. Political symbols and "revolutionary politics" were replaced by hard struggles for wages and benefits and influence and power within the framework of the bourgeois democratic state at all levels of governments. The economism characteristic of the post-World War Two democratic period owed its existence primarily to the recomposition of the working class and worker consciousness and needs (in the context, of course, of economic growth and Cold War propaganda and repression). In effect, the modern working class inherited liberal democratic forms from the combined development of generations of "old" worker struggles and bourgeois revolutions and injected them with new

[67] See for example Robert J. Bezucha, "The 'Preiendustril' Worker Movement: The Canuts of Lyon," in Robert J. Bezucha, ed., *Modern European Social History* (Lexington, Mass., 1972), 118; Arthur J. Penty, *Restoration of the Guild System* (London, 1906).

[68] Louise A. Tilly, "I Fatti di Maggio: The Working Class of Milan and the Rebellion of 1898," in Bezucha, ed., *Modern European Social History*, 127.

contents which became indispensable in the making of modern social democracy.

During the 1960s and 1970s, the modern working-class economic struggle increasingly combined and conflicted with struggles around the issues of national, race, and sex oppression within the workplace, political system, and society as a whole. The growing consciousness of blacks and other oppressed minorities, women, other ascriptive groups, and "foreign workers" led to or continued the dual struggle by these "reserve armies" to unite along ascriptive lines and "join" the working class as full-fledged members; that is, to force the white, male industrial working class to unify along class lines, a contradictory and woefully incomplete process which was subject to setbacks, trial and error, backlashes, and modifications rooted in many conjunctural processes, above all, the period of American aggression in Southeast Asia.

Less important historically were the simultaneous deskilling/skilling processes which occurred when new industries were developed at the same time as old industries were rationalized. In the late nineteenth and early twentieth centuries, skilled workers in the USA were often retrained for new kinds of industrial work because of the unusual rate of expansion of new industries in that period. The great majority of industrial workers were, therefore, recruited from the immigrant population and countryside rather than from the "decayed" old crafts and trades. A similar process, whereby latent reserves of women were recruited from the home and into the new industrialized service sectors, occurred in the 1960s and 1970s. Meanwhile, craft and skilled labor processes were recomposed into mass production processes in industry, commerce, finance, and other branches of the US economy more rapidly than in any other industrial capitalist power. Since World War Two, changes in the international division of labor have created new layers of research and development, finance, real estate, administrative, and services capital in the USA (and other advanced capitalist countries). There also occurred a relatively large expansion of state activities and employment. Not only traditional trades such as building and printing, but also teachers, social workers, secretaries, computer programmers, and other "new" skilled occupations have been increasingly "proletarianized" in ways roughly similar to those found in the traditional nineteenth- and earlier twentieth-century work described above. Perhaps we can conclude that proletarianization in the USA (excluding remote possibilities of public child-raising which would free millions more women for duty in the active armies of labor, and mass immigration, legal or illegal, which would have to confront resurgent national chauvinist sentiments) is "more or less" complete. In any event, the working class is more impoverished than ever before, defined in terms of autonomous skills and occupational groups, and control of the means of production, work, product of work, and community defined in traditional ways, i.e., local ethnic and craft "indivisibility."

Conclusion

It has been argued that successive waves of capital restructuring and modernization, development of the modern working class and salariat, and bourgeois democracy and the state assumed their modern forms not only through periodic and structural crises but also through worker sruggles. In their obsessive need to restructure the circuits of capital, state structures, and cultural forms during economic crises and their after-maths, capitalist enterprises and interests, and ruling power blocs were more often than not unable or unwilling to compromise with the direct producers struggling to defend price structures, wage scales, control of work, community power, and ways of life, i.e., their individuality based on their indivisibility from forces of production and community.

In real Western history, exceptions to this simple model of accumula-tion, crisis, worker struggle, and class composition abound.[69] A major exception was the "slack" enjoyed by certain skilled trades in England in the period when that country appropriated super-profits from its monopoly on world trade in manufactured goods. Another was the series of "historical compromises" in France between the peasantry and petty bourgeoisie and big capitalist industry. Still another was the "compro-mise" between German capital in science-based industry and the skilled work force which the former depended upon.

[69] A more concrete and historically grounded model of crisis, class struggle, and class recomposition in the West would include specifically political struggles in the context of the *uneven development* of bourgeois democracy and related national imperialist rivalries. Traditional struggles by the direct producers in defense of established conditions invariably had crucial political dimensions, especially regarding national movements and struggles (see, for example, Rostislav Ulyanovsky, *National Liberation: Essays on Theory and Practice*, Moscow, 1978). More, the political nature of worker struggles was often decisive because economic issues were fought out in whole or part in political-ideological terms. The relevant literature includes: Charles Tilly et al., "The Rebellious Century: Italy," *Summary*, Con-ference on the Rebellious Century, Bielefeld, November 1974, 4; Nicos Poulantzas, *Political Power and Social Classes* (London, 1973), 175; 183–4; Henry Weissner, *British Working-Class Movements and Europe, 1815–1848* (Totowa, New Jersey, 1976); Richter, *Political Purposes in Trade Unions*; Moss, *French Labor Movement*, 157; Michael Mann, *Conscious-ness and Action Among the Western Working Classes* (London, 1973); Oskar Negt, "The Misery of Bourgeois Democracy in Germany," *Telos*, 34, Winter 1977–78; Val Burris, "Class Formation and Transformation in Advanced Capitalist Countries: A Comparative Analysis," *Social Praxis*, 7, 3/4, 1981.

However, the underlying currents of Western capitalist development are clear. Large-scale capital and the state by and large rejected a "negotiated" model of accumulation until the development of the modern working-class movement and salariat in the mid-twentieth century. Worker struggles in the nineteenth and first part of the twentieth century therefore had two contradictory meanings. From the standpoint of the relationship between the traditional work force and the modern working class, the workers' struggle may be interpreted as the Great Tradition, or the long and contradictory growth process of modern labor unions, political parties, and other worker organizations. From the standpoint of the historical process of capitalist accumulation, worker struggles had a radically different meaning. Defensive struggles unintentionally accelerated capitalist restructuring and political and cultural restructuring as well, hence capitalist accumulation in general. Capitalist and state struggles against the working class were especially fierce in times and places where counter-offensives by the direct producers were well organized, militant, and "revolutionary."

Worker struggles were "engines of accumulation" not only in the sense noted by Marx (e.g., mechanization of industry in response to the workers' struggle to reduce days and hours of work) and some contemporary Marxist writers. *Worker struggles were motors of capitalist development in the deep sense of strengthening a model of accumulation which in the course of crises periodically subverted the workers' own social bases of resistance by recomposing labor and the work force itself.* The independent farmer, craft laborer, skilled worker, and organized trades in this sense were not "living negations" of the capitalist mode of production but merely "barriers to overcome" for capital. Defensive worker struggles were *self-negations* in the sense that they accelerated innovations in production, marketing, administration, and so on, which freed capital from its dependency on the crafts, management systems which relied on the abilities of individual foremen, workers gifted with unusual strength or skill, traditional casual labor systems, and other barriers to the development of abstract social labor and the law of value. More, the political struggles of direct producers and their political allies were self-negations in the sense that they "helped" the national state to consolidate and centralize political power over and against the village, commune, occupational group, and society in general.[70] More specifically, the dialectic of economic

[70] This "self-negation" process is, needless to say, an interpretation of Western capitalist development, not the confident judgment of a professional historian, simply because in any particular situation many factors combined to create and recreate particular social outcomes. See, for example, Ralph Samuel, "Village Labor," in Samuel, ed., *Village Life and Labor*, 18–19.

crises, worker struggles, recomposition of the work force, and capitalist accumulation created a tragic historical discrepancy between the will formation and intentions of the "old" producing classes struggling to defend their economic and social life and the actual results of their actions. *This discrepancy made it appear that capitalist development proceeded in accordance with its own objective laws of motion.*

In this view, capitalism's laws of motion through the mid-twentieth century cannot be adequately described by the contradiction between value production and realization, the anarchy of market exchange, or the law of the tendency of the falling rate of profit. These traditional lines of reasoning are not so much wrong as incomplete, and in their own way fetishistic. Capitalist development in the West generally and in the USA in particular seemed to be "inevitable" because the objective and subjective conditions of the working-class struggle for reproduction and self-development were poles apart.[71] In fact, worker struggles were "class struggles" only in the ideological sense precisely because the "Marxist" working class/salariat had not yet emerged. They were struggles *outside of* and *against* the onrush of capital and the central state. The critical practice of the direct producers did not and could not produce new social knowledge about the past and present which clarified future possiblities. Instead, these practices resulted in social class and cultural recomposition, hence a kind of "social amnesia." They did not illuminate the past so much as help to purge it from historical memory.

The meaning which the direct producers attributed to their own struggles was more often than not the opposite of their actual historical meaning. The former was constructed not only from their immediate experiences in the course of their labor, life, and social struggles and their anarchistic, trade unionist, and other ideologies, but also out of the main ideological and intellectual current of the nineteenth century, the Romantic "great protest" against objectification, which dominated nineteenth-century philosophy, including extremist reactionary movements against the new "rational" industrial order. In the USA, "antimodern sentiments affected more than a handful of intellectuals; they pervaded the middle and upper classes. Aesthetes and reformers sought to recover the life of the medieval craftsman; militarists urged the rekindling of archaic martial vigor; religious doubters yearned for the fierce convictions of the peasant and the ecstasies of the mystic."[72] This kind of cultural protest, as well as worker unrest, reached a peak before and directly after World War One. It practically disappeared in the pain of the Depression, the horrors of

[71]   No teleology of "progress" or inevitability is intended in this formulation.

[72]   T. J. Jackson Lears, *No Place of Grace: Antimodernism and the Transformation of Modern American Culture, 1880–1920* (New York, 1981).

fascism and World War Two, and, afterward, the profit and power hungry mentality of the American empire.

In sum, through "felt experiences" in labor and life, "their responses ... shaped by values, traditions, and organization experiences that predated the modern industrial era" (and mediated by the protests of philosophers and artists),[73] the direct producers were in effect blind historical subjects, who "turned themselves into" more perfect historical objects; who fatefully recomposed and objectified themselves and perfected labor power as a commodity, as variable capital, and in this way helped to make their own worst nightmares come true.

The historical capacity of Western capitalism in general and US capitalism in specific to defeat the workers' struggle and "correct itself" economically and politically through crises of various kinds has been explained by traditional and neo-Marxism in well-known ways. An alternative, but not mutually exclusive, view of the failure of the working class to bring about a revolutionary transformation of society is that this failure was the result of the composition of the working class itself and its relationship with capital. Until recent decades, racism, sexism, national chauvinism, and traditional "individuality" were insurmountable barriers to "class unity." Although "antimodern" struggles are by no means dead, their social and political meaning is quite different today, because they combine with struggles against racism, sexism, etc., and vice versa. The practical critique of "individuality" presupposed the dissolution of the individual crafts and trades and traditional "community" and the emergence of modern social abstract labor and the "global village." The critique of sexism and the patriarchal family presupposed the proletarianization of women. The critique of racism presupposed the proletarianization of oppressed minorities who traditionally were exploited in various forms of rural bondage and debt peonage. The critique of national chauvinism presupposed the internationalization of labor migration and the productive circuit of capital. Not until the working class was recomposed into modern global, social labor could it be said therefore that the working class *as such* existed. Not until the traditional countryside, the division of labor between town and country, patriarchy and the family, and the ethnic community were "shaken up" by the universalization of the wage form of labor, commodity form of need satisfaction, and the state form of politics, was the struggle for unity within the working class, *the struggle against and within the law of value and against and within the state*, historically possible.

---

[73] Sewell, *Work and Revolution in France*, 1.

Part Two

Individualism, Class Struggle, and the Contemporary Crisis

3

Origins of the Contemporary Crisis

Introduction

A centerpiece of Marxist crisis theory is that each long-run or structural crisis (and related sequence of periodic expansion and contraction and sectoral change) is conjunctural in nature. This means that in any particular crisis "all the basic variables of capitalism can partially and periodically perform the role of autonomous variables – naturally not to the point of complete independence, but rather in interplay . . ."[1] Another centerpiece is that because "the capitalist mode of production develops in a contradictory manner through crises . . . the nature of these crises is a *historical* process which must be analyzed as such . . ."[2] This means that the "role of the basic variables" in particular historical crises cannot be adequately explained except in terms of the economic expansions, crises, and contractions which historically preceded them. The conclusions of historical crises constituted the beginnings not only of subsequent economic expansions, but also of succeeding crises. Every crisis was based not only on preceding expansions and crises, but also on the ways in which past crises were resolved through specific processes of capital restructuring, social struggles and class recomposition, and state intervention, as well as changes in the world market, international political relations, and the division of international labor. Strong threads of continuity through change therefore are woven into the history of capitalist crises.

More specifically, "solutions" to past crises became "problems" during succeeding ones. In economic terms, the thesis of the present work is that the "solution" adopted by capital and the state in postwar USA to historical

[1] Ernest Mandel, *Late Capitalism* (London, 1975), 39.
[2] Manuel Castells, *The Economic Crisis and American Society* (Princeton, 1980), 11, italics added.

crises of overproduction of capital slowly but inexorably created a crisis of underproduction of capital defined in terms of insufficient amounts of surplus value produced and unproductive utilization of the surplus value which was produced. In sociological terms, the argument is that the working class and salariat, large-scale capital and new forms of capitalist competition, and the state, i.e., the structure of modern US society, increasingly, albeit blindly, became social barriers to capitalist accumulation.

These theses are based on the premise that postwar class struggles operated in fields against and within a "mature" law of value, or a social economy in which the tension between reification and struggles within and against reified existence was well developed. This premise sharply differentiates modern crisis in which social struggles occurred *within* the capital form (including the "fourth and fifth circuits of capital," the consumption process and the state, respectively) from historical crises in which struggles occurred *outside* the capital form. It also differentiates the modern economic struggle, whose goal was to *advance* the economic condition of the working class and salariat, from historical worker struggles which attempted to *defend* pre-existing economic, social, and political conditions. Further, it distinguishes historical crises which were by and large systematically produced and resolved by economic forces from the modern crisis which was largely produced by social and political forces, and must be similarly resolved. Finally, it differentiates past crises which were vehicles for capital to recompose itself through struggles against the direct producers from the modern crises which became a vehicle for the working class to recompose itself through struggles against racism, sexism, national chauvinism, individualism, and a reified social and political existence in general.

Before elaborating this theory of modern crisis in the remainder of this book, it is necessary to sketch, however crudely, the historical relation between the development of the working-class and labor movement and changes in the character of capitalist crises. As described in Chapter 2, capital, the working class, and the state were forged (and forged themselves) in the crucible of economic crisis. However, the nature of successive economic crises was itself transformed by the growth of the proletariat and salariat, concentration and centralization of capital, and modern state intervention in the economy and society. The focus of this chapter is the process whereby changes in the composition of capital, the working class, and the state quietly revolutionized the character of capitalist crises. In sum, the preceding chapter studied the effects of crises and worker struggles on capitalist and working-class composition and the state. This and subsequent chapters investigate the effects of changes in the composition of capital, the working class, and the state on capitalist accumulation and crises.

Marxist economic crisis theory is based on the movements of four key variables: the organic composition of capital;[3] the rate of exploitation; the costs of the elements of constant and variable capital (raw materials and fuel); and the turnover (including circulation) time of capital. The denominators of two key variables – the composition of capital and the rate of exploitation – consist of the size and value content of the average consumption basket, or the costs of reproducing the employed work force. Further, the numerator of the rate of exploitation consists of surplus value, or surplus living labor. Also, the costs of the elements of variable capital (e.g., gasoline) and the costs of reproducing the employed work force are closely related. Finally, the turnover time of capital partly depends on, first, the ability of capital to transform labor-power into productive labor and raw materials into productive capital in the immediate process of production, and, second, average and total wages, the expenses of advertising, packaging, and other components of the "sales effort," and, last but not least, consumer credit.

Both socially necessary and surplus living labor – total employment, average conditions of production, size and value content of the consumption basket, and hours and average conditions of work – are inexplicable outside of the context of capitalist competiton and the struggle between capital and labor. Similarly, the costs of the elements entering into variable capital are partly determined by the class struggle as well as environmental, national, and other struggles. Further, the turnover time of capital depends in part on worker struggles within the production process as well as on the wage struggle, social demand for consumer credit, etc.

In turn, the workers' struggle (and, by extension, environmental, feminist, and other struggles) depends in large part on the composition of the working class, its militancy and organization, historical and cultural development, the particular political conjuncture, and, last but not least, the hegemonic national ideology, i.e., in the USA, individualism. This means that crisis theory needs to be historicized to be a useful tool of historical-theoretical analysis. The formal logic of crisis theory needs to be "packed" or "weighted" with the real historical development of the working class/salariat, class struggle, and political development, including the development of the dominant ideology.

The first step in this "weighting" process is to show how logical possi-

---

[3] The organic composition of capital consists of the technical composition of capital times the value composition of capital. The former is defined as the ratio of machinery to total employment (or total consumption). The latter is defined as the ratio of the value content of machinery to the value content of the average consumption basket.

bilities of economic crisis resolved themselves into historical probabilities in the course of capitalist development through the increase in capitalist concentration and centralization, proletarianization/salariatization of the direct producing classes, the development of state intervention in the economy and society, and the growth of the world market and international capital. The second step is to explain why capitalism increasingly became subject to the "inevitability" of severe crises through the effects of preceding crises on the composition of capital and working class, role of the state, and so on, hence the changing character of the workers' struggles and the effects of these changes on the rate and mass of profit.

Latent Crisis Tendencies in Western Capitalist Development

Economic crisis is always latent within the capitalist mode of production, hence within any particular capitalist social formation. The reasons are twofold: first, the anarchy of the market threatens equilibria within and between the circuits of capital, e.g., between money capital and the supply of labor-power, physical requirements of production and available raw materials, and commodity supply and effective demand. Second, the capital-labor relationship itself creates economic (and social and political) contradictions between conditions of value and surplus value production, on the one hand, and effective demand and value realization, on the other. In the Western capitalist social formation, latent crisis tendencies historically became increasingly manifest for two general and closely related reasons: first, the development of the world market; second, capital concentration and centralization and the development of the proletariat (which, as we have seen, crises themselves accelerated).

The growth of world commodity markets in the nineteenth century speeded up increases in the number and kinds of commodity transactions, hence magnified possiblities of ruptures in the commodity circuit of capital. Similarly, the growth of more complex raw material and labor markets exaggerated possibilities of disorder within the money and productive circuits of capital. The development of the international market for money capital and the proliferation of credit instruments and institutions increased crisis potentials within the money and commodity circuits. Meanwhile, urbanization expanded "social density" and the complexity of commodity and money exchanges, hence increased crisis risks. Increases in the technical composition of capital and urbanization also created a "permanent" physical and spatial structure of capital which created new inflexibilities in the form of fixed capital, hence more crisis possibilities.

The growing fragility of the circulation sphere, in particular, was historically prefigured in the growing money and credit crises of the late nineteenth and early twentieth centuries, and was finally registered on a catastrophic scale in the Great Crash of 1929.

The same historical epoch witnessed increased concentration and centralization of capital and proletarianization. The polarization of capitalist classes and life chances (modified by the development of the "new middle class" or salariat and the growth of state employment) magnified the difference between "the conditions of exploitation and those of realizing exploitation," or the production and realization of surplus value. As Marx showed, capitalist development *itself* therefore increased the risk of traditional overproduction of capital. Capitalist development also increased related dangers of disproportionality crises. This danger was exacerbated by the growth of oligopolistic and monopolistic pricing policies. In sum, the risk of capital overproduction grew in proportion that productive capital increased in relation to the consumption power of society (the opposite danger of underproduction of capital, defined in the traditional sense of the diversion of capital to circulation expenses at the expense of productive capital, also potentially increased). This potential for a huge rupture between capital value production and effective demand and value realization increasingly exposed the capitalist system to the danger of a massive crisis – an economic time bomb historically presaged in the post-World War One crisis, but which exploded in the years 1929–33. It was the fragility of the sphere of circulation, combined with the growing disproportion between economic sectors and the contradiction between value and surplus value production and effective demand and value realization, which made the economic disaster of the 1930s so deep and long-lasting. It was also these economic processes (and Fascism, the war, postwar worldwide revolutionary movements, and the rise of Soviet power) which were the occasion for the massive restructuring of the Western capitalist system in the late 1940s and 1950s, as well as the reorganization of economic and political relationships with the old colonial world.

In this way, during the nineteenth and twentieth centuries, logical possibilities of crisis and expansion of the proletariat and capital concentration/centralization were more and more transformed into historical probabilities. *There was a greater probability of increased crisis/proletarianization and related tendencies precisely because of increased crisis/proletarianization.* Crises progressively resulted in more proletarianization, increased commodification of needs, expanded markets, increased capital concentration/centralization, etc., hence increased chances of more frequent and/or more severe crises. Increase in capital and proletariat and crisis risks were dialectically related historical processes. In this general sense, "the limit of capital" was in fact "capital itself."

Crisis Tendencies During Western Capitalist Development

Historical probabilities of crisis are by no means the same as historical "inevitabilities." In the West, the former presupposed the growth of the world commodity and money markets and concentration/centralization of capital and increase in proletariat. In orthodox Marxist theory, the latter presupposes the tendency of the falling rate of profit. The main reason that the rate of profit tends to fall is the increase in the organic composition of capital in the economy as a whole without offsetting increases in the rate of exploitation, cheapening of the costs of the elements of constant and variable capital, and/or reductions in the turnover time of capital. Movements in the composition of capital and rate of exploitation, in particular, need to be analyzed during the period of capitalist development within the general problematic of the theory of crisis, capital, and proletariat developed in the last chapter.[4]

In the early decades of Western capitalism, most branches of economic life were organized by small producers, organized trades, and village cooperatives, as well as capitalist workshops and manufactories, and rural "proto-industries." The amount of money capital required to establish a manufactory or small factory was relatively small; technology was underdeveloped, and labor processes in most branches of production and exchange were based on craft skills, heavy manual labor, and/or simple cooperation.

Under the impetus of growing European and New World colonial markets, more and more branches of the economy were capitalized and recapitalized. In this period, relatively large amounts of money capital found their way into undercapitalized industries and regions, or economic sectors in which the organic composition of capital was relatively low; relatively small amounts were advanced in sectors which already had become capitalized. The result of this pattern of capital accumulation was the expansion of sectors with a low and/or constant organic composition of capital relative to those sectors with a high and/or rising organic composition. The average organic composition in the system as a whole therefore increased relatively slowly.

This process of capital widening permitted Western capitalism to main-

---

[4] The crisis model used in this chapter is crude and meant to be suggestive only. A detailed and creative account of orthodox crisis theory is David Harvey, *The Limits to Capital* (Oxford, 1983).

tain a favorable rate of profit.[5] Capital widening inhibited the outbreak of economic crisis and, when crises did break out, acted as a kind of "insurance" against sharp and/or prolonged economic declines, as did the prevalence of local monopolies, inefficiencies in transportation, and other barriers to competition. Another result of the process of capital widening investments, in particular investments stimulated by economic hard times, was a relatively rapid increase of the proletariat. In newly capitalized industries in which labor was subject to deskilling and/or increased specialization, and which were increasingly integrated into the world market, there occurred an increase in proletarianization in the qualitative sense. Especially in sectors where the direct producers resisted crisis-induced capitalization, production became governed by the impersonal law of value more rapidly.

The major result of the capital widening model of accumulation was the *quantitative* growth of the proletariat. The proletariat increased in sheer numbers; more precapitalist and non-capitalist producers were displaced than were absorbed into capitalist wage labor in certain branches of agriculture and such industries as clothing, leather, woodworking, textiles, pottery, and household implements.[6] In these and other industries where the composition of capital was relatively low, post-crisis market expansions effectively increased the demand for labor-power and the absolute number of workers employed. However, the growth of the demand for labor-power was in diminishing proportion to the growth of the supply. Unemployment thus increased hand in hand with the expansion of employment. When material production hitherto organized on an independent or cooperative basis was swept aside by the tides of crisis and replaced by wage labor organized in capitalist workshops and factories, the result was the growth of a latent reserve army of labor which lacked organization and effective political ideology and fighting capacity.

The general effects of this model of early accumulation were reductions in the value of the average consumption basket; looser labor markets

[5] In terms of the *technical* composition of capital, capital widening means an increase in machinery with no increase in productivity (i.e., a quantitative extension of production), hence a proportional increase in employment given any increase in production. Capital deepening means an increase in more "productive" machinery, hence a decrease in the number of workers per unit of output.

[6] Certain branches of agriculture and raw material processing were the first sectors of the economy placed on a capitalist basis (see, for example, Raphael Samuel, "Workshops of the World: Steam Power and Hand Technology in Mid-Victorian England," *History Workshop*, 1976). In Western Europe, "deurbanization" in the seventeenth and eighteenth centuries was associated with the rise of capitalist agriculture and an agricultural proletariat, and the rapid population growth therein. The capitalization of wage goods industries typically followed (Richard Tilly, "Emerging Problems in Modern European History," MS, Jan. 1971).

which permitted capitalists periodically to increase hours and intensity of work; and a politically weak working class. Growing industrialist power within representative institutions and the state bureaucracy strengthened capital politically. Capitalization of raw materials production and processing reduced the cost of the elements entering into constant and variable capital. Increasing regional and world markets (grounded in colonial expansion and conquest and the growth of the white settler capitalist countries), together with improvements in transportation and communications, reduced the turnover time of capital. In sum, increases in the rate of exploitation more than kept pace with the moderate rise in the organic composition of capital, and the rapid spread of capitalism around the globe and into the countryside in the industrial countries, together with the conversion of profits into more and more productive capital, maintained relatively high levels of effective demand. Western capitalism was relatively crisis-free, and those crises which did break out were mild and/or short-lived compared with later ones.

This simple model, while not directly applicable to any particular country or region, highlights some of the important features of Western capitalist accumulation and crisis through the first two-thirds of the nineteenth century. However, during the "second Industrial Revolution" in the last decades of the nineteenth century, there occurred changes in both the composition of capital and the rate of exploitation which threatened the system with more frequent and/or deeper crises. As we have seen, in early capitalism, workers exercised considerable power in branches of the economy fabricating means of production ("branches" which were often simply departments within consumer good firms). In turn, worker power in consumer good industries presupposed that the technical composition of capital in means of production industries remained relatively low. "In the first century after the Industrial Revolution the organic composition of capital in [means of consumption industries] was, generally speaking, higher than in [means of production industries]. The genesis of industrial capital . . . must in fact be described as the machine-industrial production of consumer goods by means of hand-made machines."[7] While handmade machines permitted capital to subvert more traditional worker control of the labor process in consumer good industries, the development of the "real subsumption of labor" (abstract social labor) in these industries required higher degrees of capitalization of means of production industries.

During successive historical crises, capitalist competition (including national competition) and worker defensive struggles "forced" capital to increase the composition of capital in means of production industries.

---

[7] Mandel, *Late Capitalism*, 185.

"The point was reached when machines produced machines to construct other machines."[8] Post-crisis expansions of the world market which stretched existing productive capacity to the limit had a similar effect. The expansion of capacity in capital goods sectors in turn permitted rapid increases to occur in the technical composition of capital in consumer goods industries, so that consumer commodities were produced more cheaply. Precisely because the labor movement was weak and undeveloped, the effect was a dramatic increase in relative surplus value and the rate of exploitation. Meanwhile, larger portions of total money capital were advanced in the consumer goods sector where the composition of capital was relatively high. At the same time, new branches of both means of production and consumer goods industries were developed on a more advanced technical basis.

The general result of these trends was that the accumulation process increasingly assumed the form of capital deepening. The average organic composition of capital increased, which tended to depress the average rate of profit. The major offsets were twofold: first, the persistent economically and politically weak position of the proletariat in mass production industries, which permitted capitalist firms to increase absolute surplus value; second, capital deepening in capital goods (i.e., "the mechanization of machine-building"), which resulted in large increases in productivity in consumer goods, with the result that relative surplus value increased sharply in the system as a whole.

Agriculture and raw material production were partial exceptions. In England, excepting the threshing machine, harvest tools and methods were about the same in 1850 as in 1750.[9] By contrast, the USA, from an early date, experimented with many advances in agricultural technology. Then "a transformation occurred in the technology of the sub-department of [means of production industries] producing *circulating* constant capital – the production of raw materials." Ernest Mandel describes this change as "the transition from the production of raw materials by handicrafts to their production on the lines of manufactures or early industry."[10] The capitalization of raw materials, increase in the technical composition of capital, and recomposition of the work force occurred when consumer

---

[8] Ibid. Capitalization of machine-building and other means of production industries was greatly aided by the cycle of imperialist rivalries, during which nation-states periodically played an active role in rationalizing production in shipbuilding, metals, and other war-related sectors. The full capitalization of agriculture (historically delayed because of the relatively long turnover time of capital in food and raw material production) also depended on the growth of capital goods industries producing farm machinery, chemicals, etc.

[9] David H. Morgan, "The Place of Harvesters in Nineteenth Century Village Life," in Raphael Samuel, ed., *Village Life and Labour* (London, 1975), 30.

[10] Mandel, *Late Capitalism*, 186.

good industries were relatively capitalized, hence when the capitalist system as a whole required mass-produced foodstuffs and elements of constant and variable capital – that is, when proletarianization and urbanization as a whole reached a certain critical mass. Finally, the capitalization of raw materials production, together with capital deepening in fixed capital goods production, "determined – to a varying degree – a significant increase in the organic composition of capital in [means of production industries as a whole]."[11]

By the last decade of the nineteenth century, the growing integration of science into industry, concentration and centralization of bank capital, external economies of scale, forward and backward "linkage" effects, and the growing world market reinforced capitalist accumulation both in relatively advanced and in backward sectors, with the result that the organic composition of capital increased to higher and higher levels. During economic booms, industrial workers temporarily benefited from their structural power within big capitalist enterprises, which, in turn, encouraged capital to expel more living labor from production, increasing the organic composition of capital still more. "The fundamental element of this tendency towards the rise in the organic composition of capital is . . . the predisposition of the capitalist to save the greatest amount of variable capital and to replace it progressively with constant capital. And this is due essentially to the *development of the labor movement*, to the emphasis on class struggle, to the deterioration of capital's power vis-à-vis labor."[12] Subsequently came a transformation in the mechanics of the system as a whole. In early stages of capitalist development, capital increased the rate of exploitation to offset unfavorable effects of increases in the composition of capital on the rate of profit. In later stages, capital began to increase the composition of capital to offset unfavorable effects of reductions in the rate of exploitation. The contradictory result was to increase risks of overproduction of capital.

Difficulties in raising the exploitation rate were exacerbated by changes in the make-up of the reserve army of labor. During successive crises in the last half of the nineteenth century, the composition of the unemployed shifted. There were relatively more experienced wage laborers and relatively fewer fresh recruits from the latent labor reserves in the countryside. This was the result of the general process of capitalist accumulation and proletarianization, increasingly pronounced cyclical movements because of growing fixed capital investments, and the "structural crisis" of the late nineteenth century. Meanwhile, cities grew faster and the proletariat became a bigger fraction of city populations. Bourgeois struggles against

[11] Ibid., 187.
[12] Castells, *Economic Crisis*, 18.

feudal and Absolutist traces sometimes assumed the form of "urban versus rural" ("modern versus pre-modern") conflicts and urban bourgeois/ worker alliances against landed wealth/peasant/rural populations. The urban labor reserves, and urban workers generally, thus were more experienced and geographically concentrated, and sometimes better situated politically. These changes, among others, made it harder for capital to increase the rate of exploitation to offset the growing value composition of capital.[13] Meanwhile, growing competition between national capitals periodically increased "overproduction" of commodities and the turnover time of capital. All these factors, together with the persistence of craft and skilled worker resistance to increased exploitation when the rise in value composition of capital threatened the rate and mass of profits, increased crisis risks and the dangers of prolonged crisis. In the USA, between 1873 and 1920, capital deepening in manufacturing dramatically pushed down the rate of profit.[14] However, crises remained the main mechanism which periodically weakened traditional worker resistance and also "modern" working-class economic struggles. Meanwhile, two other offsetting factors to the tendency of the rate of profit to fall came into play. The first was the development of new sources of foodstuffs, agricultural raw materials, minerals, and fuels in the white settler capitalist countries and the colonies. The second was the survival of traditional communities, the reproduction of independent production, small-scale capital, the "competitive sector," and classic "self-exploitation," which maintained traditional conditions of reproduction of labor-power, hence reducing the amount of money capital required to be advanced for variable capital.

In sum, Western capitalism developed as a *relatively* crisis-free system (although less and less so as time went on) until the twentieth century, especially until the 1930s, when both capital and consumer goods industries were highly capitalized, that is, when the industrial proletariat and salariat were more or less "fully" formed.[15] Because the internal contradiction of capital is "capital itself," the great crisis was postponed until the "full" development of the traditional model of industrial capitalism. The "break-down" of capitalism in the 1930s was, therefore, the result not only of the absence of clear national leadership in the imperialist world system but also of the organic composition of capital in capital goods catching up

[13] Giovanni Arrighi, "Towards a Theory of Capitalist Crisis," *New Left Review*, Sept.–Oct. 1978, 6.

[14] Mike Davis, " 'Fordism' in Crisis: A Review of Michel Aglietta's *Régulation et Crises: L'Expérience des Etats-Unis*," *Review*, 2, 2, Fall 1978.

[15] The completion of the development of the modern working class/salariat did not occur until the 1960s and 1970s, when there developed rapid capitalization of services previously produced within the household and community economy. This development lowered the average organic composition of capital, hence was a factor holding up the rate of profit.

with, and finally surpassing, consumer goods capitalization. Despite the fact that in the 1920s consumer good capitals rapidly increased circulation or selling expenses with the aim of reducing circulation time, the expansion of capital goods production resulted in a big increase in capital's share of total values. The fresh purchasing power thrown into the market by the "new middle class" or salariat was not enough to prevent the development of classic conditions of overproduction of capital, which culminated in the great devaluation of capital in the Great Depression. It was only in the post-World War Two period that an "intensive regime of accumulation" developed in forms which, at least for two decades, solved the traditional problem of capital overproduction.[16]

Conclusion

This rough sketch of Western capitalist accumulation and crisis has neglected the role of individual nation-states and their uneven development and imperialist rivalries. In any particular period, the conjuncture of capital composition, working-class composition, circulation time of capital, and costs of the elements of capital differed in particular countries and regions. In this way, there developed different conjunctures of worker struggles, rates of exploitation and profit, and risks of crisis. Crucial determinants were the form of the nation-state, the relation between the state and the national economy, and the relationship between imperialist states, which played different roles in different countries at different times in capitalist accumulation, and processes of crisis prevention, crisis management, and crisis resolution. The model of "crisis-induced modern-ization" presented in the last chapter and the model of "modernization-induced crisis" sketched in this chapter thus cannot be applied directly to particular conjunctures in different regions, countries, and historical periods. However, the model of "crisis created proletariat/proletariat created crisis" (and "crisis created capitalist concentration/centralization/vice versa, etc.") may be regarded as an underlying structural process in Western capitalist development, which was played out through the media-tions of politics and state policies, international rivalries, and cultural and

[16] See Davis, " 'Fordism' in Crisis ." Aglietta's pathbreaking work insists on the importance of worker struggles in the transition from what he calls "extensive" accumula-tion to "intensive" accumulation after World War Two. The weakest part of his thesis is the claim that the former corresponded roughly to the phase of absolute surplus value produc-tion, while the latter is associated with relative surplus value production. The most powerful part is his focus on the revolution in the conditions of reproduction of labor-power under "Fordism," i.e., the mass development of the commodity form of need satisfaction, product competition, etc.

other changes. Concrete analyses of concrete situations thus require careful study of regional, sectoral, and national-state developments and the connections between these developments in different countries and regions within the world capitalist economy as a whole.

Despite widely different, typically crisis-inspired state initiatives in different countries, the unbearable tension between massive overproduction of capital and massive proletarianization everywhere matured in the late 1920s and early 1930s. This tension and its resolution in the crisis of the 1930s also manifested itself differently in different countries. The ways that the crisis was politically administered was also widely disparate. New forms of government and state structures developed in the Depression ranged from fascist blood purges to the first systematic attempts in the USA to soften the dominant ideology of "natural rights individualism" with "utilitarian individualism," and to politically and culturally integrate the working class. Finally, the economic crisis was resolved by World War Two, which resulted in the massive slaughter of capital values in proportion to the massive slaughter of people. Under the hegemony of the USA, the West's tragic groping toward a new economic and political international order gave capitalism a new lease on life despite the "loss" of China and East Europe. The massive restructuring of economic organization, political systems, state structures, world markets and monetary systems, social life, and international political relations, from the end of the war through the mid-70s, placed Western capitalism on a new and increasingly contradictory footing. As we will see, in the same way that the proletariat and capital concentration/centralization became less "crisis-created" and more "crisis-creating," state structures, programs, and policies which were the result of historical economic crises became by the 1970s "relatively autonomous" causes of crisis.

4

The Money and Commodity Circuits of Capital and the Modern Economic Struggle

Introduction

In the postwar period, the development of capitalist concentration and centralization, abstract social labor, and the modern state placed American capitalism on new economic, social, political, and ideological footings. The focus of the present study is the new social-ideological conditions of reproduction of the working class/salariat within the productive circuit of capital and the so-called fourth and fifth circuits of capital (private household consumption and public or social consumption). The aim is to show that these new conditions of economic and social reproduction resulted in a growing crisis of underproduction of capital; first, in the traditional sense of insufficient productive utilization of surplus value; second, in the "revisionist" sense of insufficient surplus value production.

An essential preliminary task is to analyze the development of modern working-class economism. Economism is defined as the struggle for higher wages and shorter hours in the money circuit of capital; the fight to lower prices and increase consumer and mortgage credit (as well as to expand public credit destined for social services and transfer payments) in the commodity circuit of capital; and the relationshp between these struggles and the accumulation crisis.[1] A second preliminary task is to analyze the

[1] The analysis of economic struggles and their effects on profits and accumulation falls into the tradition established by such modern writers as Andrew Glyn and Bob Sutcliffe, Giovanni Arrighi, Robert Rowthorn, Thomas Weiskopf, and Samuel Bowles and Herbert Gintis. Key texts include Glyn and Sutcliffe's *British Capitalism: Workers and the Profits Squeeze* (Baltimore, 1972); Rowthorn's Review of *Late Capitalism*, in *New Left Review*, 98, July–Aug 1976; Thomas Weiskopf's "Marxian Crisis Theory and the Rate of Profit in the Post-War U.S. Economy," *Cambridge Journal of Economics*, Dec. 1979; and Bowles and Gintis' "The Crisis of Liberal Democratic Capitalism: The Case of the United States," *Politics and Society*, 11, 2, 1982. Also, the "autonomia" tradition is essential to the following analysis. For example, Bruno Ramirez, "The Working Class Struggle Against the Crisis: Self-Reduction of Prices in Italy," *Zerowork*, 1, Dec. 1975.

closely related development of large-scale capitalist exchange relationships in the commodity circuit of capital, in particular, the development of
product competition, and the relationship between product competition,
working-class economism and the accumulation crisis.

The Labor Market and Modern Working-Class Economic Struggle

The theoretical point of departure for the study of working-class economic
struggle and its relation to the mass and rate of profit and capitalist
accumulation is the premise that the wage demand, demand for credit,
struggles to lower prices, and so on are "independent of the process of
capital," or an expression of "necessary labor for itself" rather than that of
"labor for capital."[2] The opposing premise of Marxist orthodoxy is that
the rate of accumulation and the reserve army of labor regulate the wage
rate in favor of capital, and that capitalist crises periodically reproduce the
reserve army. This was a reasonable position in the epoch of Western
capitalist development, i.e., proletarianization of the direct producing
classes and the creation of a latent reserve army of labor. It remains a
reasonable position in relation to the analysis of present-day world capitalism as a whole. However, the possibility that economic struggles combined with the expansion of consumer and public credit and new forms of
capitalist competition and technical change might effectively increase the
consumption basket and/or its value content – thereby creating risks of a
crisis of underproduction of capital – was never considered by Marx and
remains alien to modern Marxist orthodoxy.

"Necessary labor for itself" may be defined in both quantitative and
qualitative terms. The quantitative definition pertains to the struggle to
"get more for less," i.e., to reduce labor-time to a minimum, meanwhile
expanding money income and commodity consumption to a maximum.
The qualitative definition of "necessary labor for itself" pertains to struggles
against reified production relationships and capitalist concepts of space
and time and life meanings. In the following chapters, "necessary labor for
itself" will be analyzed in terms of the operation and self-negation of:
dominant managerial ideologies and practices of individualism within the
production process; the satisfaction of needs in the commodity form; and
ideological forms of reproduction of the working class/salariat by and
within the state. However, at the "phenomenal" level of the money
and commodity circuits of capital, the working-class struggle to self-
valorize its labor-power depends, in the first instance, on the supply and

[2] Toni Negri, *Marx after Marx*, English translation, unpublished MS, ch. 7, 6.

demand for labor-power, the degree of solidarity and organization within the working class, and the legitimacy of the working class in the state and society as a whole.

In the present model of postwar US capitalism, the analysis of the demand and supply of labor-power presupposes that latent labor reserves were exhausted or in various ways economically neutralized, i.e., that the working class in effect monopolized the supply of labor-power. The major reason was the more or less full capitalization of agriculture, hence the contraction of latent labor reserves in the countryside, and the "capitalization" of the household economy and proletarianization of women. This analysis also presupposes that productivity increases were insufficient to replenish the reserve army and/or that social and political conditions changed in ways which caused the reserve army to cease to function as the "lever of accumulation."

On these assumptions, capitalism lost its " 'normal' flexibility,"[3] which created upward pressures on wages and salaries, prices, interest rates, and budgetary deficits. Moreover, declining latent labor reserves combined with the politicization of unemployment undermined the function of unemployment as a basic mechanism of capitalist accumulation in relation to wage rates and structures, worker motivation and incentives, labor discipline and social integration generally.[4] This loss of flexibility and the development of an "increasingly reliable indigenous working class"[5] was highly significant from the standpoint of the traditional Marxist theory of accumulation, which defines the reserve army as the "lever of capitalist accumulation."

The size of the reserve army may be regarded as the "background variable" in the analysis of wages, prices, and profits. Historically, tight labor markets were necessary but not sufficient conditions for successful economic struggles. In postwar USA, the "key variables" were the degree and kind of cooperation or unity within fractions of employed and unemployed workers and between the employed and unemployed as a whole and the legitimacy and power of the working class in the state and society as a whole. The crucial role of coordination and direction of worker organizations in determining wages has been documented by many

---

[3] The expression " 'normal' flexibility" is Samir Amin's ("Some Thoughts on Self-Reliant Development, Collective Self-Reliance and the New International Economic Order," unpublished MS, undated, 25).

Some writers stress the short-run relationships between supply and demand for labor-power. It has often been said that short-run expansions which bring high or full employment in *modern* capitalism are inconsistent with maximum profitability because real wages grow and labor productivity falls owing to growing absenteeism, quit rates, and problems of labor discipline (e.g., J. Crotty and L. Rapping, "The 1975 Report of the President's Council of Economic Advisors," *American Economic Review*, Dec. 1975, 796).

historians.[6] Sociologists have also stressed the importance of labor organization and political strength (rather than tight labor markets, which were more conjunctural) in wage struggles.[7] It has been shown that strikes and economic conflict depended less on the phase of the capitalist cycle than on the mobilization of working-class organizations, organizational capabilities, and political acceptability.[8]

In the USA, there were many attempts in the nineteenth and early twentieth centuries to establish the rudiments of national labor unity. However, the preconditions of working-class unity defined in terms of the development of abstract social labor were not present until the 1920s. Not until the 1930s was industrial worker unity established in principle, albeit not always or often in practice. Another factor affecting the analysis of working-class unity in the USA was the form and content of union alliances with other classes and class fractions. In the USA, organized labor at times sought the political support not only of minorities and the poor, but also of farmers, small business, and professional groups. Still another factor is that any full evaluation of the forms and goals of worker organization has to take into account the cycles of international struggles within the framework of world capitalism and imperialism.

In the USA, three general points may be mentioned in relation to the development of worker unity within and between productive workers and the reserve armies of labor. First, the dominant ideology of individualism and its identification with the American nation militated against class consciousness and praxis oriented to non-economistic working-class goals. A second and closely related point is that the absence of the commune tradition and guild system, which defined in many ways the meaning of European socialism, freed the American working class to concentrate on economic gains and economic reform (business unionism, job consciousness, etc.). Until the 1940s, nowhere else was the slogan "take politics out of the unions and unions out of politics" so prevalent. Third, the populist

---

[4] Bowles and Gintis, "Crisis of Liberal Democratic Capitalism."

[5] S. Markovits and S. Kazarinov, "Class Conflict, Capitalism, and Social Democracy," *Comparative Politics*, April 1978, 384.

[6] For example, see Edward Shorter and Charles Tilly, *Strikes in France, 1830–1968* (London, 1974), 338.

[7] Marino Regini, "Changing Relationships Between Labour Unions and the State in Italy: Towards a Neo-Corporatist System?" in G. Lehmbruch and P. Schmitter, eds., *Variations in the Pattern of Corporatist Policy Formation*, vol. II (London, 1980). If wage advances come about merely because of tight labor markets, planned recessions are enough to correct any "disequilibriums" which ensue.

[8] David Snyder, "Institutional Setting and Industrial Conflict," *American Sociological Review*, June 1975, 40. Snyder tested this thesis for different periods in the USA, Italy, and France.

and imperialist nature of the development of the USA nation-state meant that the developing proletariat was not only multiethnic, multiracial, and multicultural in character but also divided in relation to America's "imperialist destiny." This helps to explain the defeats of early worker struggles in mass production where the labor force was primarily made up of women and/or oppressed ethnic and racial minorities, and hence not regarded as "mainstream labor." Worker struggles were thus relatively isolated, lacked political resources and goals, and were easy to defeat. The major exceptions were early industrial conflicts which occurred within ethnic communities where workers were able to win local support for their struggles with capital. However, oppressed nationalities and minorities normally received little if any support (and were often the objects of antagonism) from "nativist" craft unions and organizations. Other cultural differences may also be mentioned. European-American skilled workers typically earned a "family wage," and a "wife at home" was included in the skilled male worker's standard of living. This was not normally true of oppressed minorities and new ethnic/national groups, hence relations within the family and community were established on a different material basis in new immigrant communities. While the relationship between the ethnic/racial and the industrial/occupational composition of the work-force began to break down in the 1920s, intra-ethnic/national unity was often established outside of the framework of "mainstream" labor.

The transition to "full capitalist" worker organizations and economic struggles occurred in the period between the early 1900s and the 1930s. These were the years when capitalization in capital goods industries began to catch up with and/or surpass capitalization in wage good industries and also when new wage good industries developed on a mass production basis. The result was the development of abstract social labor across industrial boundaries, hence new possibilities of cooperation within the ranks of the employed and between the employed and unemployed. In the 1920s, however, "welfare capitalism," ethnic divisions, and "Red scare," among other factors, made these possibilities more formal than real.

The pressing need for working-class cooperation was not obvious until the 1930s precisely because of the consequences of its absence in the 1920s. In that decade, workers became increasingly conscious of their collective potential, although it was not exploited effectively because of the absence of generalized economic crisis.[9] Very briefly, the explanation is

[9] "While the foreign born, the semiskilled, and the unskilled had accepted their lot in silence, in the twenties this docility began to change. The inferior workmen began to recognize that they constituted an overwhelming majority of the labor world and that they were a potential power" (Joseph G. Rayback, *History of American Labor*, New York, 1963, 346).

that wage payments in capital goods relatively to wage goods industries did not increase enough to prevent a deadly combination of realization and disproportionality crises (both insufficiencies of total demand and disproportionalities between the demand for and supply of wage goods) and an overall shift to profits in the 1920s.[10] Besides sectoral disproportions between wages, employment, production, and profits, the weakness of the working-class movement inhibited increases in average wages, which exacerbated both realization and disproportionality crisis tendencies. The failure to transform incipient class consciousness into organized economic and political power in the 1920s in this way helped to create the conditions (the crisis of the 1930s) in which the need for collective worker power became overwhelmingly manifest.

In the early years, the Depression divided the working class even more deeply, forcing workers to accept large-scale unemployment, wage reductions, and speedups, at the same time strengthening traditions reinforcing white male supremist and racist attitudes and practices. In 1933–34, however, the struggle for mass working-class unity across ethnic/national boundaries (albeit in a context in which issues of the specific conditions of women workers and oppressed minorities were unresolved) began to develop. These included the general strikes of 1934; the new organizations of the unemployed led by the Communist Party; the struggles against racism, speedup and wage cuts and deterioration of working conditions (also led by Communists, among others); John L. Lewis and Roosevelt's mutual aid pact and the mutual aid agreement between Lewis and the Communists. The struggles of the working class in coalmining and the clothing industry, where small capitals were eager to control price competition directly, and also indirectly through wage regulation, prefigured the explosions of workers in large-scale industry. The result was Sidney Hillman and John L. Lewis' support for the corporatist National Recovery Act (NRA) and the new beginnings of industrial acceptance of wage stabilization and unionism. The CIO, organized by these corporatist leaders, among others, was legitimated by the New Deal in the mid-1930s. The Wagner Act ratified and reinforced the corporatist victories in the garment trades and soft coal mines. Besides the pivotal role of Hillman and Lewis, two overlapping processes developed as both cause and consequence of the Wagner Act: first, the workers' autonomous struggle against capitalist "laws of motion," i.e., wage reductions, speedup, reproduction of

[10] Sidney Coontz, *Productive Labour and Effective Demand* (New York, 1966), 151. This underrated book shows, among other things, that stagnation in the capital goods sector and associated displacement of labor inhibited increases in consumption. Also reinforcing crisis tendencies hidden in the accumulation process in the 1920s was the rise in the composition of capital in the consumer goods sector.

the reserve army as a lever of accumulation, etc., in large-scale industry; second, the union-organizing drives to channel these struggles into collective bargaining and (by 1944) formal political action. The capitalist class opposed the Wagner Act because it provided the framework within which workers were able to sell their labor-power collectively without also permitting capitalists to combine to fix supply prices – as they were able to do under the NRA. The Wagner Act was thus a great victory for unorganized labor because it established the ground rules for the collective determination of wages and organization of unions. Other fractions which made up the New Deal supported (failed to oppose) the Wagner Act because it held out possibilities for social peace, increased consumer spending and the revival of commerce, and industrial recovery.

The Wagner Act and the National Labor Relations Board helped to prevent the development of labor as an independent political force. The victory of industrial unionism and collective bargaining, in particular, prevented the development of a labor party. Collective bargaining, however, did not simply "integrate" the working class into American capitalism. The power of the working class expressed itself in other forms. Struggles in the labor market and workplace in the late 1940s, 1960s, and early 1970s dispelled the myth that collective bargaining and the "regularization" of labor-management relations would end militancy and strike action. To the degree that industrial unions presented themselves as mechanisms of social and political integration, they acquired considerable political influence. Furthermore, the disciplinary functions of industrial unionism *within* the working class (or the struggle against competition in the labor market and in production, which utilized organization, persuasion, mutual aid, and, at times, violence) should not be overlooked.

Unity at the level of industrial unionism was the pivotal change in the history of the class struggle in the USA. First, industrial unionism weakened capital's control of the length of the working day, week, and year. Until World War One, "for the vast majority of workers throughout the world there was virtually no limitation on hours of work other than that arising out of custom."[11] Capital opposed shorter hours "not only because of their possible cost and economic consequences, but also on the grounds that leisure for workers was dangerous."[12]

The demand for an eight-hour day (six-day week) originated in the nineteenth century (Robert Owen, First International, etc.). However, not until World War One did political conditions force most capitalist governments to grant the 48-hour work week *de jure*; by 1930, most European

[11] Archibald, A. Evans, "Work and Leisure, 1919–1969," *International Labour Review*, 99, 1, Jan. 1969, 36.
[12] Ibid., 35.

industrial workers had won this demand *de facto*. In the USA, during the Depression, while most unions rejected work-sharing at the plant level, the 40-hour week established by Fair Labor Standards legislation helped to put a floor on wages, meanwhile exemplifying labor unity at the political level. After World War Two, all the advanced industrial countries established the "normal work day," "weekends," and "vacations." Weekly hours were reduced to 40 hours (from 59 hours in 1899)[13] not only because of increases in productivity, but also because of the development of social abstract labor and industrial worker unity. After the war, the "struggle against work" appeared as the demand to work fewer days per year and for more frequent breaks, increases in medically sanctioned absenteeism, and earlier retirement and longer school years. These struggles universally "raised the economic ante" as well as laying the groundwork for the demand for a 35-hour week.

Second, industrial unionism created the basis for the "limitless" demand for higher wages and consumption (which may be contrasted with early wage struggles to protect traditional wage levels and income differentials and to maintain "customary standards"[14]). After World War Two, the strikes of 1945–46 reminded large-scale capital and the state of the new power of the industrial working class. Industrial labor quickly won "peace wages" which were equivalent to wartime wages (capital replied with Taft-Hartley in 1947, which included a ban on secondary boycotts and hence tried to "illegalize" class solidarity). Third, the struggle to normalize the intensity of work, which tended to "freeze" absolute surplus value production, reaped its first successes after the war.

Even in the shadow of Taft-Hartley, there developed annual wage increases, cost-of-living adjustments for the strongest unions, the detailed elaboration of fringe benefits, regular grievance procedures, and successful resistance against compulsory arbitration. Older capitalist welfare ideologies were discredited and rejected. Industry-wide bargaining (which in the 1970s was increasingly undermined by the growth of conglomerate capitals and the internationalization of production) helped to fight capital's attempts to undercut union scales. Informal cooperation mechanisms such as loose amalgamations of locals of international unions, district councils, joint boards, and trade councils were replaced or supplemented by more

[13] John Durand, *The Labor Force in the United States, 1890–1940* (New York, 1948), 21.

[14] In early capitalism, "many saw money as something to be saved and consolidated so as to replenish and revitalize their connection to a customary means of survival . . . For the non-industrial people who came to populate industrial America, the wage system represented an intrinsic violation of a basic assumption, customarily derived from a sensual proximity to nature. Hence, the common compulsion among early immigrants to *save*, to appropriate money as *if it were land*" (Stuart and Liz Ewen, "Americanization and Consumption," *Telos*, 37, Fall 1978, 44, 45).

formal cooperation, especially forms of coalition bargaining, which established common termination dates on all labor contracts signed by a single
corporation or industry.[15] "Leapfrogging" of wage demands and settle-
ments increased with more intense union rivalries, and also increased
union sensitivity to wage differentials between occupations and industries,
which was one source of inter-union competition.[16] By the late 1970s,
when unions were once again on the defensive, more worker organizations
were considering the utilization of "pension fund power" as a weapon in
the economic struggle.[17]

Meanwhile, "tandem" salary adjustments protected the economic position of some white-collar workers, although wage and salary differentials,
in fact, significantly declined. Seniority became more important for job
security, stable income, and higher wages; no longer did capital have such
a free hand to use the reserve labor army as the "lever of accumulation."
Meantime, with the formation of the Committee of Political Education in
1944, local labor political action committees, financial support for "labor"
elected officials, the development of big labor's veto over Democratic Party
presidential candidates, and the growth of state agencies and bureaucrats
beholden to labor clientele, among other changes, the working class,
typically within "interest-group liberal forms," began to employ political
means to advance the economic struggle in more systematic ways. Politically, the working class expressed itself as such in national elections; not
symbols or personalities, but hard economic issues were the magnets
which attracted working-class votes.[18] Mediated by family, ethnic, and
religious loyalties, workers seemed to develop an unshakeable economistic
class consciousness (albeit in individualistic and nationalistic forms) in the
labor and commodity markets, and also in politics in so far as political
struggles were means to individualistic/familist economic ends. The effect
of these changes, even in the face of the diffusion of deskilling into office
work and the rise of low productivity service industries, was substantial.
Average real wages increased by more than one-third between 1947 and
1965; wage and salary income expanded even more in large-scale industry;
real wages rose even during recessions.

These victories, however, were won in part at the expense of workers in

[15] William N. Cernish, *Coalition Bargaining: A Study of Union Tactics and Public Policy*
(Philadelphia, 1969), 11, 29, 31.
[16] Joan Robinson favorably cites labor economist Phelps Brown, who writes that "when
some earnings move up sharply and others are left behind the disparity is usually felt to be
unfair. Those who try to catch up are seen not just as demanding 'more for me' but as trying to
right a wrong" (quoted in "Latter Day Capitalism," *Contributions to Modern Economics*,
New York, 1978, 235).
[17] "More Unions Brandish Money as a Weapon," *Business Week*, Feb. 26, 1979, 47.
[18] Richard Hamilton, *Class and Politics in the United States* (New York, 1972).

small-scale industry and trade, the labor reserve army, and peasants and workers in the Third World. Inflation of wage good prices combined with relatively low wages in small-scale capital and even lower welfare incomes to impoverish unemployed, subemployed, and underemployed workers relative to unionized workers.

Awareness of inequalities within the working class – inequalities closely associated with racism and sexism – increased apace. Gathering force in the late 1950s and early 1960s, the reserve army of labor exploded politically in the mid-1960s and 1970s. Unlike earlier stages of capitalism, when radicalism sprang from the "debased trades" rather than the new, urbanized surplus population, in the 1960s the radical economic struggle was organized by the urban masses. The class issue was raised in race, national, and gender forms. The struggles of blacks and other oppressed minorities, women, the elderly, handicapped, and other ascriptive groups constituted in effect a massive political recomposition of the working class in the 1960s and 1970s. The result was the rapid expansion of the welfare state in the 1960s and early 19760s rooted in rioting, new forms of organization, and new protest movements. The McGovern candidacy exemplified these new historical conditions of the struggle for working-class unity in which oppressed minorities and women in particular were becoming more "legitimate" groups in the state and society.

In this way, underemployed and unemployed workers joined workers in large-scale industry in voicing the demand for "more," which strengthened union control of money wages, hence economic struggles generally. "What we have witnessed over the last 40 years has been the phase of militant economic struggles by the working class and the assimilation of blacks into these economic struggles . . . All each group is interested in is 'more' – more wages, more benefits, more goods . . . as each group has become more incorporated into the system, its members have become more individualistic, more consumer-oriented."[19] New struggles of grocery-chain workers, teamsters, hospital workers, and, above all, state workers, for unionization, better wages and fringe benefits reinforced the vitality of working-class economism. Between 1958 and 1968 there was a 46 per cent rise in white-collar union membership. Although the unionization rate of clerical workers generally remained about 10 per cent, by 1981 roughly one-half of state and local government workers were unionized by the State, County and Municipal Workers; Teachers; and Service Employees. Farm workers, social-industrial complex employees, professional and semiprofessional groups, and others discovered the power of collective and political means to individual economic ends. These combined gains

[19] James Boggs, "Beyond Militancy," *Monthly Review*, 26, 4, Sept. 1974, 41.

more than made up for the loss of union members in declining industrial sectors in absolute terms (union membershp rose from 19.8 million in 1970 to 20.5 million in 1978), albeit not in relative terms (union members in relation to total employment dropped from 28 to 23.6 per cent during the same period).

In the 1970s and early 1980s, new "rainbow coalitions" (including attempts to resolve conflicting seniority and affirmative action claims), community and Church coalitions, local unity between trade union locals and minority organizations (and, at times, international solidarity groups), community organizing approaches to unionizing workers, and steps toward national unity between hitherto antagonistic national unions, civil rights and women's organizations, and reformist political groups exemplified new attempts to forge "cooperation between employed and unemployed." Structural economic changes which led to an expansion of employment in weakly organized industries and a decline in jobs in well organized branches of the economy compelled organized labor to try to extend its political influence and base into the "community" (today less "ethnic" than "working-class").[20] These moves, in turn, inspired some unions to support local political action, especially demands to defend social services. Some unions were also pressed to try to represent the marginal work force in order to maintain their legitimacy and political strength in the context of rising employment in the "informal economy" and small-scale industry and declining employment in large-scale industry. By the late 1970s, every fraction of the working class, including workers employed by small-scale capital and in branch plants of large-scale capital located in new regions of accumulation, developed richer and more complex, albeit more contradictory, union-community-ethnic-gender consciousness.

At the same time, however, new anti-working class forces and tendencies gathered strength. These included the computer revolution, which produced not only more rapid and complex communications but also new "strike breakers" which destroyed the air controllers' union and weakened the communications workers. Blue Cross workers were outmaneuvered by communications satellites which shifted insurance accounts from struck offices to facilities in strike-free cities. Control of technology and its deployment thus became more of a "class issue" than ever before. Moreover, the development of new industry in anti-union States, the inter-

[20]   In recent years in the USA "ethnic identifiers [people who identify themselves in terms of their membership of a given ethnic group] are increasingly individuals with mixed ethnic ancestry, who are likely to have a muted ethnic identity" (Richard D. Alba and Mitchell B. Chamlin, "A Preliminary Examination of Ethnic Identification Among Whites," *American Sociological Review*, 48, April 1983, 240).

nationalization of capital, growing resentment by many white workers against the welfare system, fatal weaknesses in the political machines in the older industrial cities, and the destruction of traditional Democratic Party coalitions also undermined established union power and the influence of welfare rights, women, and other organizations and movements which developed in the 1960s and 1970s. These sharp reversals in large part originated in the accumulation crisis itself, as well as the closely associated revival of racism and "male" and "welfare backlash."

This rough sketch of half a century of economic struggle underscores the changes which came about with the development of a "full capitalist" working class. Unionism in the USA (like British laborism, German social democracy, Italian communism, and many other national working-class struggles) was by and large economistic. Economic demands replaced political demands because of the recomposition of the working class and because workers acquired more political legitimacy and political and social rights. This does not mean that the workers' movement, broadly defined, ceased to be political. However, politics consisted of collective struggle, bargaining, and compromise for individual/familist material ends, hence was ultimately self-defeating.

The universal demand for more wages, more money, and more commodities restructured the capitalist economic apparatus, including economic incentives and social motivations. The center of this restructuring process was "consumerism" and the preponderance of wage good industries and services in the economy. Economic restructuring, in turn, had independent effects on class composition which reinforced economism. The growth of the salariat and working class in sales, advertising, public relations, finance, real estate, and related employments was, in part, the result of the wage and economic struggles of the industrial working class and reserve armies. Similarly, the growth of state workers and employees, especially in the welfare bureaucracies, was largely explicable in terms of the welfare struggle and political attempts to contain the black movement and other movements for social change. In turn, workers and salariat in these new growth sectors expanded demand for money and wage goods, employment in consumer good industries, and the circle of economistic demands generally.

The Commodity Market and Modern Capitalist Product Competition

As we saw in Chapter 2, capitalist enterprises historically modernized production processes and organizational and other structures in the crucible of economic crises. Chapter 3 set out to show that crisis-inspired revolutions in the productive forces and production relations expanded productivity, lowered the cost of wages, and increased potential relative surplus value. Because the working class was undeveloped and weak and engaged in defensive struggles, productivity growth was reflected only sporadically in higher wages and improved conditions of work. For this reason, it became common for potential increases in surplus value, based on technical changes which lowered the value content of the average consumption basket, to be realized in fact.

In the last section, it was shown that the modern, organized working class overcame the limits of earlier struggles and established annual wage increases, moderated the ups and downs of the capitalist cycle, reduced hours of work, etc. Meanwhile, concentrated/centralized capitalist enterprises became permanent "bureaucracies." Capitalist accumulation increasingly depended on organizational coherence, long-term planning, political stability, cooperation between large corporations and the state, and most importantly in the context of the present argument, new consumer product development and product competition. Capitalism's inner compulsion to revolutionize the productive forces remained as powerful as ever. However, the form which this compulsion assumed changed markedly in the modern epoch. First, large-scale capital's struggle to monopolize "technological rents" resulted in various kinds of monopolies of new technology, which inhibited not technical change per se but rather the diffusion of technique and hence generalized increases in productivity. Second, traditional price competition became incompatible with modern large-scale capital. The development of technological discontinuities in production "generate[d] an industrial structure . . . congenitally incompatible with [price] competition. . . . If . . . all concerted action among oligopolies . . . [was] abolished, the result would not be price flexiblity but price chaos."[21] More, price competition became incompatible with large-scale capital's drive for monopolistic market power independent of the degree of technological discontinuity within a particular enterprise or industry.[22] Finally, price competition was modified or abandoned when the working class began to exercise significant power over wages.

The result was that the main form of competition between large-scale capitals in consumer commodity markets became product competition, including competition in service and quality.[23] The systematic development

[21] Paolo Sylos-Labini, *Oligopoly and Technical Progress*, revised edn (Cambridge, Mass., 1969), 147.

[22] This line of analysis is stressed by Paul Sweezy, Harry Magdoff and the "*Monthly Review* school."

[23] Paul Sweezy, "Theories of the New Capitalism," *Monthly Review*, July–Aug. 1959.

of new or differentiated products, and style and model changes transformed the economic and social meaning of technology and productivity.

The major change in the strategy of large-scale capital was to combine new production processes (recomposition of workers) and new product development (recomposition of needs) into a single unified process. In some industries, monopoly power inhibited process innovations which threatened market price structures and existing capital values. However, no such inhibition prevented product innovation. This was so because consumers more or less bore the financial burden of obsolete commodities; consumer product obsolescence forced down the market value of existing wage goods, hence protected the value of capital goods (for example, model changes in automobile production reduced the value of used cars, rather than the value of capital employed in producing cars).

In branches of the economy in which monopoly power in product markets was difficult to establish, there remained considerable pressure to introduce new output-increasing and/or cost-reducing production processes. However, it became increasingly common to introduce new processes to manufacture new consumer products rather than merely to cheapen the production costs of existing ones. As early as the 1890s, "to retain its sales pre-eminence . . . Eastman Kodak discovered that 'continuous innovation became a more effective strategy' than patents." In the early twentieth century, "Western Electric, Du Pont, Squibb, General Electric, Goodrich, Corning Glass and other large companies were also finding that 'improving products and processes' was a more practical tool than patent laws for maintaining dominance over markets in concentrated industries."[24] A specific example was double-knit weaving facilities, which accelerated the redundancy of older plant and equipment and oriented new productive forces to new product development alone. The most dramatic example was microcircuitry and microprocessors, which were used as means of production (e.g., automated warehouses) and also as means of reproduction of labor-power (e.g., pocket computers, TV games, digital watches). (In the early 1970s, Texas Instruments' most profitable semiconductor products were wage goods, not capital goods.) New materials – for example, ferrite, a basic magnetic metal - were used to manufacture new wage goods (e.g., ferrite cores and magnets used in TVs, videotape recorders, radios, audio equipment). New means and objects of production were often developed which simultaneously permitted the production of new wage goods and lowered the value of existing wage goods (for example, applications of genetic engineering to industrial processes, which potentially reduced production costs of chemicals by con-

[24] Richard B. DuBoff and Edward S. Herman, "Alfred Chandler's New Business History: A Review," *Politics and Society*, 10, 1, 1980, 95, citing Alfred Chandler.

trolling reactions with bacterial enzymes, increased metal recovery by leaching with bacteria, etc.). In short, science-based industries such as electronics, chemicals, and aircraft developed new production processes *and* new consumer products. This was reflected in the fact that product innovation monopolized a large portion of research and development expenditures. In the early 1970s, as much as 70 per cent of research and development funds in West Germany was spent on product development.[25] In the USA, General Motors spent "about three percent of its sales on research and development, with most of its spending directed towards developing new products [which] primarily mean new cars . . . "[26]

Michael Shanks summed up the issue in this way: "first, there was rapid growth in research and development primarily to develop new products but also to make existing products cheaper or better or simply 'different.' This development went hand-in-hand with a growth in marketing techniques and methods of all kinds. Second, there has been a remarkable growth in the techniques of automation, in the broad sense of the substitution of sophisticated capital equipment for labor."[27] As large-scale capital organized new technology for product innovation, new contract research enterprises specializing in consumer good technology appeared on the scene. "Little [Corporation] claims to have been the first commercial organization in the world to engage primarily on contract research on technical processes. Today, the range of inquiry which it handles is bewildering. Its inventions include instant breakfast foods and missile fuels, hot-drink paper cups and low-temperature crystals, nylon fishing lines and atomic-fallout shelters."[28]

Whether large-scale capital developed its own new products or purchased them from specialized research companies, new products were often placed on the market at higher prices than old products. Costs of research and development, new marketing expenses, retooling, retraining workers, extra burdens on management, and new and different raw materials (especially for disposable products) were incorporated into the value of the commodity. New products which replaced old products were sometimes more elaborate or wasteful; fixed costs were relatively high because of limited production runs; financial burdens were greater because borrow-

[25] Hartmund Neuendorf passed on these results of his group's study of science policy in West Germany, conductd at the Max-Planck-Institut in Starnberg, to the present writer in 1975.

[26] "How GM Manages Its Billion-Dollar R and D Program," *Business Week*, June 28, 1976, 54. Meanwhile, the US machine tool industry's new research and development spending has practically stagnated. See also, "Where Private Industry Puts Its Research Money," *Business Week*, June 28, 1976, passim.

[27] Michael Shanks, *The Innovators* (Baltimore, 1967), 43.

[28] Ibid., 48.

ts rose with the expansion of demand for energy and raw
ed to fuel and manufacture new consumer products. For
easons, new products often "contained" more direct and
oor than old products, hence their values were higher. The
ew commodities were produced for which living labor
d a growing share of total production costs ignores all
sary labor besides direct factory labor. In the modern
ductive labor and semi-productive and indirectly produc-
de many activities within the white-collar work force,
h state bureaucracies as higher education, agriculture, and
er prices thus partly reflect the semi-productive labor of the
er taxes partly reflect the indirectly productive labor
organized by branches of the state engaged in material and related activities.

The tendency outlined above had especially significant economic effects
when older and/or relatively simple wage goods were *deliberately* taken
off the market to make room for more elaborate, costlier substitutes.[29]
Another strategy was "value engineering." Products were offered at lower
prices as a result of new techniques which used lower-cost materials,
redesign of packaging to give less protection, sacrifices in durability to save
weight, substitution of welds for bolts, stampings for cuttings, clips for
screws.[30] This strategy did not cheapen the cost of production of existing
commodities so much as it "cheapened" the commodity itself. The result
was less an increase in potential relative surplus value and more an
expansion of replacement demand as a consequence of the production of
inferior use values. "Value engineering" thus might have increased, rather
than reduced, socially necessary labor-time. A related point may be made
about capitalist strategies dealing with adverse consumer reactions to new
products, which often led merely to repackaging of the products,[31] or an
increase in marketing budgets which had potential unfavorable effects on
the production of relative surplus value. In the food industry, for example,
a typical strategy was to sell the same product in new and different forms,
e.g., expensive convenience foods which required more packaging.[32]

The "product cycle" reflected more than any other practice the systemic
process of self-expansion of new wage goods and needs, hence the self-
expansion of reproduction costs: "When production is the crucial element,
ownership of plant and equipment may be essential for control. But where
product design becomes the dominant element, investment in develop-

[29] E. J. Mishan, *The Costs of Economic Growth* (New York, 1967), 110.
[30] Graham Bannock, *The Juggernauts* (London, 1971), 74.
[31] Asim F. Firat, *The Social Construction of Consumption Patterns*, Ph.D. Dissertation,
Graduate School of Management, Northwestern University, June 1978.
[32] A US Department of Agriculture economist, cited in *Seven Days*, March 30, 1979, 34.

ment and marketing is the more important . . . modern business has come more and more to think in terms of product cycles lasting perhaps from two to fifteen years. At any one time, they have projects in the initial stage, products in the middle stage, and products in the final stage. Their strength comes from being able to deal with all three at once and to *couple* the various stages of research, production and marketing by integrating information."[33] As market demand for older products leveled out, new products were introduced to maintain and expand the circulation of capital in its consumer commodity form. In the words of Nestlé's managing director, "the underlying purpose of our diversification is, first and foremost, to ensure the replacement of those of our products which are growing old, so as to maintain the overall growth rate of the company."[34] Companies faced with a decline in profits developed new products, which, if successful, made the company "profitable" again.[35] Even in the recession year of 1975, about 1,000 new food and drug products were introduced in the USA, an increase of ten per cent over 1974.[36] Perhaps 40–50 per cent of these products failed, and in addition to the cash costs, "product failures tie up time and talent that might have gone into profitable projects."[37] (The same is true of new production processes; cost overruns, technical bottlenecks, and other factors mean that new processes at times cost too much to compete with old processes.)[38]

In the first stage of the product cycle, potentially successful new products had slow rates of diffusion in the mass market; hence it may pay to suppress new products requiring large-scale changes in production and marketing. Sales of actually successful products expanded dramatically as they traveled from the "middle-class" to the mass market, and from the national to international market, and as increasingly differentiated products penetrated more refined submarkets. *Ideally*, for capital as a whole, the product cycle, product differentiation, planned replacement demand ("the disposable economy"), and associated mass media illusions "guaranteed" permanent expansion. The danger of price wars was minimized, the growth rate of large corporations maintained, science and

[33] Stephen Herbert Hymer, *The Multinational Corporation: A Radical Approach* (New York, 1979), 249. Edwin Mansfield argues that capital will strive for a payoff on new products in five years or less (*The Economics of Technological Changes*, New York, 1965, 92–115). Shanks claims that two years is a more accurate figure (*Innovators*, 64). Ernest Mandel argues that the life cycle of fixed capital has been shortened from ten years to four or five years. This might be related to the product cycle.

[34] "How Nestlé Revives Its Money-Losers," *Business Week*, Jan. 27, 1973, 44.

[35] "Eli Lilly: New Life in the Drug Industry," *Business Week*, Oct. 29, 1979.

[36] Bernard Wysocki Jr, "Disastrous Doubts," *Wall Street Journal*, March 23, 1976.

[37] Ibid.

[38] "The Catch-up Game at Owens-Illinois," *Business Week*, Oct. 5, 1974.

technology "fully employed"; "through the creation of a spectacle of *change*, frustrations and boredom within the context of industrial society might be mobilized to maintain and sustain that order."[39] However, the cost was an enormous yet "essential" waste of human labor-power and the subversion of capital as a whole in proportion as the growth of individual capitals was geared to new consumption.

Two or three specific examples will underscore the central role of product innovation and the product cycle in post–war US capitalism. In 1970, 4.8 million electric and gas ranges were sold in the USA. By 1975, sales had declined to 3.6 million. Meanwhile, sales of microwave ovens grew from zero in 1970 to one million in 1975. Most of these new products were bought by households already equipped with electric or gas ovens (the dealers advertised microwave ovens, which cost roughly $100 more than traditional ovens, as a "third appliance"). No wonder that one manufacturer stated that "microwave is saving the day for a lot of appliance dealers."[40] Manufacturers expanded capacity; there was the appearance of "profits"; from the standpoint of value realization, this was an ideal situation for individual manufacturers. The old product was not replaced; a new one was added which cost more than the old.

Traditional gas and electric ovens were called "mature products." The Model T Ford was a mature product by the late 1920s; black-and-white TV was a mature product in the 1960s. Perhaps the chemical industry handled the problem of mature products more systematically than other manufacturers. "The chemical companies well know that in their game the great rewards have always gone to the swift, to those who have boldly pushed out on the frontiers of technology toward *ever more sophisticated end products* – 'downstream' in the industry's terminology."[41] Chemical capitals had to face the problem of adequate productive capacity as well; in 1976, chemical companies invested "upstream" owing to shortages of basic building blocks for chemical products. However, capacity was expanded to permit the production of new products; upstream investments were needed because shortages "put something of a crimp on expansion down nearer the consumer."[42] In other words, new capacity was not built primarily to cheapen the production of old products but to provide materials for new products. Synthetic fibers, for example, had already become "mature products" in the 1970s when they commanded 70 per cent of the total US fiber market. Consumer resistance inhibited new investments oriented to cheapening the production of synthetic fibers,

[39] Stuart Ewen, *Captains of Consciousness* (New York, 1976), 87.
[40] "Sales are Sizzling for Microwave Ovens," *Business Week*, Feb. 9, 1976, 32.
[41] "Capital Boom in Chemicals," *Fortune*, Feb. 1976, 98, italics added.
[42] Ibid.

forcing the chemical industry to exploit and/or manufacture new needs and new possible markets. Similar mechanisms were at work in many other branches of capitalist production.

The product cycle presupposed enormous amounts of social labor-time utilized in ways which created new needs, and which made the working class and salariat more aware of needs already established within the general context of individualist ideologies and practices in the labor and consumption processes (see chapters 5 and 6). Moreover, the smooth functioning of the product cycle meant that capital had to suppress forms of collective consumption which economized on social labor-time. Existing collective consumption facilities which posed a threat to the commodity form of need satisfaction were, if possible, eliminated (e.g., the infamous case of the destruction of the Los Angeles interurban electric railroad). Resistance to railroad reconstruction, mass transit, social forms of health care, and cooperative housing testified to capital's need to maintain and strengthen the commodity form and to produce differentiated commodities in accordance with the rules of market segmentation. Last, but not least, the product cycle appeared to be accompanied by faster turnover of new means of production.

Also essential to both the expanded value of wage goods and the growth of money capital in the sphere of circulation was the increase in realization labor, including advertising. In Stuart Ewen's words, capital supplied "mass produced visions of individualism by which people could extricate themselves from the mass."[43] As capitalist enterprises increasingly became product innovating and marketing units,[44] the need for the product cycle and product differentiation presupposed an "idea cycle," or new images associated with new commodities or new forms of the old ones. Product differentiation, market segmentation, and forced obsolescence presupposed idea differentiation, idea segmentation, forced obsolescence of ideas. In this sense, style and model changes, packaging and similar strategies, as well as advertising, were merely different forms of symbols to communicate ideologies of commodity individuation. Since "commodity ideas" were typically inseparable from the commodity itself (e.g., the ad from the TV program, the package from the use value, the car model change from the basic engineering, etc.), realization labor of all kinds became embodied in, and entered into, the value of the commodity.[45]

Perhaps the same conclusion may be drawn about other forms of

[43] Ewen, *Captains of Consciousness*, 45.

[44] Paul Baran and Paul Sweezy, *Monopoly Capital* (New York, 1964).

[45] Even "selling costs . . . grow unceasingly, making bigger and bigger the price the ultimate consumer has to pay for commodities" (Ernest Mandel, *Marxist Economic Theory*, vol. I, New York, 1968, 201).

circulation labor. First, the commodity labor-power became fully subject to market exchange. Workers selling labor-power had to guard its value by combining together, employing bargaining agents, etc. The capitalist buyer of labor-power had to employ guard labor to "protect the payroll." A second reason that circulation labor expanded was that more products became commodities, hence more circulation activity was required generally, e.g. more buying and selling and more labor organized to protect the commodity form of objects. A third reason was that because the commodity has a twofold nature as use and exchange value, there was more and more speculation in money itself, which was bought and sold, circulated independently of the circulation of commodities, and grew independently through the process of credit expansion. It became possible, therefore, for circulation labor to expand without a comparable expansion of productive labor; hence the possibility of large amounts of labor being organized within the money market itself, i.e., through financial institutions which proliferated with the development of "full capitalism."[46]

Most important in the present context, "financial services" for workers and salariat became essential elements of reproduction costs. In 1975, roughly one-half of total labor in US banking and insurance served individual consumers.[47] Financial, real estate, and retail services, in fact, tended to grow more rapidly than total value production. Real estate and financing services were especially important in housing costs, making "housing a costly and complex commodity which is not likely to be easy and inexpensive to provide under any system."[48] Furthermore, "product competition" penetrated money markets as well as wage good markets; banks and other lending institutions offered increasingly complex loan packages. Finance charges, administrative expenses required to differentiate loan packages and to market "creative financing," land costs, real estate expenses, etc. in this way entered into the value of labor-power. These should be analyzed as socially necessary costs under modern capitalist conditions of production and distribution rather than as deductions from surplus value. Finally, the relatively rapid growth of consumer services generally reduced average productivity because of the difficulty of

[46] On the growth of exchange labor, see John D. Gurley and E. S. Shaw, "Financial Structures and Economic Development," *Economic Development and Cultural Change*, 15, 3, April 1967, passim.

[47] Harry Greenfield, *Manpower and the Growth of Productive Services* (New York, 1976), 11. "With our low savings rate and high usage of consumer credit, America has a banking system that is all too good when it comes to servicing the consumer. What we need is long-run investment funds" (Lester Thurow, "How to Rescue a Drowning Economy," *New York Review*, April 1, 1982, 3).

[48] Stephen E. Barton, "The Urban Housing Problem: Marxist Theory and Community Organizing," *Review of Radical Political Economics* (*RRPE*), 9, 4, Winter 1977, 29.

mass producing services (although in the 1980s, computerization of bank, hotel, travel, and other services began to increase productivity sharply). The growth of services expanded the value of labor-power because many services which previously had been self-provided had to be purchased as commodities. Moreover, "services" were also subject to product competition; hence the tendency for high-value to replace low-value services. For example, medical companies updated drugs and equipment, while consumer groups demanded better medical care; financial services became fancier and wider-ranging, while borrowers demanded still more "creative financing."

In sum, in postwar US capitalism, there was a strong tendency for the system to produce more wage goods and services in relation to capital goods, and also more capital goods designed to produce new wage goods in relation to those designed to cheapen the cost of existing wage goods. This was also a kind of "product innovation: an old machine is idle because a new-design product requires a new-design machine to produce it or requires a smaller number of the existing type machine."[49] It is uncertain whether this process of obsolescence of machinery required new constant capital outlays exceeding old levels. "This is partly a matter of . . . the question of capital-using and capital-saving innovations and partly a matter of the production possiblities available for producing the new-design product."[50] Further, there was also a tendency for more potentially productive capital to be invested in prevention and cleanup of pollution, as well as in energy supplies, which tended to increase with the expansion of the various forms of product competition. Also, retail trade, advertising, and banking and credit activities, based on value realization rather than value production, expanded in relation to productive capital. Within the block of total capital, these structural changes tipped the scale in the direction of "consumption and sales" and against "productivity and production."

The Economic Struggle and Modern Capitalist Crisis

The next step in the present argument is to analyze the ways in which the modern economic struggle and capitalist product competition converted traditional Marxist accumulation and crisis "laws" from historical trends to theoretical tendencies. At the level of the wage relationship and economic

[49] Royall Brandis, "Obsolescence and Investment," *Journal of Economic Issues*, Sept. 1967, 171.
[50] Ibid., 172.

struggle, the main problem is to develop the historical connection between unionism, welfarism, wage struggles, and so on, and profits and the profit rate, hence accumulation and the rate of accumulation. The first step is to investigate the relationship between working-class organization and struggle and total and average wages and the wage structure, presupposing that profits were inversely related to unit labor costs. Robert Ozanne and others have shown that in US capitalism an expansion of demand for labor-power was historically a necessary but not sufficient condition for wage increases. The sufficient condition during recoveries and booms was collective worker action, especially unionization.[51] Further, the necessary and sufficient condition for the prevention of wage *reductions* during crises and contractions was working-class organization and struggle.[52]

Wage stabilization during economic contractions and wage increases during recoveries and expansions meant that average wages grew secularly, albeit at lower rates than during cyclical expansions. As we have noted, according to Marxist orthodoxy this new phenomenon had little significance for the classical laws of capitalist accumulation because the rate of accumulation is thought to determine the rate of wages, not vice versa, i.e., wages supposedly depend on the amount of capital advanced for variable capital, which, in turn, depends on expected profits and accumulation.[53] In the model of full capitalism, however, the working class/salariat was able to appropriate a larger share of the total product than that determined by direct wages and salaries. *The reason is that the whole system depended on the expansion of consumer credit, home mortgage credit, fringes, and what may be called "social credit," i.e., state deficits to finance transfer payments, social services, and collective consumption facilities.* The growth of state debt (all levels of government) by 340 per cent between 1950 and 1980, and the expansion of private debt by 1,624 per cent during the

---

[51] In his study of wages paid by International Harvester, Ozanne showed that booms accompanied by bursts of worker agitational and organizational activity led to average wage increases of 3.5 per cent yearly; during booms in which workers were relatively quiescent, wage increases averaged only one-third of one per cent yearly. These kinds of wage patterns could be found in the US economy as a whole (E. Robert Livernash, "Wages and Benefits," *Review of Industrial Relations Research*, 1, 1970, 99).

[52] Although both Hoover and Roosevelt requested big business not to cut wages during the Depression, "it was not until the post-World War II period that large corporations ceased cutting wages during recessions, partly because they had learned the errors of their ways, but mainly because the big industrial unions were by then strong enough to prevent wage cuts" (James O'Connor, *The Fiscal Crisis of the State*, New York, 1973, 36, n. 23).

[53] More specifically, wages are thought to depend on the demand for labor-power, which, in turn, depends on the rate of accumulation. Further, the supply of labor-power (reserve army of labor) supposedly depends on the rate of accumulation as well. Hence it is thought that the accumulation process itself regulates the wage rate.

same period, highlight the significance of this new mechanism of modern capitalism.[54]

Traditional Marxism's argument is that wage bargains were made in money, not real, terms and that large-scale capital's monopoly pricing policies and inflation tended to cancel out money wage increases. Second, the claim is that the growth of real wages, in so far as money wage increases were not offset by inflation, had little significance because real wages were constrained by increases in productivity. Third, traditional Marxism argues that the expansion of productivity through increases in the technical composition of capital recreated the active reserve army, hence engendered downward pressures on money wages.

The first comment which can be made about traditional Marxism's analysis of wage struggles is that when money wages were advanced in proportion to increases in labor productivity, *ceteris paribus* relative surplus value did not increase, but remained unchanged. Further, when productivity growth was associated with consumer product innovation, the composition of total values shifted from capital goods to wage goods, which tended to reduce relative surplus value and the rate of exploitation in the economy as a whole (see below). The second comment pertains to the role of workers in production where they were free to organize their own autonomous resistance against productivity drives and alienated, reified labor in the context of the dominant ideologies of control. This struggle within the production process created disjunctures between wage and productivity changes (see Chapter 5). Workers viewed unions as "service organizations"[55] limited to regulating the price of labor-power, hence there arose the need for worker autonomy within production itself. Possibilities of worker autonomy were enhanced because the reserve army tended to be absorbed in state employment, state dependency relations, and employment within small-scale capital, and hence ceased to regulate worker discipline in organized branches of the economy in traditional ways.

Another point concerns the relationship between wages and productivity at the level of the economy as a whole. From the standpoint of bread-and-butter economic issues, many and perhaps most workers in the USA were not *for* the union and *against* the company, but either for or against both the union *and* the company. Definite mutual, albeit fragmented, interests were perceived to exist within what Saint-Simon once called the "produc-

---

[54] Paul M. Sweezy, "The Economic Crisis in the United States," *Monthly Review*, Dec. 1981, 2.

[55] John H. Goldthorpe et al., *The Affluent Worker in the Class Structure*, Cambridge Studies in Sociology, No. 3 (Cambridge, 1969), 170. In the USA, workers also typically see unions as instruments to raise wages, i.e., as collective means to individualistic ends.

tive classes." Labor and capital within large-scale enterprises and/or industries in effect constituted different kinds of interest groups, albeit typically in terms of economistic issues alone. Workers often supported the marketing, pricing, and other economic policies of the enterprise and/or industry. Enterprises and/or industries often supported relatively high wage policies, increased fringes, and stable employment. Thus, at the level of the relations between large-scale capitals and/or industries, a kind of interest-group pluralism flourished. The result was regular wage and salary increases, which were the unintended result of the free play of interest-group competition. In turn, the expansion of wages and salaries had an unplanned expansionary effect on aggregate demand, production, and employment in consumer goods and service industries. As we have noted, the basic structure of industry shifted against capital goods and in favor of wage goods and services under the pressure of rising money wages and salaries, the expansion of social security, welfare, and other forms of the "social wage," the dramatic growth of mortgage and consumer credit, and also "social credit" in so far as state deficits financed the "social wage" in its various forms. Further, the growing importance of wage good and service industries was due not only to the effects of wage and salary agreements on aggregate demand for consumer goods but also to the relatively low composition of capital in the consumer goods and services sector, hence the relatively rapid increase in employment in this sector.

This process steered the system as a whole on a path of rapid expansion of employment, which had further expansionary effects on total and average wages and salaries. Increases in underemployment and unemployment were largely the result of the flood tide of women and youth entering the work force for the first time. Increases in average wages in particular industries or sectors indirectly expanded the demand for labor-power and average and total wages in the system as a whole. These, in turn, fueled expansion of demand and employment, hence indirectly increased wages even more. This occurred through the Keynesian multiplier and also the "political multiplier" which underwrote the growth of the social wage. Meanwhle, the shift from consumer commodities to services weakened the classical "accelerator" effect, which theorizes the process whereby increases in consumption are supposed to stimulate new capital goods spending. In sum, the opaque Keynesian-type economic mechanisms at work in US interest-group capitalism systematically "distorted" the relationship between consumer and business credit, and so on, and in these ways impaired the capacity of the system as a whole to produce relative surplus value.

As has been noted, Marxist orthodoxy claimed that large-scale capital adapted to the wage struggle and wage agreements and protected profit margins through oligopolistic control of prices. Large-scale capital used monopoly pricing to transfer increases in unit labor costs to consumers in the form of higher prices, in this way protecting money profits.[56] However, inflationary expasion of money profits was perfectly consistent with a *contraction* of surplus value to the degree that money profits were a form of speculative return ("fictitious" profits), technological or other forms of rent, merchant profits, and bank profits disconnected from the process of valorization itself. This interpretation suggests that inflationary pricing helped large-scale capital to dig its own grave because of the adverse effects of inflation on interest rates and the costs of replacing inventories, and also because credit expansion increased the financial vulnerability of the system as a whole.[57]

Moreover, the economic struggle was fought on an increasingly broad front with the intention and effect of protecting and advancing real wages and incomes. The most powerful unions tied money wages to the cost of living, and social struggles and the process of political legitimation extended inflation insurance to old-age pensioners, veterans, and other groups.[58] Of course, only one-third or so of the working class was employed by large-scale capital, hence potentially able to protect real wages. In small-scale capital, while money wages increased during cyclical upswings, inflation tended to inhibit increases in real wages. Growing differentials in real income between workers in large-scale and small-scale capital, however, tended to increase worker militancy at the base and to extend union activity, however tentatively, into unorganized and weakly organized

[56] One standard line is that oligopolistic pricing and inflation had the effect of reducing real wages, hence functioned as an alternative mechanism to the reserve army of labor (Maurice Dobb, "Inflation and All-That," *Marxism Today*, 9, 3, March 1965, 86).

[57] In 1978, for example, consumer debt repayment in relation to disposable income reached an all-time high (almost 21 per cent). ("The New Debt Economy," *Business Week*, Oct. 16, 1978, 89.)

[58] In the USA, "the combination of first-year increases and subsequent cost-of-living adjustments 'leads to virtually complete indexing of wages to consumer prices' over the life of three-year contracts" (Brookings Institution economist, D. J. B. Mitchell, quoted in "Economic Diary," *Business Week*, Jan. 8, 1979, 10). Of all current workers and retirees, "a striking 93% . . . strongly favor cost-of-living adjustments in private pensions" ("A Growing Disillusion with Social Security," *Business Week*, March 12, 1979, 26). In 1970, less than three million union workers were covered by cost-of-living escalators; in 1975, six million. Another two million non-union workers were also covered. Since the early 1970s, cost-of-living adjustments were introduced for pensions (31 million social security recipients); allotments to about 19 million food stamp users; military and Federal civil service retirees (2.5 million); Federal lunch subsidies (25 million children) (Jonathan Lang, "On the Escalator," *Wall Street Journal*, March 1, 1976, 1).

sectors. John Goldthorpe sums up the general issue this way: "Money bargains are in general made in terms which reflect the parties' expectations as to their real value; thus, under conditions of steady inflation, with the 'money illusion' dispelled, expectations (of prices, wages, etc.) will be more or less accurately adjusted to the rate at which inflation is going on."[59] Further, while it has been argued that the growth of consumer credit muted workers' wage demands, credit expansion was itself inflationary, hence demands to maintain real wages may have been even greater.

In addition, during the 1970s the wage demand was not limited to inflation adjustments, but was extended to wage expansion in real terms. The so-called revolution of rising expectations (a cultural phenomenon based, as will be seen, on the development of abstract social labor, the commodity form of need satisfaction, modern product competition, and the legitimacy of the working class/salariat in society and the state) underwrote rising wage levels, employment security, fringes, and, last but not least, state transfer payments, social services, and collective consumption facilities. The expansion of the "social wage" (or "citizen wage," in Bowles and Gintis' terms) was especially important. By the 1970s, it is a fair estimate that the full range of social benefits including welfare, medical, other assistance, and public housing exceeded average factory wages.[60] More specifically, in the USA, welfare and social programs were tilted to the bottom end of the income scale.[61]

Some writers have characterized this "revolution of rising expectations" as the adaptation of the bourgeois spirit of acquisitive gain to the working class's own purposes. An alternative but not mutually exclusive view is that the working class became more mature; older status orders which restrained demands broke down, and workers became more conscious of their citizenship rights (which, until the 1980s, restricted the capacity of the state to deflate the economy through unemployment).[62] Some writers have argued that individuals demanded satisfaction of material needs as a

[59] John H. Goldthorpe, "The Current Inflation: Towards a Sociological Account," in Fred Hirsch and John Goldthorpe, eds., *The Political Economy of Inflation* (London, 1978), 192.

[60] Welfare checks themselves made up a relatively small part of the "social wage." Besides social security, medical aid, food stamps, and housing subsidies of various kinds were the most important components. In the late 1970s, an estimated one in twenty-five families was aided by various housing programs (housing subsidies rose from about $2 billion in 1974 to $5 billion in 1979, and subsidized housing units rose at the rate of about 10 per cent yearly). By 1979, Medicaid had become the largest Federal welfare program.

[61] "Almost half of the aggregate income of the bottom fifth of the population is derived from social welfare benefits. The poorest people in the country are now as much dependent on the government for their subsistence as they are on the labor market" (Francis Fox Piven and Richard Cloward, *The New Class War*, New York, 1982, 15).

[62] Goldthorpe, "The Current Inflation."

civil right and "constitutionally guaranteed status."[63] In short, demands
for rising real wages tended to be not only inflation adjustments, but also
"normal phenomena" until the end of the 1970s.[64] To the degree that
governments were powerful enough to engineer small recessions when
money wages rose faster than prices, productivity growth rates slowed
down, costs rose, and profits were threatened. To the degree that governments were able to use indirect taxes and inflationary policies to lower real
wages, unions tended to increase the demand for money wages to recapture
income losses.[65] When the state tried to control wage demands through
income policies, labor demanded reduced wage differentials or other
trade-offs.

The crucial point is that the demand for higher real wages and working-
class income resulted in the diffusion of the economic struggle into all
spheres of circulation, including the credit sphere. Labor unions increasingly tried to represent workers in the sphere of circulation of consumer
goods and services not only because particular unions had different kinds
of workers within their jurisdiction, but also because the growth of social
abstract labor meant that more people became more vulnerable in more
ways to economic changes initiated by capitalist enterprises. Decisions by
large-scale capital, in particular, affected workers in their role of consumers in an ever-widening circle, e.g., land use, pollution, auto safety,
food and drug regulation, interest rates, unemployment, etc.[66] Also, outside the world of large labor associations, workers in community organizations, renter groups, consumer groups, environmental groups, and
ascriptive groups of all kinds became involved in the struggle for "public
values" and higher real wages and/or income. These struggles, which were
more complex, unorganized, and inchoate than the struggle for money
wages, developed across a broad front which included struggles for price
controls and against inflation, as well as demands for more social wages.
The struggle for real income also consisted of flanking actions and guerrilla
strikes to maintain or reduce individual prices. Credit default became a

[63] Hans Peter Dreitzel, "On the Political Meaning of Culture," in Norman Birnbaum, ed.,
Beyond the Crisis (New York, 1978).

[64] Goldthorpe, "The Current Inflation," 201: "one may see the decay of the status order as
having released ... distributional dissent and conflict at a new level of intensity – reflecting ...
a clearer, more hardheaded, indeed *more* rational appreciation of the nature of class
inequalities ..."

[65] James Harvey and William McCallum, "Problems of Inflation," *Marxism Today*, 9, 4,
April 1965, 127; Emile Burns, "Problems of Inflation," *Marxism Today*, 9, 8, Aug. 1965,
249–50.

[66] David Greenstone, *Labor in American Politics* (New York, 1969), 389. Greenstone
calls union actions around these and related issues the creation and preservation of "public
values."

form of resistance to rising interest rates. Consumer boycotts and struggles against consumer fraud and consumer issues generally may also be mentioned in this connection, as well as those for rent control and against housing and land speculation (which became important in the late 1970s), and also for "lifeline" utility rates and for lower interest rates in forms ranging from Congressional populism to strategies of establishing state banks and local financial cooperatives. The struggle against taxation, typically organized by local and regional petty bourgeoisies, also, in effect, contained the demand for more real income.

In these ways, the economic struggle assumed a totalizing character exemplified by the unspoken demand for "money that is worth something." This struggle was not consciously organized, coordinated, or unified. Precisely because it was waged by workers and salariat as owners of different forms of property, it was individualistic, pluralistic, and fragmented. Theoretical, not practical or political, connections may be made between the struggle for money wages, struggles over commodity prices, and so on. The only practical unity possible in the highly individualistic context of US capitalism was the development of political means to individual ends. To the degree, therefore, that working-class struggle broadly defined created unfavorable conditions for capitalist accumulation, the result was unplanned or unintended. It follows that the struggle for money and credit in all their forms did not spell the end of capitalism itself, but rather foreshadowed the growing danger of system crisis. The economic struggle itself "upped the ante" rather than changed the game. Signs that the stakes were being raised included the fact that, until the late 1970s, wages were increasingly insensitive to the unemployment rate;[67] higher unemployment rates were needed to fight inflation; structural shifts from capital goods to wage goods and services and shortages of inflation-free savings and profits were more intractable;[68] working-

[67] "The size of major three-year wage agreements, many of which come up for 1979 negotiations, is 'virtually' insensitive to unemployment," according to a Brookings Institution study by D. J. B. Mitchell (cited in "Economic Diary," *Business Week*, Jan. 8, 1979, 10).

In bargaining units of over 1,000 workers (which include one in every nine workers) annual rates of wage increase for the first nine months of 1975 and 1976 were: 1975, first year of contract, 10.2 per cent, total life of contract, 7.8 per cent yearly. 1976, first year of contract, 8.9 per cent, total life of the contract, 7 per cent. The inflation rate was less than 5 per cent in that period. When fringes are included, the percentage increases over the life of the contract were: 1975, 8.1 per cent; 1976, 7.2 per cent. (Department of Labor Survey, cited in *San Fransisco Chronicle*, Oct. 23, 1976.)

[68] In 1950, consumption and government spending combined accounted for 88 per cent of gross national product; in 1960, 91 per cent; in 1974, 95 per cent. During the 1950s, which have been labeled "the years of the consumer," more than 100 per cent of all increments to gross national product were allocated to consumption and government at the expense of an

class progress in the spheres of wages and income, continuity of employment, income maintenance, and working conditions resulted in less system flexibility and less variability of labor-power. Finally, urbanization with its concentration of fixed capital, high rents and congestion costs, more rigid social stratification, and "geographic inertia" had similar effects.[69]

Product Competition and Capitalist Crisis

The preceding analysis strongly suggests that the traditional Marxist theory of exploitation, relative surplus value production, accumulation, and crisis is excessively "functionalist." It was argued in Chapter 3 that the traditional theory more or less fit the "facts" during the period of Western capitalist development. In the context of the "full capitalist" money and commodity circuits of capital, however, the possibility arises that technical change and product competition tended to increase average and total variable capital and reduce relative surplus value for capital in general. The economic meaning of technical change, product competition, and the economic struggle, therefore, did not appear to be confined merely to the completion of what Marx called the "consuming circle within circulation."[70] Instead, there appears to have developed a new tendency for the

absolute decline in investment (and this was a period in which the military budget in relative terms was stagnant or declined), according to a report James Tobin gave J. F. Kennedy before his electoral victory in 1960.

Put another way, the result of the economic struggle broadly defined through the 1950s and 1960s (together with increased labor force participation or demand for wages) in the USA has been a growth rate of per capita consumption faster than per capita production (1954–66, 2.6 per cent compared with 2.5 per cent; 1966–73, 3.1 per cent compared with 2.7 per cent. In the recession of 1973–75, per capita production fell by 2.7 per cent while per capita consumption fell by only 0.7 per cent) (Joan Robinson, "What Has Become of Employment Policy," in *Contributions to Modern Economics*, New York, 1978, 265, Table 1). As late as 1977–78, wages were rising three to four times faster than productivity.

[69] Good discussions may be found in: Enzo Mingione, *Social Conflict and the City* (New York, 1981), chs. 2–3; David Harvey, *The Limits to Capital* (Oxford, 1982), 418, 422, 427–9. Harvey stresses the importance of crises in the coordinating mechanisms of world capitalism arising from extreme tensions between fixity and mobility of capital; the possible failure of global reforms of these mechanisms; and the probable consequences – global crisis.

[70] Marx developed an argument to the effect that competition between individual capitals is not only one mechanism for distributing produced surplus value in accordance with the absolute size of particular capitals, but also a vehicle for forcing capitals to adopt production process innovations or "labor-saving" technological changes which increase "technological rent" and, everything else being equal, indirectly reduce the value of the average consumption basket, hence, increase relative surplus value in the system as a whole. In Marxist orthodoxy, increases in the technical composition of capital not only reduce the value content of the

system as a whole to expand the "consuming circle" beyond the "circle" of the production of surplus value.

The line of reasoning that points to this conclusion begins with the observation that product competition and forms of modern technology were determined by both the capitalist wage labor relation in the money circuit and capitalist exchange relations in the commodity circuit. First, as we have seen, the working class and salariat imposed a kind of "private Keynesianism" on large-scale capital, which was reinforced by monopoly pricing and the "economy of high wages." Worker resistance to wage cuts during crises, labor union implementation of supplemental unemployment benefits which expanded demand, "job creating benefits" which shortened hours of work, expansion of consumer credit, earlier retirement and increased pensions, and rank-and-file resistance to rationalization of production, among other factors, increased employment and working-class demand for wage goods, with the consequence that markets for older and new consumer commodities were strengthened and expanded.

Second, the "anti-recession strategy" imposed by the working class was reinforced by large-scale capital's plan of developing new products and accelerating replacement demand for old products, which independently raised aggregate demand. Until the 1980s, capital's classical strategy of liquidating labor, slashing wages and employment, and reducing costs was modified and/or replaced by one of expanding demand and markets. In the

---

consumption basket, but also increase the organic composition of capital, which ultimately lowers the profit rate. It should be stressed, however, that throughout most of his analysis of competition and accumulation, Marx assumed that workers consumed a *given* basket of wage goods, hence that capitalist accumulation was a process whereby the average value content of the consumption basket declined, which tended to offset the unfavorable effects of the rising organic composition of capital on the rate of profit.

In traditional Marxism, the process of circulation of capital as a whole (as distinguished from capitalist competition which refers to relations between individual capitals) is regarded as deeply contradictory. Circulation of capital is considered to be necessary for the production of capital and, at the same time, a barrier to the growth of capital. As Michael Lebowitz writes, the reason is that "every moment capital [exists] in the sphere of circulation [is] 'pure loss,' time outside the sphere of production of capital" (Michael Lebowitz, "Marx's Falling Rate of Profit: A Dialectical View," *Socialist Review*, 38 (8, 2), March–April 1978, 76–7). Reductions in circulation time thus increase the time that capital can be put to productive uses. However, from the point of view of "each capitalist, the total mass of all workers, with the exception of his own workers, appear not as workers, but as consumers" (*Grundrisse*, Baltimore, 1973, 419). The contradiction therefore arises that while capital seeks to reduce circulation time to a minimum, it also tries to widen the sphere of circulation as a whole by increasing needs and expanding markets.

In Marx's view, new branches of production and new products which fulfill new needs are developed from surplus value produced on the basis of older industries and products. "The mass of social wealth, overflowing with the advance of accumulation, and transformable into

long run, the effect was a high-cost, high-consumption economy which increasingly ran into trouble in international markets. In the short run, crisis tendencies generated new needs, new demand for credit, and new products in place of deflation, devaluation of capital and economic collapse.

Third, in modern capitalism, the self-expansion of capital meant the "self-expansion" of new means and objects of reproduction as well as protecting the value of existing means of wage good production. Since new product development and production presupposed new or modified means of production, and since the latter were typically output-increasing as well as cost-reducing, the growth of physical productivity did not necessarily reduce the value of labor-power.

The process of expansion of reproduction costs and expenses may be described in more detail supposing that technical change was oriented to new wage good development. When new products passed the test of the marketplace, the innovating capital reaped a "superprofit" or what may be termed "market rent." Competing capitals subsequently produced and marketed the new commodity, which sooner or later compelled the innovating capital to develop new production processes designed to lower product costs. Meanwhile, product competition compelled the innovating capital to make real or imagined "improvements" in the new product. In turn, competing capitals were likely to try to match these "improve-

---

additional capital, thrusts itself frantically into old branches of production, whose market suddenly expands, and into newly formed branches . . ." (*Capital* I (Kerr edn, New York, The Modern Library, 1906), 632). More specifically, the production of relative surplus value requires "production of new consumption; requires that the consuming cycle within circulation expand as did the productive cycle previously." This consists of "firstly, quantitative expansion of existing consumption; secondly, creation of new needs and discovery and creation of new use values." For Marx, the importance of expanding needs and creating new use values is that these are essential not only to expand markets, but also to preserve the value of existing capital. "If, through a doubling of productive force a capital of 50 can now do what a capital of 100 did before, so that a capital of 50 and the necessary labor corresponding to it become free, then, for the capital and labor which have been set free, a new, qualitatively different branch of production must be created, which satisfies and brings forth a new need. The value of the old industry is preserved by the creation of the fund for a new one in which the relation between capital and labor posits itself in a *new* form" (*Grundrisse*, Baltimore, 1973, 408–9). This passage proves that Marx did not believe that the development of new branches of industry in the wage good sector presented any difficulties for the theory of accumulation. On the contrary, Marx's capital theory depends on the assumption that the creation of new industries is necessary to preserve capital values in old industries. Technical changes which reduce the reproduction costs of labor-power (hence which potentially increase relative surplus value) liberate money capital and labor-power, which in turn become the basis for the development of new industries.

This brief exposition suggests that Marx's argument was historically specific to his epoch. One implicit premise is that capitalists in means of production industries (and associated

ments." Subsequently, there ensued a race to manufacture and market new and "improved" products at standard or lower costs. Every cost-reduction step taken by the competing capitals had the potential effect of raising relative surplus value in the system as a whole. This tendency, however, was more or less matched by the counter-tendency that every new product development and product improvement may be regarded as the development of new or expanded needs, hence the basis for new wage, salary, credit, and other demands for more money, which, in turn, tended to raise reproduction costs and lower the production of surplus value.

It remained true that each capital unit attempted to minimize the amount of money capital advanced for variable capital. The process described above, however, tended to increase average variable capital outlays, a trend reflected in the growth of average wages paid by large-scale capital. Meanwhile, each capital sought to *maximize* its share of total variable capital advanced by capital as a whole and expended as wages and salaries. Each capital also tried to maximize its share of total consumer credit, i.e., tried to recover variable capital equivalent to the amount it expended and also as much in addition as possible. New money capital was required not only to modernize and expand constant capital, but also to introduce new consumer products and new capital goods required to produce new consumer products. Each capital, therefore, exploited every conceivable real and potential need, and meanwhile attempted to develop new needs by

---

bank capital, etc.) constitute the dominant capitalist fraction. The possibility of the development of new capitalist class alliances between wage good industries, merchant capital, and bank capital servicing the first two sectors is neglected. Another premise is that new needs and branches of industry spring up alongside and in addition to old needs and industries. The possibility that new industries replace old industries or that new high-value wage goods replace low-value wage goods within any particular industry is also neglected.

The same criticism can be made about Marx's theory of technological change. New technology may be oriented to the development of new wage goods rather than to reducing the value of existing wage goods. The contradiction between surplus value production and realization may, in fact, manifest itself in contradictions pertaining to the form of technological change.

Science and technology may also be used as vehicles for the concentration and centralization of capital and monopoly, or for enhancing the value of existing capital rather than lowering the value content of the consumption basket. Furthermore, there is no analysis of the possibility that circulation expenses might become part of the reproduction costs of labor-power and raise its value, hence either reducing surplus value or lowering real wages below the value of labor-power. The possibility, therefore, that the value content of the average wage good and/or consumption basket may increase is ignored. In short, Marx did not consider the problem of the "management of the reproduction of labor-power" which implies the management of wage good capitals by capital as a whole, i.e., the "control of the whole of production of Department II" (Aboo T. Aumeeruddy, Bruno Lautier, and Ramon G. Tortajada, "Labour-Power and the State," *Capital and Class*, 6, Autumn 1978, 58).

promoting new products which competed not only with the products offered by other capitals but also with its own products, at the same time fixing prices of old products despite excess productive capacity. However, these new products typically required extra outlays of total capital for retooling, purchases of new raw materials, new research and development, and so on. Yet each capital expected that its share of new money capital laid out by capital as a whole, or the share which it recouped for itself, would cover its own expected future capital needs. With each capital unit functioning in similar ways, total money capital advanced, including average variable capital outlays, tended to expand. Assuming that the total supply of money capital and consumer credit remained unchanged, the average capital unit obviously could not recoup more than it laid out. Under these conditions, the combination of process/product innovation neither raised nor lowered the rate of exploitation. However, the whole system of product competition and product cycles presupposed regular increases in the demand for and supply of business and consumer credit.

This expanding "paper economy" permitted the tendency for the value of labor-power to increase to be realized in fact. Credit expansion (new money, including new loan packages and product competition in the money market) was clearly essential for financing the production of new means both of production and consumption. Credit expansion was also essential for financing consumer purchases of new means of consumption. Business loans were extended on the basis of traditional collateral. Working-class/salariat loans were extended on the basis of the only collateral that the working class was able to offer – its own exploited labor-power: the worker's job. In this way, the credit system tended to freeze the division of labor and also to expand the demand for labor-power and employment. Product competition thus unintentionally had the effect of raising the level of employment which, in turn, maintained more or less favorable conditions for the wage struggle. The effect on the system as a whole was the development of the permanent debt economy, fiscal and liquidity crisis, and high inflation and taxation, which capital required to maintain some control of the rate of real wage increases and volume of working-class purchasing power.

Meanwhile, new constant capital functioned to produce new products as well as new production processes; the substitution of new for old means of reproduction presupposed the substitution of new for old means of production, or, at least, modifications in old means of production. The value of existing constant capital thus tended to decline correspondingly, especially when individual capitals destroyed old markets to make way for new products. The very concept of the organic composition of capital in this way became problematic. There was no "necessary" tendency for the composition of capital to increase, hence no "necessary" tendency for the rate of profit to fall in accordance with traditional Marxist theory. Instead, the pressure on the rate of profit emanated from the self-valorization of labor-power, struggles against prices and productivity, and the unintentional effects of the expansive credit system and product competition, which combined to reduce surplus value absolutely and relatively, or, at least, to prevent capital from raising surplus value. The systemic contradiction thus arose: the system as a whole required more surplus value to develop and produce new products and new means of producing new products; but to the degree that consumer credit raced ahead and new products entered the value of labor-power, surplus value tended to fall.

This mechanism of replacement and expansion demand for means of reproduction, growth of credit, and expansion of the value of labor-power required a secondary mechanism to expand demand for old means of reproduction or used products. This demand originated within strata of the working class expelled from large-scale capitalist enterprise together with new workers whom big capital could not absorb, i.e., the reserve army of labor, or the unemployed, underemployed, unemployable, and subemployed, or workers fully employed at less than a "living wage." Large-scale capital's expulsion of living labor reproduced the conditions for the renewal of small-scale capital, whose survival depended on relatively high rates of exploitation and low wages. In effect, large-scale capital "supplied" both the cheap labor-power and the cheap use values required by small-scale capital. Without the sector of small-scale capital and the "secondary labor force" on which it depended, there would have been significantly fewer markets for older, deteriorated housing, used cars and trucks, used appliances, second-hand furniture and clothing, damaged goods, "seconds," and so on. In this, among other senses, the reproduction of small-scale capital and a relatively low-paid work force was indispensable for the reproduction of large-scale capital and a relatively high-paid work force. However, this large (and growing) reserve army did not pull down the labor-power value of workers in large-scale capital, but rather maintained or expanded it. This occurred indirectly through the mechanisms described above, and also directly through the "second-hand standard of living" within the secondary work force, which became a source of union organizing drives in small-scale capitals and new wage struggles.

In sum, taken as a whole, there developed a contradiction not only between the interests of individual capitals in wage goods and capital as a whole, but also between those of wage goods capitals as a whole and capital as a whole. The shift in economic, social, and political power in favor of wage goods capitals, merchant capital, and related capitals, combined with the rise of working-class economic power, solved realization crisis tendencies in US capitalism, and neutralized the traditional falling rate of profit tendency, and, precisely for this reason, generated a new tendency for surplus value and profits to decline.

Conclusion

The preceding analysis of working-class and capitalist struggles in the money and commodity circuits of capital throws some light on the origins of the modern accumulation crisis in the USA. This analysis, however, is largely "economistic" in that it abstracts from the social conditions of reproduction of labor-power and the working class/salariat, hence from the social conditions of valorization and accumulation. In fact, economic struggles in the money and commodity circuits were "epiphenomena" of the process of social and material reproduction, which will be analyzed in the next three chapters. The general argument advanced is that, in the context of the hegemonic ideology of national 'individualism and its various practices, social conditions and struggles within the production process, the process of consumption, and the process of the state and reproduction of working class/salariat undermined the variability of labor-power and capital and underwrote the crisis of accumulation. As will be seen, US capitalism lost much of its flexibility in six broad areas: the size of the consumption basket and its value content; the size of the social consumption basket (social wage and services) and its "value content"; variability of the production of absolute surplus value; and variability of the fixed and circulating components of constant capital. Qualitative changes in "socially necessary labor," including reconceptualizations of capitalist space and time within direct production, the household and community, and politics and the state lowered the real rate of exploitation, hence of accumulation. Further, modern social conditions and struggles changed the social meaning of profits, exploitation, and accumulation.

Not merely labor-power, but the whole system became more inflexible, which has been pointed out in different ways by various theorists. Max Weber argued that developed capitalism would become more rigid and perhaps ossified because of the historical process of rationalization and routinization. Joseph Schumpeter predicted that institutionalized capitalism would become less innovative, more cautious, and less dynamic. In relation to traditional bank and industrial capital in the old US industrial zones, this proposition obviously contains more than a germ of truth. More recently, Samir Amin has argued that the "present crisis . . . is the crisis of a system that is less flexible and capable of adjustments than was previously the case."[71] David Harvey has written that excessive centralization of capital means that the "system stagnates, becomes bogged down, held captive by the weight and complexity of its own organizational structures."[72] Harvey has developed the perceptive thesis that the greater the ratio of fixed to circulating capital (especially the greater the importance of "immovable" capital and "built environments" as "composite commodities"), the greater the inflexibility in the system as a whole, or the less is the capacity for creative changes in technology and organization.[73] In these and other ways, the development of abstract social labor – in the sense of the objectification of labor-power and labor subject to the blind workings of the law of value and the tendency toward institutionalized reification – negated itself. Historical crises had the effect of creating not only more social abstract labor, concentrated/centralized capital, etc., but also new conditions of social and material reproduction which threatened economic system domination/integration and capitalist accumulation and also social domination/integration and social order.

As we will see, struggles *within* the working class toward a kind of class unity representing anti-racist, anti-sexist, anti-national chauvinist, and anti-individualist forces validate the thesis that the crucial variable in the modern accumulation process ceased to be the composition of capital and instead became the composition of the working class and the rate of exploitation. Two points may be made in this connection. First, it was precisely the political integration of the working class into the consumption-based economy and society which made it difficult for US capitalism to avoid problems of capital underproduction and unproductive utilization of capital and the fictitious profits, inflation, and stagnation (and ultimately unemployment) which were the hallmarks of the underproduction crisis. Second, it was the struggle against the wage, commodity, and state forms of material and social existence (i.e., the struggle against reification) which transformed the social meaning of "socially necessary labor." In short, underproduction of capital generally, and inflation in particular, were inexplicable outside the context of quantitative and qualitative struggles for reproduction within and outside the circuits of capital and the effects of these struggles on wages, prices, taxes, state expenditures, private and public credit, etc. on the rate and social meaning of exploitation and profits.

[71] Samir Amin, "Towards a Structural Crisis of World Capitalism," *Socialist Review*, 5, 1, (23), April 1975, 37.

[72] Harvey, *Limits to Capital*, 154. Harvey adds that "excessive decentralization . . . can create . . . a climate of uncertainty . . . gaps between production and realization . . ."

[73] Ibid., 323–5.

The roots of inflation, in particular, which was the surface manifesta-
tion of the underproduction crisis, were incredibly complex. Inflation was
the result of the expansion of the demand and supply of consumer credit,
the state debt, and business credit required to develop and market new,
higher-value commodities, finance mergers and acquisitions, real estate
speculation, and so on. Inflation was also caused by high unit production
costs in a period of relative stagnation and excess capacity. Another source
of inflation was the periodic weakness of the US dollar and the "energy
crisis." Still another was high real interest rates or a seemingly permanent
large differential between money interest and inflation rates. Inflation was
also used as a deliberate strategy to attempt to keep prices in advance of
wages and social benefits, albeit an increasingly counterproductive one.
Inflation was also due to the monetization of claims on the economy which
became less and less possible to meet with the given rate of exploitation,
rate of profit, and capitalized economic resources.[74] In sum, the modern
conjuncture of economic class struggle, capitalist competition, and state
policy were at the root of modern inflation.

One reason that inflation was limited as a crisis-management strategy
was that differentials in inflation rates strengthened some national currencies relative to others, hence gave some capitalist countries competitive
advantages over others. Moreover, worldwide inflation expanded international debt, generated greater supplies of dollars and other currencies
which were not subject to national monetary controls, and hence created
more financial and social instability in world capitalism as a whole.
Further, inflation became a source of fictitious capital and fictitious profits.
Inflation was increasingly needed to reproduce fixed and circulation
capital and the employed labor force, restock inventories, and reproduce
the state apparatus and the working class/salariat as a whole. Profits
became fictitious to the degree that higher inflation and credit expansion
"upped the ante" and required greater revenues to reproduce the system as
a whole. US capitalism, in effect, had to run faster to stay in the same place,
which was reflected in the collapse of the long-term US capital market and
the dramatic growth of short-term borrowing inspired by financial institutions' fears of permanent inflation. The more capital expanded in the
absence of "real" profits, the greater the inflation rate, and the more
difficult it became to expand productive capital in the future.[75]

[74] See, for example, Sam Rosenberg and Thomas Weisskopf, "A Conflict Theory
Approach to Inflation in the Postwar U.S. Economy," *American Economic Review*, 71, 2,
May 1981.

[75] As Mandel points out, capital is not fictitious to the degree that it is used to purchase
new means of production and labor-power and "thereby converted into productive capital"
(Ernest Mandel, "The Industrial Cycle in Late Capitalism," *New Left Review*, 90, March–
April 1975, 6).

Inflation and fictitious profits did not, therefore, arise because of unproductive utilization of capital for military spending and circulation expenses alone – a view which is well established within both modern Marxist orthodoxy and "Keynesian Marxism." In the model of full capitalism, underproduction of capital and inflation were also determined by insufficient production of surplus value, not only by its unproductive utilization. A low and/or falling rate of exploitation became structurally embedded in the conditions of social life in general, and conditions of reproduction of the working class/salariat in particular. Moreover, the concept of "the rate of exploitation" itself became problematic because of the qualitative changes in the relationships of production which accompanied political integration and ideological control and resistance of the working class and salariat.

As will be seen, the working class and salariat developed individualistic economic and social needs, pluralistic forms of economic and social struggles and political organization and activity which incrased the size and value content of the consumption basket and altered the social meaning of "labor-power." The combined development of capital concentration/centralization and proletarianization and modern social struggles resulted in new forms of state intervention in the reproduction of society and capital (administered society, political capitalism), which reinforced and exaggerated these trends. In the 1980s, the process of capital restructuring thus became, first and foremost, a social, political, and ideological question – one which the growth of the working class and salariat, and the structure of capitalist enterprise and the state and political system, made it increasingly difficult to resolve unambiguously in favor of capital and at the same time retain liberal bourgeois democratic forms and practices. As we will see, of the many potential tools of state crisis-resolution, the most effective, but also the most difficult to implement, were programs to reorganize the social conditions of commodity production, reproduction of labor-power and the working class and salariat, and the nature of capitalist competition with the purpose of lowering variable capital outlays, i.e., cheapening the costs of reproducing the working class. The rise of neo-conservatism and neo-liberalism in the 1980s (i.e., Reagan's contradictory attempt to restructure social and economic life respectively along traditional patriarchal normative and classical market lines) starkly revealed the social, political, and ideological barriers to statist/corporatist solutions to the problem of restructuring and planning social and material life.

Meanwhile, American individualist ideologies and practices also became more expensive in economic, social, and psychological terms for the working class and salariat themselves. On the one hand, the individualist obsession with the wage and income struggle pushed up prices of commodities in the workers' consumption basket. On the other hand, the struggle for less costly living standards in effect put a limit on the wage and salary increases. Older workers looking out for themselves helped to limit life chances of younger workers, e.g., possibilities of home ownership and adequate social security retirement income. White workers and men looking out for themselves limited economic opportunities of blacks and women. These and related contradictions arising from the development of collective means to individualist ends reinforced the economic expenses and social and psychological costs of "full capitalist" social life. The working class was, in this sense, compelled to begin the arduous historical task of independently reorganizing social life, which began within the context of ethnic revivalism and struggles for self-identity along ascriptive lines (e.g., the new social movements of women, minorities, the elderly, youth, etc.). The subsequent ideological, material, and political struggles over the aims, principles, processes, and results of social reorganization – and, last but not least, over political reorganization and state structures – in this way became the determinant forms of the modern class struggle.

The new and contradictory processes outlined above may be regarded as revolutionary ruptures in the structure of capitalism. The coming of age of the US working class and salariat *within the ideological individualistic context of "full capitalism"* constituted a major rupture in the inner nature of economic crisis itself; the working class/salariat became a seemingly insurmountable barrier to capitalist accumulation. In broader terms, political capitalism, the social factory, and administered society themselves became their own limit. The resulting crisis was, therefore, a crisis of capitalist relationships with the working class in particular and the state and society generally. In these senses, the limit of accumulation may be regarded as the process of accumulation itself.

5

The Productive Circuit of Capital

Introduction

In Marxist theory, the quantitative meaning of "proletariat" is simply the work force engaged in wage labor. "Proletariat" in the qualitative sense requires a more complex definition. The word implies, first, the "real subordination of labor to capital," and, second, the notion of "abstract labor." The "real subordination of labor" means that the *labor process* is subordinated to the *valorization process*. The material process whereby concrete labor produces use values is subordinated to the social process whereby abstract labor produces exchange value. Put another way, "real subordination" means that humankind's appropriation of nature and the knowledge and skills developed therein are subordinated to the process of producing and realizing surplus value and converting surplus value into productive capital.

"Abstract labor" means that the *production process* (the combination of the labor and valorization processes) abstracts from any and all *autonomous* ascriptive, cultural, and technical attributes of individual workers which capital may have at one time depended upon. *Individual* technical and cultural skills which characterized pre- and semicapitalist labor and which developed in whole or in part *independently* of the capitalist production process are replaced with *social* technical and cultural skills developed *within* the capitalist production process in particular and capitalist social reproduction in general. "Labor remains a productive force," Marx writes, "but in a different form, from direct to scientific labor, from individual to social labor."[1] The individual laborer is transformed into the abstract social laborer who exists in the context of the "development of a large-scale collective labour process within which

[1] Karl Marx, *Grundrisse* (Baltimore, 1973), 705–6.

specific forms of skills and competencies may be lodged."[2] Within the many-sided skills of the social labor force, there may be found one powerful unifying element. Each concrete labor-power and labor process is the same in the sense that individual labor capacities and work tasks appear and disappear within the process of the production and reproduction of capital as a whole. "Individual" skills and capacities therefore confer little or no independence, that is, no "individuality" in the traditional sense of the independent small producer or semi-independent craft worker.

The many varieties of labor, means and objects of labor, products of labor, and labor-power in developed capitalism are both "cause and effect" of the functioning of the law of value on a world scale. The more extensive the operation of the law of value, the greater the tendency for capital to transform individual labor into social labor. The greater the development of social labor, the wider the field of operation of the law of value. The regulation of labor by the blind workings of the law of value defines "proletarian impoverishment" (which may or may not imply reductions in the consumption basket and/or more brutalized, routine, or monotonous work), which means the loss of any sense of traditional individual and/or communal historical subjectivity, or any sense of individual and/or communal control of material and social life.

The crucial aspects of the development of abstract social labor were, as we saw, economic crisis and class struggle, the development of the world market, the integration of science into industry, and the growth of detail labor and standardized albeit variable "routines" within the process of direct production. The latter were the result of machine production and automation, work specialization and the division of industrial labor, the separation of conception and execution of work, and functional specialization within and between capitalist enterprises.[3] Standardized, yet variable, routines are associated with machine-tending, assembly line work, and continuous process production and electronic communications and information processing,[4] among other operations. Machine-like manual

[2] Tony Elger, "Valorization and Deskilling: A Critique of Braverman," *Capital and Class*, 7, Spring 1979.

[3] The standard work is: Harry Braverman, *Labor and Monopoly Capital: The Degradation of Work in the Twentieth Century* (New York, 1974). The role of technology and science in the development of mass production is discussed in David Noble's *America by Design: Science, Technology and the Rise of Corporate Capitalism* (New York, 1977).

[4] Representative literature includes: Philip Kraft, *Programmers and Managers: The Routinization of Computer Programming in the United States* (New York, 1977); Andrew M. Pettigrew, "Occupational Specialization as an Emergent Process," *The Sociological Review*, NS, May 1973; H. A. Shepherd, "Engineers as Marginal Men," *Journal of Engineering Education*, March 1957; "The Consciousness of Being Declassed," *International Socialist*

tasks are designed the better to expel living labor from production by transferring physical tasks to real machines. Machine-like mental tasks are designed the better to transfer counting, memorization, and other mental tasks to computers which can perform any well defined cognitive routine.[5] The collection, transmission, and interpretation of symbols denoting material and financial processes are found both in the office and on the shop floor. Automated material and mental processes thus tend to transform skilled blue-collar labor into a species of office labor, and skilled office labor into a species of machine operation. In sum, the development of abstract labor and the "real subordination of labor" to capital is the result of "the reorganization of the whole complex of the capitalist labor process,"[6] including the individual worker's relationship to production.

The General Contradiction of the Regime of Modern Industry

In Marxist theory, mass production and the social laborer are regarded as profoundly contradictory developments. Abstract social labor is interpreted as capital's basic weapon in the class struggle and at the same time as the capitalist system's Achilles' heel. "There are two realities in capitalism – one analyzed by bourgeois economics in which labour is just one factor of production and the other expressed by Marxism within which labour becomes conscious of itself as the whole basis of production."[7] The general meaning of the two-sided nature of the production process is that there is a constant struggle by capital to impose wage labor (or the capitalist form of work activity) and by workers to reassert anti-bourgeois, social forms of production relations, or "social individuality."

Journal, 4, 24, Dec. 1967; Floyd Mann and L. Richard Hoffman, *Automation and the Worker* (New York, 1960), 160.

The effective elimination of production labor and the recomposition of detail labor into technical labor engaged in repair, monitoring, and maintenance occupations appears to be confined to industries processing fluids and gasses, e.g., oil refining, chemical processing, and glass. These three industries alone have automated all or most of processing material handling, and control simultaneously, hence abolishing the "economy of labor-time" (cf. National Commission on Technology Automation, and Economic Progress, *Technology and the American Economy*, Appendix vol. VI. Statements Relating to the Impact of Technological Change, Washington, 1966, 257).

[5] The scope for the mechanization of mental tasks in the USA may be appreciated when it is realized that perhaps one-half of all jobs are "information occupations, from data processing to investments to insurance to real estate, compared with 17 percent in 1950" (Robert Fierro, "Real Estate, 1981," *Mainliner*, Feb. 1981, 67).

[6] Elger, "Valorization and Deskilling," 66–7.

[7] Andrew Giles-Peter, "The Problem of Scientific Marxism," *Arena*, 37, 1975.

Modern industry and the law of value are regarded as capital's basic weapon because they establish the real or "systematic" domination of labor. At the level of the capital as a whole, individual workers are pawns in the grip of the law of value, i.e. a reified material world over which they exercise no control. At the level of the workplace, deskilled workers in particular are deprived of any trace of subjectivity when machinery paces living labor and when labor is reduced to unit labor-time which, in turn, permits quantitative comparisons between living labor-time and machine-time. This makes possible rational capitalist cost accounting, capital budgeting, and financial reporting, which facilitate the domination of the law of value on an ever wider scale.

The reduction of individual workers to interchangeable parts in the processes of production and circulation makes capital more "fluid" and workers more "versatile." In this way, competition between workers in the labor market (and also in the "internal" labor market within the capitalist enterprise) is intensified. Competition within the working class is further intensified by the periodic recreation of the reserve army of labor through cyclical, structural, and sectoral economic crises. In traditional theory, the reserve army is the lever of accumulation in the sense that it remains in a state of alert for tours of industrial duty during periods of economic expansion, and also in that it "regulates the wage rate," or disciplines and/or replaces rebellious workers, in times of crises and contractions. Also, in theory, capital uses the reserve army as a lever to downgrade jobs during economic crises. In these ways, modern industry permits capital to treat individual labor-powers as if they were com-modities, or mere objects of exchange and labor. Capital units thus are in principle free to vary individual concrete labors and deskill and reskill individual workers in accordance with changes in market conditions, technical conditions of production, forms of worker resistance, and so on. This is facilitated by part-time and temporary work which offers capital greater flexibility in work scheduling and layoffs, reduced unit labor costs, and cheaper training costs.[8] In sum, modern industry theoretically makes labor power into "variable capital," which is the basic condition for the unrestrained operation of the law of value.

The other side of the contradiction constituted by social abstract labor is that the working class, i.e. the labor movement, is also capitalism's Achilles' heel. Theorists in the "class struggle" tradition of Marxism in

---

[8] Larry Hirschorn, "The Theory of Social Services in Disaccumulationist Capitalism," *International Journal of Health Services*, 9, 2, 1979; anon. "Off the Job: The Renewed Struggle to Shorten the Working Day," *The American Owl*, 5, March 1979, 3–4. The writers of both of these accounts are keenly aware of the contradictions inherent in part-time and temporary work.

particular regard the "mass worker" as the "only unplannable element of capital," i.e. as the only factor of production which is irreducibly autonomous within the labor process, and hence potentially a collective historical subject. The empirical premises of the "class struggle" tradition are cycles of wildcat strikes, slowdowns, plant seizures, working to rule, rank-and-file revolts against contract violations and union bureaucracy, "counter-planning on the shop floor," and related forms of resistance and struggle. The theoretical premise is that the law of value itself is stamped by worker struggle. "If the autonomous workers' power forces reorganization and changes in capital, then capital cannot be understood as an outside force independent of the working class. It must be understood as the class relation itself . . . Capital seeks to incorporate the working class within itself as simply laborpower, whereas the working class affirms itself as an independent class-for-itself only through struggles which rupture capital's self-reproduction."[9]

Different writers have stressed different sources of working class solidarity and power within the regime of modern industry. One source is the sheer size and complexity of the modern capitalist enterprise,[10] which necessitate structured labor processes and a stable work force, which in turn create possibilities for worker unity.[11] These possibilities are reinforced by the stabilization of market structures, vertical and horizontal economic integration, and state policies favoring economic expansion, among other factors. The premise that capital suffers from "geographic intertia" and that work in large-scale capital is regularized and relatively secure depends, of course, on conditions in world capitalism as a whole, hence is conjunctural in nature.

Another feature of large-scale capital which permits workers in the same

[9] Harry Cleaver, *Reading Capital Politically* (Austin, Texas, 1979), 53. The Introduction to this work includes a comprehensive summary of the development of the theory of the working class as collective subject beginning with C.L.R. James and Ray Dunayevskaya and culminating in the works of Raniero Panzieri, Mario Tronti, Sergio Bologna, and other theoreticians associated with, or inspiring, the Italian New Left.

[10] Dean Morse writes that "in a world of certainty, a manufacturing plant should be designed for a constant flow of output, interrupted only rarely by maintenance requirements, wherever the scale of production and the state of technology makes this pssible. Installations of this type usually require very heavy investments of capital. Interruptions of production for whatever purpose entail heavy costs" (Dean Morse, *The Peripheral Worker*, New York, 1969, 89). A good discussion of the characteristics of "primary" and "subordinate primary jobs" in large-scale capital can be found in Richard Edwards, *Contested Terrain: The Transformation of the Workplace in the Twentieth Century* (New York, 1979), 158, 170–4; 181–3.

[11] David Harvey (*The Limits to Capital*, Oxford, 1982) focuses on the inflexibility of fixed capital, especially in centers of capitalist "agglomeration," and capital's objective need to make alliances with workers.

enterprise to establish closer bonds is the abolition or "subsumption" of craft labor and traditional craft status distinctions, which may create closer horizontal ties between workers in different enterprises and industries. The argument is that mass production weakens the influence of custom and traditional equity concepts on wage structures, and also undermines traditional connections between individual skills and effort and productivity and wages. It is also argued that mass production subverts the ideology that low wages are rooted in low levels of individual productivity, i.e., that substandard wages and living conditions are the fault of individual workers. For these reasons modern industry makes possible strong "mechanical solidarity" between workers in large-scale enterprises.[12] Possibilities of "mechanical solidarity" are reinforced by the elimination between workers and management of personal or paternal ties which were not uncommon in earlier stages of capitalist development. In earlier industrial regimes of hierarchical control, close supervision, and "foremen's empires . . . frequent threats and often mass firings and layoffs" were commonplace. But increasing worker organization meant that, while the firm could still safely dismiss recalcitrant *individuals* with relative impunity, it could not easily do so with rebellious *groups* of workers.[13]

There is a more general sense in which Marxism regards the development of the regime of modern industry as a potential boost to working-class solidarity. For the first time the possibility arises of "regular cooperation between employed and unemployed workers," which Marx thought was the "basic condition of working class unity" (but which it is more accurate to say is the actual labor of unity; if mechanical solidarity is the condition of cooperation, cooperation itself is the condition of *organization*).

It is also thought that regular cooperation between employed and unemployed is facilitated by the decline in latent labor reserves, which everywhere occurs in developed industrial capitalism.[14] In theory, exhausting the recruitment of labor-power from the countryside and home creates a more experienced, urban, and homogeneous work force. Common

---

[12] James O'Connor, "Emile Durkheim's *Division of Labor*," *Insurgent Sociologist*, 9, 3, Winter 1979.

[13] Edwards, *Contested Terrain*, 57. Edwards concludes that the control systems of early large-scale capitalist industry failed because of the absence of traditional personal ties between workers and employer. However, he ignores changes in class composition, hence the fact that personal ties and paternalism were impossible with the advent of large-scale industry, not merely because of the size of the capitalist unit, but mainly because the worker's individual or personal attributes ceased to be a productive force.

[14] Mandel refers to the "gradual reduction of the industrial reserve army in the metropolitan countries and a gradual swelling of the reserve army in the underdeveloped lands" (*Late Capitalism*, London, 1975, 363).

industrial experiences, conditions of life, and social status may be regarded as necessary preconditions for regular cooperation within the working class through industrial unions, political parties, community organizations, and the like.

The development of working-class power in these and related ways becomes a fetter on the forces of production and process of accumulation. It is thought that there exist three forms of capitalist counterattack. The first two consist of expelling living labor from production. The third involves subdividing manufacturing units and replacing workers in older "core" industries with workers from the reserve army of labor in the world as a whole, hence fragmenting the work force.

The first form may be described as the replacement of paid by unpaid work in the guise of "self-service," e.g., food and gasoline distribution, telephone communications, automobile transportation, and similar activities. While the contradictions within self-service activities have not been explored either theoretically or practically, self-service may be regarded as the creation of common experiences within the sphere of reproduction, hence may result in new forms of social unity (see Chapter 6).

Capital's second counterattack is capital restructuring in the form of automation or continuous process production, miniaturization of production processes, and so on, which transform employed workers into a more or less permanent unemployed "surplus" population. In turn, surplus labor recreates conditions for the reproduction of small-scale capital based on high rates of exploitation and maximum flexibility in utilizing labor-power, which occurs both spontaneously and also in the form of subcontracting strategies of large-scale enterprises.[15] Workers employed by small-scale capital, where there is an absence of "elaborate employer-imposed work structures"[16] and worker rights, constitute a so-called secondary work force whose labor-power is "unfettered and unencumbered by any job structure, union, or other institutional constraints" and may hence be treated as if it were a commodity.[17] "It is the lack of job security and the ever-present possibility of immediate replacement by others from

[15] Morse, *Peripheral Worker*, 90–1; Robert Averitt, *The Dual Economy: Dynamics of American Industry Structure* (New York, 1968), passim; James O'Connor, *The Fiscal Crisis of the State* (New York, 1973), chs. 1 and 2; Andrew L. Friedman, *Industry and Labor: Class Struggle at Work and Monopoly Capitalism* (Atlantic Highlands, NJ, 1978), passim.

[16] Edwards, *Contested Terrain*, 167.

[17] Ibid. Edwards' treatment of divisions within the working class is in one sense inadequate. According to Edwards, the essence of the secondary labor market is the "casual nature of employment," little training or education, low pay and little job security, and dead-end jobs. The problem with Edwards' approach is that his criterion for defining labor-power as a commodity is the nature of the concrete labor in question, which he tends to assume is fixed and unchanging. For example, he includes in the secondary labor market

the reserve army that marks a secondary job."[18] One result of the reproduction of small-scale capital and the "secondary work force" is the
"redivision and segmentation of the American working class"[19] which the
internationalization of production, the marginalization of a fraction of
the urban population, and growth of the "informal economy" intensifies.
Another result is that the burden of economic and social changes (i.e.
variability of capital and social reproduction) falls on ascriptive groups
overrepresented in the sector of small-scale capital, e.g. women, youth,
retirees, ethnic small businesses and subcontractors, etc.

The contradictions within the secondary labor market and small-scale
capital have begun to be explored theoretically and practically in the
developed capitalist countries. The basic contradiction is that the reproduction of small-scale capital helps to give rise to so-called new social
movements, which explains why labor market segmentation and marginalization of a large fraction of the work force are not unmitigated
blessings for capital. In the first place, while it is true that "secondary
workers" in the USA typically discipline themselves in the dark corners of
modern capitalism, there is little evidence that they regulate the average
money wage or hours and conditions of work. Until the 1980s, there were
few signs of the traditional inverse relationship between money wages and
unemployment. Second, the "periphery" of irregular workers employed
by large-scale capital during cyclical expansions are normally organized
into industrial unions, hence are not a reserve army which regulates the
wage rate or disciplines regular employed workers. Third, the expanded
reproduction of small-scale capital reproduces conditions of wages, hours,
and work condition struggles, hence the need for labor unions (usually
allied with community or ethnic, women's, or other ascriptive groups) to
organize and establish normal wages and working conditions – as for
example in parts of the garment trades, soft coal mining, and construction.

Surplus labor which is not unemployed or subemployed within small-
scale capital or the "informal economy" is typically utilized within, or

---

hospital orderlies and part-time teachers, i.e. public employments where labor-power cannot
by definition function directly as capital. He also includes guard labor, or labor-power used
to prevent any threats to the commodity form, which is paid for out of revenues, not capital.
Edwards argues that the basis for the division into labor market segments is "to be found in
the workplace, not in the labor market" (178). But the "workplace" is defined in terms of
"control systems" (simple, technical, bureaucratic control – see below for a critique of this
approach) not in terms of the social relations of the production and the production and
circulation of value and surplus value.

[18] Ibid., 169.
[19] Ibid., 163.

enlisted by, the state sector of the economy.[20] Thus, irrespective of differences in the value of labor-power exploited within small capital, large-scale capital, and the state, it appears that wages, hours, and working conditions in all three sectors are increasingly politicized. This happens because permanent inflation forces labor unions and other working-class organizations to politically confront wage controls or income policies and restrictive fiscal and monetary policies. It also happens because political legitimation requires direct or indirect state-provided supplements to workers exploited by small-scale capital. Further, worker struggles compel big capital to nationalize, hence politicize, some forms of variable capital outlays. Also, wages and conditions of work of state employees and state client income are politically determined in direct ways.[21] Finally, the politicization of the economy transforms unemployment from a function of blind and impersonal "market forces" into a political-administrative issue subject to the technical expertise of economic planners.

Some Marxists believe that these trends create common economic and political experiences and expectations within the three main fractions of the working class, i.e., that the political and ideological context and the relation between political and work socialization as well as the industrial system itself help to shape working-class consciousness and institutions. The argument is that political-administrative determination of wages, working conditions, and social welfare modifies the law of value in the sense that the amount and kind of "socially necessary labor" is subject not only to economic, social, and political struggles, but also to judicial decree, competition between political parties, the results of chaotic state administration, and so on. The displacement of impersonal and spontaneous "market forces" into the spheres of politics, administration, and the court system is thought to increase chances of political cooperation between productive workers in big capitalist firms, subemployed and unemployed workers, and state workers.

In the USA, this was exemplified in the 1960s and early 1970s by labor union support of the welfare state; local political alliances between community and ascriptive groups organized by the unemployed and sub-employed and labor in large-scale industry; organized labor's support for organizing drives within the state sector; post-McGovern unity moves between blacks, women, and organized labor within the Democratic Party; new forms of organization betwen urban and rural workers drawn from oppressed minorities; and so on. The power of such movements is measured by the force of the backlash – capital's sharp political turn to the

[20] O'Connor, *Fiscal Crisis of the State*.
[21] Ibid., chs. 1–2, 5–6.

right in the late 1970s and early 1980s. It seems unlikely, however, that the rudiments of cooperation between "employed and unemployed," including the pivotal role of state workers in preventing competition between the two groups, will be destroyed in the 1980s. The reasons include the fact that employment and unemployment no longer expand together; competition and conflict with the socialist countries and the Third World creates the political need for "recovery programs" and more or less high levels of employment; the conversion of the active reserve army into a new kind of latent urban reserve is of limited use to capital; state transfers and subsidies tend to break down the connection between productivity and income and undermine competition within the working class based on individual motivations and incentives, meanwhile subverting the so-called achievement principle.[22]

Capital's third counterattack in its struggles with the industrial working class is to enlist "undocumented workers" and married women, and/or Third World workers through the vehicle of "increasing segmentation of previously integrated production processes into separate, specialized phases, coordinated through the market or more directly through sub-contracting," in short, the interregionalization and internationalization of the productive circuit of capital.[23] In fact, in the USA, most labor force growth since World War Two has consisted of adult women, especially married women. Until the early 1960s, part-time workers accounted for most expansion; since then, most new workers have been full-time. More, in recent years, the importance of "foreign workers" and "illegals" has been widely recognized.

Foreign workers, however, have been drawn to the USA not only because of capital's labor shortages, but also because of the high wages and welfare benefits established in the past.[24] Immigration, therefore, should not be interpreted solely as an "offset" to capital's loss of flexibility, but also in terms of economic and social struggles for high wages and a decent standard of life. Similarly, the proletarianization of married women, hence feminization of the working class, does not signify that women workers effectively function as a labor reserve army. In fact, women,

[22] See for example Claus Offe, *Industry and Inequality* (New York, 1977), 17–20; 135–7.

[23] Harvey, *Limits to Capital*, 184. A good summary of the internationalization of production is Folker Froebel *et al.*, "Export-Oriented Industrialization of Underdeveloped Countries," *Monthly Review*, 30, 6, Nov. 1978. A summary of the utilization of foreign workers is Santa Cruz Collective on Labor Migration, "The Global Migration of Labor," *U.S. Capitalism in Crisis*, Economics Education Project, URPE (New York, 1978).

[24] Santa Cruz Collective, "Global Migration of Labor"; Estevan T. Flores, "Multinational Mexican Workers: Their Struggles, Carter's Attack and Counterplanning," *Zerowork*, 3, 1979.

including more and more married women with children, are a permanent fraction of the work force. In other words, it has proven to be easier to recruit women into the work force than to expel them during periods of declining demand for labor-power. Most important, feminization of the work force engenders new struggles for equal rights and opportunities, revitalized demands pertaining to social and women's issues, and an economistic brand of feminism generally. Utilization of women workers is thus a contradictory process which should not be interpreted merely as a capitalist strategy to correct inflexibilities in the labor market and production process.

Roughly similar conclusions may be drawn with regard to the inter-regionalization and internationalization of production and the development of new interregional and international divisions of labor, i.e. the trend for large-scale capital to fragment and decentralize and export older and newer industrial processes to the "periphery" at home and abroad.[25] This process too should not be regarded as an unmitigated blessing for capital. First, when manufacturing units become subdivisions of larger enterprises and specialize in producing particular product components, workers no longer produce a useable final product. This is one factor which tends to lead workers to abandon anarchist and other traditional "workerist" ideologies and to adopt more class conscious attitudes, values, and organization. Other factors in the world of transnational corporations are the global process of labor deskilling and the loss of significant worker bargaining power in individual plants of integrated transnational firms. Second, the decentralization of industry and internationalization of production also seems to be creating, independent of the traditional union movement, a worldwide revival of regional and local movements, as well as combinations of nationalist-regionalist and union movements.

Meanwhile, capital concentrates administrative and management services, financial operations, research and development, public relations, and related activities in the largest cities (and also, because of "gentrification" of urban office space, in the suburbs) of the developed countries. The result is the development of new capitalist hierarchies and specialization of spatial functions and forms according to location.[26] Much urban labor

[25] It is in petrochemicals, steel, and engineering, including autos, that most decentralization of industry occurs. The same is true of traditional labor-intensive industries (e.g., textiles and garments) as well as new high-tech industries. The "export of industry" is to a large degree motivated by congestion costs, high labor costs, and lack of flexibility in labor utilization due to union rules, grievance, mediation, and arbitration provisions in labor contracts, etc. (Barry Bluestone and C. Bennett Harrison, *Capital and Communities: The Cause and Consequence of Private Disinvestment*, Washington, DC, 1980).

[26] See the work of Steven Hymer and, more recently, Manuel Castells and the "world city" theorists, and David Harvey.

118   *Individualism and the Contemporary Crisis*

thus tends to be marginalized, with the effect of expanding the informal or "underground" economy and "self-work" – which is the result not only of automation but also of the new international divisions of labor. (Or urban labor is absorbed in the growing service sector, as well as office work, and to a lesser degree, new "high-tech" industries.) While the "underground economy" has not been adequately theorized, it would appear that it and "self-work" help to reinforce "new social movements." These trends also result in new kinds of inflexibilities and immobilities based on new forms of social fragmentation and hierarchy.[27] In the new "world city" administrative and financial capitals of big business, organization of office workers spearheaded by women workers and state employees, community and ethnic organizations of marginalized workers, and militant labor groups in the service sector seem to be the most important elements in the "new labor movement" which creates new forms of resistance to large-scale capital. For all these reasons, the export of production and new international division of labor should not be seen *merely* as offsets to labor shortages, declines in productivity and profits, and related trends in the "first world."[28]

In sum, in modern Marxist theory, the regimes of mass production and abstract social labor, however globally differentiated and fragmented, retain their status as deep contradictions of developed capitalism. Attempted cooperation between workers in big industry, employed and unemployed, private and state workers, native and foreign workers, and oppressed minorities and women workers; the expansion of wage goods relative to capital goods industries; regularization of work; the growth of fixed capital; and other factors to be discusssed "freeze" the contradiction at the levels of lived experience and the workings of capitalist political economic structures. Even in the face of the dispersion of production and four years of neo-liberalism and neo-conservatism, the contradictions of the regime of modern industry have been resolved neither into unrestricted competition between workers, the full transformation of labor-power into variable capital, and the triumph of the law of value, nor into "proletarian revolution" and socialism. In the postwar period, until the 1970s, they have rather been associated with superficially crisis-free processes of economic expansion, social integration, and political legitimation.

[27] Enzo Mingione, "Social Reproduction and Informalization: A Preliminary Attempt to Interpret the Contemporary Social Crisis," University of Messina, unpublished MS.
[28] We should mention, as Harry Magdoff and Paul Sweezy stress, that the bulk of foreign investments are made in the industrial countries, thanks mainly to the continued struggle for market domination. Perhaps the most important offset is the intensification of "unequal exchange" against the Third World (oil, of course, excluded), which shifts the terms of struggle from within to between countries.

The Technical-Managerial Salariat and Ideological Control of Workers

Further elaboration of the modern capital-labor contradiction in the production process requires a brief account of the concepts of "system integration" and "social integration/domination." The former designates the integration of specialized system functions into one another. The latter designates the social integration of particular individuals and groups into system functions. In the regime of modern industry, system integration means that the valorization process and the law of value govern the labor process. This presupposes the utilization of labor-power as variable capital, flexibility between and within economic sectors, adaptability to internally generated technological and other changes, production of sufficient quantities of surplus value and their conversion into productive capital, and determination of socially necessary labor-time within the matrix of capitalist competition.

It is important to stress that system integration defined in terms of "capital in general" presupposes the social integration of workers into system functions, i.e. that individual workers and salariat live their lives in accordance with the deep rules of the law of value, or that commodity and capital fetishism and capitalist individualism are universal. The integration of system functions without the social domination of workers and their integration into these functions is an empty abstraction, or a paper theory. Real, historical system rationality, especially within large-scale integrated firms, requires the real integration of real people into system functions, which in turn requires some form of social legitimation and political consensus. (In Marxist theory, this was apparently first recognized by the Italian Communist Party in the 1950s.)

A basic problem of US capitalism since World War Two was that, although the economic system presupposed social integration, the law of value could not by itself produce social integration. The traditional ideology of "equal exchange of equivalents" based on the perceived exchange of wages for labor services (rather than labor-power) did continue to have a powerful hold on worker consciousness. Social integration, however, also presupposed the capacity and willingness of individuals and groups not only to allow the system to work but *to make it work* by forcefully performing new and changing system functions. As Durkheim showed, material production and exchange presuppose some kind of social bonding; as Mayo showed, worker morale and solidarity are productive forces; as Weber proved, social bonding presupposes some kind of legitimate authority. The integration of the US working class into systematic processes of production, distribution, exchange and consumption thus required capital to mobilize political legitimations and symbols and moral-normative traditions and forms of aesthetic sensibility as weapons in the class war.

This was particularly true in that the regime of modern industry magnified the problem of managerial control of labor and the "consensual foundations of normative integration," and reintroduced the question of the social meaning of work in dramatically new ways. Different traditions, symbols, and legitimations, of course, play more or less important roles during different historical conjunctures (e.g., patriotism during World War Two). At times, legitimations are politically manufactured or appear in the market as the product of the culture industry. In developed bourgeois democracies, however, the transcendental ideologies, hence legitimations, are based on universalistic concepts of the dignity and rights of individuals, or the "self." As we know, in American history, and postwar US capitalism in specific, the dominant national ideology was "individualism." It was precisely the cultural deification of the "self" which underwrote ideologies of individualism and individualist practices in US capitalism generally and the production process in particular.

Specifically, within the production process, system integration presupposed the concept of labor-power as the object of exchange and labor while social integration presupposed the concept of labor-power as the subject of exchange and labor. System integration refers to the instrumental process of appropriating and valorizing labor and nature, while social integration pertains to the social process of developing "intersubjectivity" and normative structures of action. The first falls into the category of science and technology as means and objects of valorization; the second into the category of experience, authority, aesthetics, and morality as means and objects of social domination. Within the reified world of capitalist valorization in the USA, therefore, it appears that system and social integration were structurally contradictory.

This contradiction between the worker as an objectified "factor of production" and as an historical subject of exchange and work was expressed in the contradictory conditions of utilizing labor-power as variable capital. Theoretically, a basic condition for the use of labor-power as variable capital is that individual workers are capable of performing many (if not most or all) concrete work tasks. This condition is met when specialization within mass production develops to the stage where every worker can be used to replace every other worker within broad ranges of qualification. Another condition is that individual workers actually perform different concrete tasks in accordance with unpredictable system and subsystem changes. This condition is fulfilled by establishing structured production processes and work regularization, as well as by making employed workers substitutable for one another, depending on types and levels of production, kinds of bottlenecks, absenteeism, turnover, technical change, and so on. The extreme form of this tendency is limitless specialization and division of work on the one side, and total abolition of specialization of workers and division of workers on the other. Less extreme forms have been called "job rotation," which means that individual workers and work groups shift from one concrete labor task or tasks to others depending on a variety of factors which change from day to day and week to week. Under these conditions, the potential for the "social laborer" to autonomously develop alternative divisions of labor and task specalizations is greatest (the realization of this potential of course requires the labor of unity, or self-management).[29]

The important theoretical point is that when labor-power is simultaneously reduced to variable capital and elevated to collective labour, it is impossible to distinguish "capital" defined as the real domination of labor from "working class" defined as autonomous and emancipatory activity within society. Variable capital becomes in effect capital and anti-capital simultaneously. Variable capital interpreted as anti-capital means specialization of work, but not workers. The latter remains a mere concept because it cannot be materialized in specialization of workers. This contradiction (discovered by Marx) may be regarded as the basis of the contradiction between worker competition and cooperation; working-class division and unity; consumption of labor-power as variable capital and class struggle; and variable capital and the working class as such.[30]

[29] In a famous passage, Marx writes that the regime of modern industry finally requires the creation of "fully developed individuals, capable of managing material production and distribution themselves." His crucial point is that capitalism requires "variation of work hence fitness of the laborer for varied work, consequently the greatest possible development of his varied aptitudes. It becomes a question of life and death for society to adapt the mode of production to the normal functioning of this law. Modern industry ... compels society, under penalty of death, to replace the detail worker of today, crippled by lifelong repetition of one and the same trivial operation, by a fully developed individual, fit for a variety of labours, ready to face any change of production, and to whom the different social functions he performs, are but so many modes of giving free scope to his own natural and acquiring powers' (*Capital* I, Kerr edn, New York, The Modern Library, 1906), 534.

[30] Job rotation should be distinguished from job enlargement, misnamed job enrichment, which often is designed to increase the number of tasks a worker must accomplish in a given period of time. Job rotation or potential self-management or production planning, co-ordination, and control is typically interpreted by "capital logicians" as the internalization of capital, hence as self-alienation. Here it is seen, however, as a contradiction between capitalist labor and primitive forms of socialist labor. The essential point is that when labor-power is variable capital, in the sense we have described, the objective conditions are created for workers to collectively advance their own autonomous social needs.

In US capitalism, the contradiction between capital and labor generally and the problematic status of social-cultural labor-power in particular required the development of ideological forms of organization of labor and worker discipline and self-control. Capital manufactured not only commodities as means and objects of system integration, but also "worker consent"[31] as means and objects of social integration. This was particularly the case when valorization depended more on the productive capacity of society as a whole and correspondingly less on individual labor-time. The ideological organization of consent was required even when divisions between workers were embedded in the "technical division of labor." It appeared to be a general rule that the more developed the reskilling of the collective laborer, the more specialized concrete labor tasks, and the less extensive the division of laborers, the greater was the need for internal ideological control mechanisms. In short, in modern US capitalism, the development of the general productive capacity of society, the collective laborer, structured and regularized concrete labor, malfunctioning of the mechanisms of the reserve army, political-administrative determination of the social wage and employment levels, and the impossibility of distinguishing experientially between necessary and surplus labor (because workloads ceased to be customary) made ideological control systems within the capitalist enterprise absolutely imperative (see next section, pp. 127–135).

Orthodox Marxism has attached little importance to ideologies of control of workers. Weberian-Marxist tendencies, however, have suggested the importance of bureaucratic impersonality associated with abstract labor; bureaucratic routine related to the development of the permanent capital unit; and the rise of administrative functions within highly integrated corporations which hitherto were exchange or market functions. Weberian-Marxism has stressed the indispensability of political-ideological control systems within the enterprise as well as the development of state programs and policies saturated with control ideologies, which have been widely discussed under the rubrics of "political legitimation" and "symbolic politics." In fact, the "Weberian question" of the conditions of legitimate authority within the enterprise as well as in civil society and the state became central ingredients of the processes of accumulation and crisis themselves. "Legitimate" capitalist authority and ideologies of control functioned to prevent and/or undermine worker unity, including independent unionization, and to minimize the costs of unions, worker turnover, shop floor militancy, and so on. The premises behind these

---

[31] Michael Burawoy, *Manufacturing Consent* (Chicago, 1979), xii. "Activities on the shop floor cannot be understood outside of the political and ideological realms of the organization of production" (4, 27).

ideologies were that while capital and labor were partners, workers assumed competitive relationships with one another. Capital in this way attempted to unite what was "naturally" divided and divide what was united. The "internal state" or the ideology of "industrial citizenship" in this way *individualized* workers and their needs and problems.[32]

The infrastructure within which these ideologies and control systems developed was the enterprise staff departments and bureaucracies managed by the "middle-class" technical-managerial salariat.[33] The historical development of the salariat (in the USA the ratio of supervisors to workers has doubled since World War Two) was closely related to the expansion of social abstract labor and the real subordination of labor to capital, the concentration and centralization of capital, and state economic and social regulation. On the one hand, the salariat was the technical brain which exercised "classical authority" over the industrial working class. It assumed work planning, control, and coordination functions which the direct producers and capitalists once performed directly. The salariat was, in this sense, the domination of mind labor over the productive forces. On the other hand, the salariat was also the political brain which exercised "formal authority" over the workers. It assumed worker planning, co-ordination, and control functions which the workers themselves and/or capitalists at one time performed directly.[34] The salariat was, in this sense, the domination of mind labor over the production relations.

The salariat was in effect a collection of individuals whose role mobility constituted "proof" of the power of the individualistic success ethic within the context of the capital-labor partnership. "Headmen" in the double

[32] Ibid., 119.

[33] Documented in Daniel Nelson, *Managers and Workers: Origins of the New Factory System in the United States: 1880–1900* (Madison, Wisconsin, 1975), passim; and especially Edwards, *Contested Terrain*, chs. 7–8. On the origins of the salariat ("new middle class") see Val Burris, "Capital Accumulation and the Rise of the New Middle Class," *Review of Radical Political Economics* (*RRPE*), 12, 1, Spring 1980.

The reader should be alerted to the particular sense in which the word salariat is used here, i.e. as the "intermediate strata" within large-scale capitalist enterprises in the money, productive, and commodity circuits of capital. Salaried layers in non-profit activity, small-scale capital, universities, the state, etc., are ignored, or considered later in this work.

[34] Marx discussed in many places the parceling out of both productive and unproductive traditional capitalist functions to hired managers and employees. Some modern Marxists have followed his lead, stressing the assumption by the salariat of both productive and unproductive functions performed in the past by the capitalist (G. Carchedi, "On the Economic Identification of the New Middle Classes," *Politics and Society*, 4, 1, 1974). Val Burris stresses the development of the salariat in terms of *both* the production relations and productive forces ("Capital Accumulation"). Other contemporary Marxists discuss the "new petty bourgeoisie" as if it were totally unproductive (e.g., Nicos Poulantzas, *Classes in Contemporary Capitalism*, London, 1975).

sense of "best capitalist worker" and "best boss," the salariat mediated the capital-labor relationship, connecting the two extremes and embodying both while at the same time being exclusively neither. It must be regarded, therefore, not as a class but a stratum within production which embodied and managed the contradiction between capital and labor – a stratum within which self-discipline was the linchpin of social control. The status of "best worker" reinforced by salaried and relatively secure employment signified individual advancement and success, hence the salariat symbolically functioned as an ideology of control. The salariat performed subdivided and delegated entrepreneurial and working-class functions, hence it was simultaneously a productive force and production relationship. As the "holy ghost" in the trinity of capital-salariat-labor, its effectiveness as a production relationship developed in inverse proportion to its efficiency as a productive force. The self-negation of the salariat (reflected, in part, in contemporary management unemployment) originated in the fact that to the degree that it effectively organized social domination ideologically, it could not organize exchange value production materially, and vice versa; the labor process and valorization process thus was contradictory.

The salariat defined as a productive force engaged in plant and machine design and machine building, which machine production and automation presupposed, and which was accomplished at one time by manual laborers, outside "jobbers," and/or working capitalists. It also engaged in the labor of planning, coordinating, and controlling production. "The foremost fact of industrial significance that followed from an extended division of labor is that the greater the specialization the greater the problem and necessity of coordination and cooperation."[35] Large-scale capital also required complex handling systems for materials, components, and finished products; research and development, transportation and communications planning, coordination, and control; and diverse ancillary functions which could not be placed on a mass production basis;[36] hence the development of engineers, designers, production expediters, material handling experts, cost accounts, and so on, as well as administrators.[37] The

[35] Wilbert E. Moore, "The Attributes of an Industrial Order," in Sigmund Nosow and William H. Form, eds, *Man, Work, and Society* (New York, 1962), 94.

[36] In the 1970s, in the USA, about 70 per cent of scientists and technicians were employed in "non-routine industries which produce programs, plans, or one-of-a-kind items or small production runs" (George Kozmetsky, "Reflections of a 21st Century Manager," *Bell Telephone Magazine*, March–April 1979).

[37] Organizational and administrative skills become more and more generalizeable. "It is basic to the principle of modern management as with the modern worker that the same man is equally capable of running a shoe factory or a steel mill" (James A. Brown, *The Social Psychology of Industry*, Baltimore, 1954, 39).

integration of science and technology into capitalist production and the related development of the productive forces and product innovation cycles required global specialization of salariat functions, e.g., biochemists, biophysicists, geneticists, electronic engineers, etc., as well as systems analysts and technicians whose task was to integrate specialized and diverse functions into "total systems."[38]

The salariat defined in terms of capitalist production relations engaged in the planning, coordination, and control of the work force itself – tasks which in the past were self-organized or organized by the capitalist or foreman.[39] The division of industrial labor and specialization of work presupposed either the total internalization by the workers of the concept of labor-power as variable capital or the specialization and division of workers themselves, i.e. forms of worker competition within the work-place or "competitive cooperation." In turn, the division and specialization of workers presupposed the salariat's labor of division and work of specialization. The salariat organized new labor processes and trained workers to perform new social routines essential for social domination within the production process. The work of specialization and division expanded along the axis of the division of industrial labor and task specialization and the substitution of specialized market functions by salaried administrative labor organized within the capitalist enterprise.[40]

In sum, the salariat was an instrument of domination in the double sense of technical and political control. In between capital and labor, it was thus a field on which class struggle was fought. In this sense, the salariat was "classless," i.e. a "heap" of individuals hierarchically organized within social production.[41] It was a "class" only to the degree that it made itself essential in the process of the constant rationalization of the productive forces and production relationships.[42]

Finally, from the standpoint of capitalist reproduction as a whole, the salariat's "function in the social division of labor may be described as the

[38] Richard Hill, "The Coming of Post-Industrial Society," *Insurgent Sociologist*, 4, 3, Spring 1974, 39.

[39] In the USA, for example, plant engineers began to assume capitalist managerial functions in the late nineteenth century (Daniel Nelson, *Managers and Workers: Origins of the New Factory System in the United States, 1880–1890*, Madison, 1975, passim). See also Noble, *America by Design*, passim; Edwards, *Contested Terrain*, 87. New salariat occupations, e.g. personnel manager, were also created.

[40] Alfred D. Chandler, *The Visible Hand: The Managerial Revolution in American Business* (Cambridge, Mass., 1977).

[41] The salariat stands in a "contradictory class location" (Erik Olin Wright, *Class, Crisis and the State*, London, 1978, 61–79).

[42] See Nelson, *Managers and Workers*; Edwin Layton, *The Revolt of the Engineers* (Cleveland, 1971).

reproduction of capitalist culture and class relations."[43] However, its function also consisted of the production and reproduction of the social productive forces. "Higher education" was required to reproduce personality traits, norms, and values which "are a requisite for adequate job functioning in production characterized by bureaucratic order and hierarchical control."[44] It was also required to produce and reproduce productive skills and relevant social knowledge. Higher education was a process of "credentialing" which was the result of, first, capital's need to certify individuals in the salariat as reliable, responsible, and competent and, second, worker struggles for higher wages, better jobs, and greater life chances. Credentialing was in this way "overdetermined."

The typical salary received by the credentialed salariat ceased to consist of pure "capital advanced." It included a component of revenue expended with the purpose of reproducing social domination within the labor process. It therefore included a component over and above the cost of reproducing salariat labor-power narrowly defined, with the result that the size of the average consumption basket and/or its value content tended to increase.[45] Credentialing also helped to create a social milieu within production in which labor-power became less variable because the salary became to a degree a payment not for labor-power, but for labor services, including "social control" services. Because salaried labor-power was treated less as variable capital and more as a source of particular labor services, rigidities developed within the labor market and labor process. The result was that salary advances tended to increase or remain inflexible at relatively high levels and also that management productivity tended to decline. The dynamic mechanism whereby science and technology reduced the value content of the consumption basket, thereby permitting potential increases in the baskets' size without undermining accumulation, was to that degree weakened.[46]

    [43] Barbara and John Ehrenreich, "The New Left: A Case Study in Professional-Managerial Class Radicalism," *Radical America*, 11, 3, May–June 1977, 11. See Chapter 7.
    [44] Gero Lenhardt, "On the Relationship Between the Education System and Capitalist Work Organization," *Kapitalistate*, 3, Spring 1975, 138, citing the work of Herbert Gintis, Samuel Bowles, and others.
    [45] Mark Gould has written that credentialing increased the consumption basket without commensurate increases in productivity ("The Devaluation of the Value of Laborpower," unpublished MS, 1980). In the USA, salaried executives received extremely high incomes compared with other advanced capitalist countries.
    [46] Individual wages and wage differentials, individual advancement and shift transfers, and so on also reproduced in various ways ideologies of individualism. These were fortified by associated ideologies of individual inequality, divisions between oppressed minorities and "native" workers, women and men, and workers with citizenship rights and "foreign workers." The adaptation of traditional ideologies of paternalism, religion, and ethnicity to

Technological Deterministic and Individual Humanistic Ideologies of Social Domination and the Salariat

The bases of capitalist social domination over the labor process were the opposing ideologies of technological determinism and individual humanism, which divided both individual labor-power and labor into their objective and subjective sides. The former originated in the historical context of the rise of science and Enlightenment ideas of secular progress in general and the mechanization of labor in specific; the latter in the revival of the concept of the individual human being as "of nature" rather than "of faith" in the thirteenth century, i.e. in that Western "humanism" which grasped the individual as a natural being. In the USA, the natural rights tradition linking individualism with both Enlightenment thought and humanism was especially strong. Technological determinism and humanism constituted the dominant bourgeois ideology within which the class struggle was fought. Their aim was to promote working-class and salariat "self-control" in general and to internalize capital's external compulsory mechanisms consisting of valorization and the law of value in specific.

Technological determinism, or the fetishism of efficiency, became a historical force with the rise of mass production.[47] It was expressed most dramatically in Taylorism and scientific management.[48] Its one-sided premise was that workers were the objects of the exchange of labor-power against wages and that they also assumed the status of objects within the production process. Gorz writes that "the production process must be organized so that the worker experiences the coercion to maximum output as an unalterable requirement of the machine or an imperative inherent in matter itself. Inexorable and incontestable, this compulsion even seems to be one of the apparently neutral laws of a complex machine, beyond volition and dispute."[49] Edwards adds that "technical control involves designing machinery and planning the flow of work to minimize the

---

modern conditions was also used to fragment the working class, although they also remained potential sources of solidarity and militacy.

[47] Tronti dates the "theory of technological reality which is the science of labor and the enemy of the worker" to the period between 1870 and 1914 (Mario Tronti, "Workers and Capital," *Telos*, Winter 1972, 25).

[48] Reginald Whitaker, "Scientific Management Theory as Political Ideology," *Studies in Political Economy*, 2, Autumn 1979.

[49] André Gorz, "The Tyranny of the Factory: Today and Tomorrow," *Telos*, 16, Summer 1973, 61.

problem of transforming labor-power into labor."[50] The aim of the large-scale enterprise was in effect to make workers the appendages of machines.[51] In capital units insufficiently capitalized to finance technology-based production methods, management tried to choreograph concrete labor directly. "Technique" or formal and reified rules replaced "technically-determined" labor processes. At the other extreme, in automated plants, the workers' "immediate oppressor becomes the programmed control device, the programming department, the printout – in short, the technology of production."[52] In all large-scale production processes the work of data preparation was structured by formal procedures and rules. Technical specialization and technical division of workers, not only of work, thus appeared as nature-like processes, the inevitable result of integrating science and technology into production. Finally, the interpretation of technological requirements as social imperatives required the hierarchical organization of the enterprise: "The social relationship between technical workers and production workers is . . . replaced by a fetishistic relationship to the machine . . . The separation of production workers from technicians is reflected in authority relations within the plant – as the latter are incorporated into the ranks of 'management.' "[53]

Humanistic ideologies of labor control were the modern form of paternalism and the dialectical counterparts of technological determinist ideologies. Their one-sided premise was that workers were not the objects but the subjects of exchange and labor, i.e., human beings whose labor-power was not a commodity in the sense that it could not be separated from its owner and circulated independently in the world market, hence whose labor could not be reduced to a mere "factor of production." Humanist ideologies were based on various concepts of the conditions of working-class social integration, e.g., that workers were "creatures of instincts and sentiments and are obsessed with belongingness or sociability."[54] Humanistic ideologies were also based on bourgeois universalistic

[50]   *Contested Terrain*, 112, 113.

[51]   For example, see Noble, *America by Design*; Stephan A. Marglin, "What do Bosses Do? The Origins and Functions of Authority in Capitalist Production," *RRPE*, 6, 2, Summer 1974; Jon Amsden, "Scientific Management and Working Class Militancy," *History and Culture: Legitimation and Resistance in Class Societies*, Mid-Atlantic Radical Historians Organization, Fifth Annual Conference, April 16 & 17, 1977, New York, NY.

[52]   Edwards, *Contested Terrain*, 125.

[53]   Francesca Freedman, "The Internal Structure of the American Proletariat: A Marxist Analysis," *Socialist Review*, 26 (5, 4), Oct.–Dec. 1975, 63. The fetishism of science and technology is neatly summarized in John McDermott, "Technology: The Opiate of the Intellectuals," *New York Review of Books*, July 31, 1969.

[54]   Andrew Friedman, "Responsible Autonomy versus Direct Control Over the Labour Process," *Capital and Class*, 1, Spring 1977, 51.

traditions of individual rights, as well as Owenism and other utopian productionist ideologies, including Taylorism itself, which attempted to exploit the worker's "personal ambition"[55] by imposing the piece-rate system on the worker. These ideologies flowered in the regime of modern industry because, according to Mayo and the human relations school of industrial sociology, modern capitalism "with its constant change and diversity, deprived people of intimacy, consistency, and predictability."[56] Industrial psychology added that the worker "is reluctant to feel himself nothing but an *object* of rationalization . . . the recommendations of the psychologists all aim at involving the worker materially and mentally in the life of the firm and the shaping of his work in such a way as to change him from a mere object to a *subject* of rationalization."[57]

Technological determinism and humanism were two ways of "managing" workers based on the contradictory nature of workers as objects and subjects of exchange and labor. Accordingly, there developed a deep contradiction between capital's desire to eliminate worker decision-making on the shop floor and its desire for "workers who could think," or whose creative powers capital could mobilize.[58] In this sense, the objective basis of the contradiction between ideologies of technological determinism and individual humanism was not only that labor-power was regarded as both object and subject of exchange and labor, but also that capitalist production relations stamped workers as factors of production while capitalist productive forces shaped them as active subjects of labor.[59] Put another way, in the absence of omnipresent "technological imperatives," the need to consciously develop and apply techniques to humanize work would be redundant. However difficult or oppressive, labor would be transparently humanly conceived and executed.

"Technologically determined" hierarchical differences in concrete labor tasks developed hand in hand with complex job definitions, which underscored the importance of the unique attributes of particular workers while

[55] Whitaker, "Scientific Management Theory," 87.

[56] Ibid. Mayo stressed the importance of management using "informal work groups" or worker-organized teamwork to increase efficiency (Elton Mayo, *The Human Problems of Industrial Civilization*, Cambridge, Mass., 1933, 70, 111).

[57] Georges Friedmann, *Industrial Society* (New York, 1955), 291. Industrial psychology was concerned to involve workers in their work groups and/or individual tasks, but not necessarily in the life of the firm itself.

[58] See, for example, Seymor Melman, *Decision-Making and Productivity* (Oxford, 1958). An important study of this issue is Ranjero Panzieri, "Outlines of a Critique of Technology," Phil Slater, ed., *Outlines of a Critique of Technology* (London, 1980).

[59] Carol Ray stresses that control by incentive is part and parcel of bureaucratic control. She writes that "human relations styles of control fit with 'social production/cooperation' and control by incentive fits with 'individual appropriation/competition.' Thus the two are contradictory" (personal communication).

creating the illusion of potentials for upward mobility. There appeared in the enterprise "elaborate systems of job stratification . . . the proliferation of job categories and the ranking of those jobs in a status hierarchy . . . to divide the work force."[60] Job definition systems involved "finely graded division and stratification of workers . . . [tending to] break up the homogeneity of the firm's workforce, creating many seemingly separate strata, lines of work, and focuses for job identity . . . *each job slot appears individual or distinct.*"[61] The result was that "occupations" and "positions" contained ideological as well as substantive content.[62] Other practices included the establishment of false career ladders, especially with the salariat labor force;[63] the appropriation of traditional craft and white-collar standards which management retained *de jure* while abolishing them *de facto* (for example, attempts to impose craft worker ways of life on the mass work force);[64] ideologies of professionalism whereby management replaced traditional professional standards with "professional associations" and norms which functioned as legitimations of domination;[65] and different kinds of role-modeling which abolished real individuality.

Within the world of "jobs," "occupations," "positions," and "professions," there emerged humanistic ideologies of "personal growth," "careers," and "cooperation," as well as various forms of psychological seduction and behavior modification.[66] These were especially important within high-tech and automated processes which required self-discipline and responsibility on the part of workers and staff. Historically associated with theories of labor-management partnership,[67] humanistic ideologies

[60] Maria Barrera, "Colonial Labor and Theories of Inequality; The Case of International Harvester," *RRPE*, 8, 2, Summer 1976, 5. An account of the proliferation of occupational titles and task specialization is Steven Deutsch, "The Sociology of the American Workers," *International Journal of Comparative Sociology*, 10, 1 and 2, March–June 1969, 63.

[61] Edwards, *Contested Terrain*, 133, 134 (italics added).

[62] See for example Katherine Stone, "The Origins of the Job Structure in the Steel Industry," *RRPE*, 6, 2, Summer 1974; Howard Wachtel, "Class Consciousness and Stratification in the Labor Process," *RRPE*, 6, 1, Spring 1974.

[63] Fred H. Goldner and R. R. Ritti, "Professionalism as Career Immobility," *American Journal of Sociology*, 72, 5, March 1967, 502.

[64] Stephen Myer, "Mass Production and Cultural Conformity: Americanization in the Ford Motor Co., 1914–1921," *History and Culture* Conference, cited n. 51 above; "Where White Collar Status Boosts Productivity," *Business Week*, May 23, 1977, 80.

[65] Kraft, *Programmers and Managers*. A study of operation researchers discovered no evidence of independent professionalism employing criteria of role preparation, coherent group values, and membership in public reference groups established independently by the researchers themselves (communcation from Phil Kraft).

[66] Richard Sennett, "The Boss's New Clothes," *New York Review*, Feb. 22, 1979, passim; "Where Skinner's Theories Work," *Business Week*, Dec. 2, 1972.

[67] Yves Delamotte, "The Attitudes of French and Italian Trade Unions to the 'Humanization' of Work," *Labour and Society*, 1, 1, January 1976; Edwards, *Contested Terrain*, 107.

included concepts of "job enrichment" and "job enlargement," redesign of production processes with the aim of making work more "interesting," and various ideologies of "participation."[68] Andrew Friedman sums up the issue when he contrasts "direct control of workers" with "responsible autonomy," which gives the work force (especially privileged workers and groups) "leeway and encourages them to adapt to changing situations in a manner beneficial to the firm."[69] Responsible autonomy 'involves allowing individual workers and groups of workers a wide measure of discretion over the direction of their work tasks and the maintenance of managerial authority by getting workers to identify with the competitive aims of the enterprise." While the direct control strategy "sees the majority of people working as machines manipulated by centralized planning departments," in this way reducing "variability of labor power by limiting its scope for independent activity," the responsible autonomy strategy aimed to "harness" the "variable aspect of labour power for managerial ends rather than [be] subdued."[70]

The twin ideologies of technological determinism and humanism were developed and implemented by salariat labor organized within hierarchical corporate structures which were governed by "rational-legal" ideologies of domination or "legitimate authority."[71] The salariat bureaucracy combined classical and formal authority, technical domination and hierarchical control. The bureaucracy was materialized in staff and line functions (the technical and control salariat, respectively) whose structure reproduced the contradiction between the salariat as productive force and

[68] Big Flame, Fact Folder 3, "Workers' Struggle and the Development of Ford in Britain," *Bulletin of the Conference of Socialist Economists*, 5, 1, March 1976, 13.

[69] Friedman, *Industry and Labour*, 78. Friedman stresses the importance of changing capital's various strategies of control in accordance with changing conditions (ibid., 49). He writes that it is "impossible to understand changes in managerial behavior and industrial organization without explicitly taking struggle at the micro level into account" (4).

[70] Friedman, "Responsible Autonomy," 48, 51.

[71] Edwards, *Contested Terrain*, passim. Edwards argues that workers in big industry in the USA defeated both Taylorism and "welfarism" by the 1920s, hence the need for bureaucratic control (ibid., 98). David Montgomery states that "scientific management" was more often than not merely an ideology and that in the early 20th century when scientific management was the rage, little or no work regularization was actually accomplished (See, for example, "Immigrant Workers and Scientific Management," in Mary Robinson et al., eds, *Work and Society* (Detroit, 1977); "Gutman's Nineteenth Century America," *Labor History*, 19, 3, Summer 1978).

In Richard Pfeffer's *Working for Capitalism* (New York, 1979) three forms of authority and control in the factory are identified: first, hierarchy built into the design of the labor process itself; second, the formal authority structure of the plant; third, the union. If the "democratic" process of the union is interpreted as an "ideology of humanism" the scheme laid out in this section can be brought into line with Pfeffer's experiences and incisive observations in a Baltimore piston ring factory.

production relationship. The bureaucracy codified labor-power as an object of exchange and labor in the form of enterprise goals based on abstract labor, exchange value and valorization. It codified labor-power as a subject of exchange and labor in the form of job descriptions based on concrete labor, use value, and the material results of production.

The structure of domination within the enterprise presupposed the universal belief in the legality of enacted rules, which established the corporate bureaucracy as a "legally-founded, impersonal social order," together with the belief in the right of command of the salariat placed in authority positions under these rules. " 'The organization' becomes an abstract bearer of sovereign prerogatives – over and above all personal 'authorizations' of bodily individuals."[72] Within the organization, salariat legitimation changed from success in open competitive struggle to an emphasis on qualities of bureaucratic leadership.[73] The resulting "naturalness" and "permanence" of the organization fulfilled capital's desire for predictability and standardization, the salariat's status-striving drive, and the need of workers for stability and security. Richard Edwards' description of bureaucratic control is exemplary, although in the context of the present analysis he mistakenly contrasts bureaucratic with technical control.[74] Instead, bureaucratic control may be regarded as the necessary *form* of the organization of both technical and humanistic control systems.

Habermas has analyzed the internal connection between ideologies of technological determinism and administrative/bureaucratic control:

Technocratic ideology serves administered politics in a doubly effective manner. First, as the leading productive force, technology and science prescribe the paradigm for the mode of organization of behavior in large organizations. Second, by providing legitimations that cast off ideology-cum-utopian truth content and repressing ethics

[72] John Keane, "The 'Decline of the Individual' and the Problem of Legitimacy," paper, Canadian Political Science Association Meetings, Saskatoon, Canada, May 30–June 1, 1979, 2, 28.

[73] Reinhard Bendix, *Work and Authority in Industry: Ideologies of Management in the Course of Industrialization* (New York, 1964).

[74] "Two possibilities existed: the control mechanism could be embedded in the technological structure of the firm or it could be embedded in the firm's social-organizational structure. Corresponding to these two possibilities are the systems of technical and bureaucratic control" the result being that "power was made invisible in the structure of work" (*Contested Terrain*, 110). Edwards' main thesis is that there has been a shift from labor processes which make work and workers homogeneous, hence make worker unity possible, to systems which institutionalize divisions and disunity. It seems more accurate to say that bureaucratic organization, incentives and rules are simply more refined and developed than in previous stages of capitalism; i.e. there has been an increased subdivision of tasks which are formally described in increasingly codified ways.

as a category of life, technocratic ideologies foster adaptive behaviors required by administrative forms of domination.[75]

No one has made a comparable analysis of links between humanistic ideologies and administrative/bureaucratic control. It can be argued, however, that humanistic ideologies also served administered politics within the capitalist enterprise. First, these ideologies prescribed another, contradictory paradigm for behavior within the enterprise because bureaucracy is formally inconsistent with personalism, arbitrariness, nepotism, and other barriers to universalistic principles of fairness and individual rights. Second, humanistic ideologies attempted to foster not merely adaptive, but also creative, behavior required by capitalist bureaucracy which was always threatened with losing its capacity for any but routine actions.[76] The contradiction thus arose that precisely because bureaucracy abstracted from the particularity of the individual worker and salariat, its capacity to impose models of social integration, which depended on the sensuous, real individual and his/her relation with social functions, was more or less undermined.

The fact that bureaucratic control was consistent with and dependent upon both humanistic and technological determinist ideologies meant that it was deeply internally contradictory. This was true of the impersonal rules or company policy which governed the direction of work tasks, evaluation of performance, and rewards and punishments, as well as of incentive systems organized to reward behavior relevant to making the control system work (as contrasted with the reward of work itself). At high levels, humanistic ideologies were dominant. Workers at low levels were expected to follow fixed rules; their performance was evaluated in terms of work habits and personal characteristics within the framework of tech-nological deterministic ideologies. At somewhat higher levels, workers and the lower salariat were oriented to predictability and dependability and were governed by a confusing mixture of humanistic and technical control ideologies.[77]

Bureaucratically organized divisions within the work force and illusory status differences and functional specializations within the salariat exempli-fied material forms of the contradiction between labor-power as object and subject. The significance of this was that the contradiction was

---

[75] Habermas' views on this subject are summarized by Jean Cohen, "Why More Political Theory," *Telos*, 40, Summer 1979, 84.

[76] Carol Ray points out that the human relations school itself concentrated on "helping" the worker adapt to *existing* situations.

[77] *Contested Terrain*, 131, 148, 150–151. Edwards does not make the link between forms of prescribed behavior and the dominance of particular control ideologies.

displaced into the structure of the organization and its rules themselves. Layered between conflicts between and within work groups and management were conflicts between rules generally and rule legitimations specifically. This helps to explain the chaotic tendencies within bureaucratic organization in the form of contradictions between rules and norms – hence the requirement that the enterprise constantly "change the rules" or make rules so ambiguous that it became difficult or impossible to fix responsibility for actions and their results on individuals filling particular positions – as well as in the form of periodic and often senseless reorganizations of the bureaucratic structures themselves. Most important, this helps to explain widespread anomie arising from the absence of "good fits" between economic and social functions.

It seems safe to say that capital's heavy batteries of ideological weaponry, including ideological *forms* of the organization of ideologies, can be regarded as indispensable within the production process under conditions of US "full capitalism." The reason was that mass production made production more cooperative in character and at the same time required keener individualistic competition within the work force for wages and salaries, desirable shifts, promotions and positions, status, etc. to prevent or minimize horizontal unity within the enterprise. The twin imperatives of social production/cooperation and individual appropriation/competition necessarily developed together. Forms of "competitive cooperation" and "cooperative competition" within work groups and "compromise conflicts" and "conflicted compromises" between labor and capital became universal.[78] The abolition of traditional individuality (indivisibility) associated with mass production and circulation, communication, and related processes was more than matched by the development of individualist ideologies and their practices. Perhaps no more important requirement for capitalist social integration existed than the need for the worker to sell or "lease" labor-power individually and to compete individually within the enterprise. In this connection, it should be stressed that wages and salaries were advanced for the salariat labor of specializing and dividing manual workers with the aim of social domination in the work place. As Claus Offe showed in his critique of achievement ideologies, the control of labor in modern capitalism was increasingly based on normative and ideological requirements defined as necessary to specific tasks but which were unrelated to technical fulfillment.[79] Labor was organized "in terms of symbolic substitutes for performance";[80] rewards were distributed

[78]   David Riesman wrote of the "antagonistic cooperation" between corporate managers (*The Lonely Crowd*, New Haven, 1950, 81).

[79]   Offe, *Industry and Inequality*.

[80]   Ibid., Translator's Introduction, 3.

according not to achievement or technical performance, but rather to how well workers accepted given power relations. The result was not only a "freeze" in relation to the distribution of power, which hindered the development of the productive forces, but also an increase in the costs of worker and salariat labor-power to the degree that these included the costs of ideological practice.

It also should be stressed that under the regime of "full capitalism" there developed a permanent division between the working class and salariat. The great majority of workers could not realistically aspire to compete individually for salariat positions, which normally required formal credentials, degrees, licenses, etc., which denoted the acquisition of certain kinds of personality (as well as technical and managerial) skills. Instead, the salariat reproduced itself through privileged access to and control over the educational-credential apparatus.[81] Meanwhle, salariat labor itself became fragmented and wherever possible routinized, which made working-class competition for "middle-class" positions increasingly illusory. This, in turn, created ever-present dangers of the breakdown of capitalist control ideologies.

In sum, the emergence and superficial stabilization of "full capitalism" brought about significant changes in the conditions of class struggle. It also changed the forms of struggle and their effects on the law of value and the accumulation process generally, as we will presently see.

Worker Control of Ideologies

The accumulation of managerial ideological practices within the framework of "legal-rational" authority systems spawned many and diverse contradictions. So much has been obvious to critical students of corporate administration, labor organization, and law. The reasons, however, are not so obvious. These were, first, the dual nature of the worker as object and subject of exchange and labor; second, the resulting coexistence of technological and humanistic managerial ideologies; third, the bureaucratic organization of managerial ideologies. The first reason belies the Marxist functionalist argument that the consumption of labor-power was inherently productive consumption. In fact, labor-power was also self-consumed in various forms of resistance.[82] Not labor-power as a form of capital, but the class struggle inscribed work roles and relations.[83]

[81] Samuel Bowles, "Unequal Education and the Reproduction of the Social Division of Labor," *RRPE*, 4, 4, 1972.

[82] James O'Connor, "Productive and Unproductive Labor," *Politics and Society*, 5, 1975.

[83] See for example P. Crissey and J. Macinness, "Voting for Ford? Industrial Democracy and the Control of Labour," *Capital and Class*, 11, 1980.

The second reason, which pertains to the contradiction between ideologies of objectification and subjectification of workers and work, belies bourgeois functionalist arguments that social differentiation was a source of social solidarity. In fact, social differentiation based on ideological practices may be regarded as a source of social confusion and social conflict. Ideologies of individualism in the form of reified roles introduced inflexibilities and irrationalities in production, hence were dysfunctional economically. Further, these ideologies mirrored in inverted ways the reality of work, hence were also dysfunctional socially. To the degree that the role was fulfilled, it was a mirror because the individual could see his or her reflection in the role and its norms. But it was inverted because the "self" located in the role was not the social self, but the reified self, i.e. the "individual" defined in terms of "outside and against" society rather than "within and of" society. This helps to explain the prevalence of great ambiguity, self-blame, confusion and emotional distress, i.e., identity crises caused by modern capital's attempts to vary workers' reified personalities in order to make labor-power more variable.

The third reason, which concerns the conditions of "rational-legal" authority within the capitalist enterprise, belies arguments in favor of bureaucratic rationality, including internal coherence and consistency of norms and rules. Rational-legal authority systems and bureaucratic routines were in fact inconsistent with the always variable quantitative criteria governing exchange value production and valorization (one reason for the well documented breakdown in communication within US corporations).[84] Rules by virtue of the fact that they are rules based on universalistic principles negated the variability of capital. In this sense, capital necessarily manufactured and depended on "deviance" of various kinds.

These three contradictions exemplified different forms of the contradiction between system and social domination/integration. At the level of lived experience they manifested themselves in conflicts between management and workers in the workplace. These contradictions and associated political struggles in the workplace were always active, and during particular conjunctures, for example the cycle of world struggles in 1968–70, they became hyperactive. However, these conjunctures themselves were in part the result of the accumulation of "small contradictions" which can be described as the "compromised conflicts" and "conflicted compromises" inherent in the capital/wage labor relation, and which were exemplified by wage lags, buildup of grievances about working conditions, shop floor

[84] An Opinion Research Corp. survey in 1982 found that 50 per cent of workers believed that lack of communication is a "root cause" of bad morale and low productivity (*S.F. Chronicle*, Dec. 13, 1982).

inequities, inequitable wage controls, disputes about the introduction and uses of new technologies, etc.

Managerial ideologies and bureaucratic control systems negated themselves in two general ways which in practice were indistinguishable. First, ideologies of control inadvertently created inflexibilities or rigidities in the labor process (or the utilization of labor-power) which tended to undermine the valorization process. Second, management ideologies and practices and their bureaucratic organization unintentionally established legitimate bases for struggles which permitted work groups to create more inflexibilities within production, which independently subverted capital valorization. Put another way, large-scale capital's need for a stable work-force was appropriated by unions and work groups to further "immobilize" the work force. Both managerial and working-class practices threatened the status of labor-power as variable capital not only in the quantitative but also in the qualitative sense (i.e. struggles to redefine capitalist concepts and practices of space and time), and in this way made the concept of socially necessary labor as the basis of the law of value problematic. The "social laws" emerging from managerial and working-class practices did not replace the law of value; rather, they opposed and hence combined with it to constitute a determinate contradictory reality. This meant that the system's capacity to reproduce its "originating structures", ("reengender its own origins at every moment")[85] became uncertain.

Specifically, at the level of lived experience workers exchanged concrete labor services (not labor-power) for wages. This meant that the worker was hired to do, hence had a claim on, a particular "job" – a precapitalist ideology which prevailed when workers in fact sold labor services, and when the concept of entitlement had substantive as well as formal meaning. This contradiction between exchange symbols (wages for labor services) and exchange substance (wages for laborpower) was most extreme in the regime of US "full capitalist" production. The lived ideology that the work force in fact exchanged individual labor services for wages meant that capital threatened its own variability, or the capacity to make labor-power into variable capital and to produce surplus value.[86]

This contradiction was activated by managerial ideological practices within bureaucratic structures together with working-class practices. On

---

[85] Maurice Godelier, *Rationality and Irrationality in Economics* (New York, 1972), 180.

[86] A good history of "property rights in work" is Warren S. Gramm, "Property Rights in Work: Capitalism, Industrialism, and Democracy," *Journal of Economic Issues*, 15, 2, June 1981. Gramm concludes his survey with the opinion that "worker achievement of property status in the job is conservative in the sense that it merely would bring to the individual worker the essence of economic independence premised by classical liberalism" (373). On the other hand, "property status in the job" is profoundly radical in the sense that it is critical of the basic capitalist concept of labor-power as variable capital.

the one side, capital concealed class domination with individualistic status distinctions; workers were defined as "job-holders," or as persons with particular jobs and statuses. Artificial job hierarchies subverted the social and abstract nature of labor. Titles, credentials, separate career ladders, "professionalization of work," developmental psychologies applied to relations within work, etc., had the unintentional effect of limiting the enterprise's ability to vary labor concretely and exploit labor intensely, hence expand value production. So did organizational rules, norms, and structures presupposed by rational-legal authority systems within the enterprise. "A completely bureaucratized organization," Branko Horvat observed about Yugoslavia (the observation also applies more or less to a bureaucratized capitalism), "would require that the number of rules be almost as great as the number of concrete decisions. Since this is impossible . . . an important element of imprecision and unpredictability creeps into the organization. To cope with this defect, those in authority tend to multiply rules, whose sheer number and increasing inconsistency with each other have a strong negative effect on those who are required to observe these rules, and this drives them to inactivity."[87] In US capitalism, labor-power was less likely to assume the character of variable capital when rule-bound enterprises were unable to hire salariat and workers who did not meet "professional standards" and/or to raise or lower standards based on profitability criteria without the risk of appearing "unprofessional." In sum, "labor services" connoted many particular qualitative meanings (concrete labor, use values). "Labor-power" connoted one particular quantitative meaning (abstract labor, exchange value). To the degree that the former polluted the latter criterion, requirements for the labor process subverted the valorization process.

Workers, of course, have had a long history of challenging managerial domination of the production process. For example, seniority and job security demands have moderated capital's capacity to exploit younger workers, especially in branches of large-scale industry where work was regularized.[88] Particularly important in the regime of "full capitalism," however, was the appropriation of managerial ideological practices and formal organizational rules as weapons in the class struggle. Individual workers, work groups, labor organizations, and rank-and-file caucuses, as well as government agencies, lawyers, and courts charged with regulating class relationships at various levels, took ideological practices seriously. Subversive material contents and social meanings were inserted into practices and rules; the basis of valorization and accumulation was thereby undermined. "Unions turned to bureaucratization of the work-

---

[87] Branko Horvat, *An Essay on Yugoslav Society* (New York, 1969), 16.
[88] Edwards, *Contested Terrain*, 152.

place to codify and thereby defend their negotiated gains."[89] "In some cases union negotiations have provided the impetus toward detailed job descriptions [hence] the conditions for both the sale of laborpower and its consumption are thereby regulated by job descriptions."[90] "In the course of the last few decades the unions and their political inspirers have succeeded in largely re-establishing hierarchical prejudices and greatly increasing the number of work categories."[91] These and other union actions were generally considered by management in large-scale enterprises to have reduced operating flexibility.[92]

As we have seen, "technologically determined" differences in concrete labor required a system of ideological job stratification and status hierarchies, which, however, had contradictory results. "Finely graded division and stratification of workers tends to break up the homogeneity of the firm's work force, creating many seemingly separate strata, lines of work . . ."[93] At the same time, these divisions created "focuses for job identity."[94] This meant that workers fought to establish individual job rights to particular concrete tasks (a different issue than the struggle for "full employment"). These struggles occurred in tens of thousands of workplaces without any reference whatsoever to their potential effects on valorization and accumulation. Workers/salariat seeking concrete job rights in effect refused new forms of social differentiation and functional integration in accordance with the requirements of the law of value. In this way, economic functions became less integrated into one another; laborpower was robbed of some of its variable character; and the principle of workers as factors of production or inter-changeable parts was undermined. This systematic "functional disintegration" was in effect the same as the process of "social disintegration" of individuals into economic and social functions. Anomie thus appeared as the social-personal expression

[89] Ibid., 132. Edwards adds that "bureaucratic control" provides "higher pay, more rights, greater job security – to workers who accept the system and seek, by individual effort, to improve their lot in it" (146).

[90] Ibid., 138, 140. Edwards deals at length with the self-negating features of control ideologies in the context of social control or "labor control." His discussion of the self-negating qualities of control ideologies with regard to valorization is more cursory. His argument is: 1) when companies make long-term employment commitments, wages tend to become fixed costs, 2) training time required to permit workers to fit job descriptions raises costs, 3) seniority and other inflexibilities during periods of decline and lay-offs mean that high-wage workers bump relatively low-wage workers, also adding to costs (ibid., 157–8).

[91] G. Munis, *Unions Against Revolution* (Detroit, 1975), 12.

[92] B. F. Goodrich's Chairman of the Board, O. Pendleton Thomas, stated that: "Because Michelin is nonunion it has greater operating flexibility, and that gives them a competitive edge" (quoted in *Business Week*, July 26, 1976, 60).

[93] Edwards, *Contested Terrain*, 133.

[94] Ibid.

of systematic malfunctioning of the law of value, and also as the social-personal expression of both system malfunctions and processes of social disintegration/reintegration.

Similar conclusions may be drawn in relation to worker control of technological determinist ideologies of the labor process, the essence of which from the standpoint of capital was that it "manufactured consent" in the form of fatalistic working-class attitudes. Technological determinist ideologies at bottom expressed the view that machines not workers were productive and efficient. Therefore, *workers resistance to increased efficiency was nothing more nor less than acceptance of the idea that machinery was the sole source of valorization.* Worker opposition to the "pace of the *line* . . . [which] establishes a technically based and technically repressive mechanism [that keeps] workers at their tasks"[95] was in this sense inherent in the regime of modern industry. The struggle against speedup, resistance to compulsory overtime, absenteeism, labor turnover, sabotage, etc., created work environments in which "ideas for replacing assembly-line labor, similar to some that were considered 'unrealistic' when published a few years ago, are now accepted as eminently practical in Sweden, campaigned for by trade unions in America and more recently in Britain, and most recently of all have been advocated for the European Economic Community as a whole by its Commission."[96] In turn, humanist-inspired factory redesigns raised variable and constant capital costs and (everything else being the same) reduced surplus value.

Humanistic ideologies of "participation," which introduced criteria within the production process which were extraneous to profitability, ran the risk that worker demands might surpass normal trade union demands.[97] This possibility arose because participation schemes and job redefinitions which aimed to make work more "human" relied on assessments of the personality and individual attributes of the worker. When workers adapted concepts such as the "development of the individual's aptitudes" for their own uses (when use value polluted exchange value criteria), they increased the danger that valorization ceased to be the only goal of production. Job enrichment and job enlargement schemes motivated by humanistic ideologies restored productive knowledge to the workers, albeit not individually, but in groups or teams, which created new chances for resistance (even though job enrichment from capital's standpoint was motivated by the

[95]   Ibid., 118.

[96]   Alasdair Clayre, *Work and Play: Ideas and Experiences of Work and Leisure* (New York, 1974), 184.

[97]   See, for example, André Gorz, "The Tyranny of the Factory: Today and Tomorrow," *Telos*, 16, Summer 1973; Paul Blumberg, *Industrial Democracy: The Sociology of Participation*, 1969; Big Flame, "Workers' Struggles," 13.

desire to deskill the remaining skilled workers, meanwhile stretching out the work of unskilled and semiskilled workers). The significance of these schemes from the workers' standpoint was that they gave workers chances to recombine and recompose tasks in more creative ways than merely "doubling-up." Also, workers with "enlarged" higher-skill jobs became more concerned with control over job content and work methods[98] and more dissatisfied with their relations with superiors (even though they identified more with enterprise goals).[99] This also made the practical application of the concept of labor-power as variable capital more uncertain. Capitalist humanism meant in effect that subjective states of individual workers were incorporated into labor management.

In sum, technological and humanistic ideological practices exemplified respectively by worker fatalism and individual volition meant that "efficiency resistance," "unmotivated resignations," "voluntary absenteeism," "moonlighting in the underground economy," etc., were doubly determined. The practical meaning of the humanistic ideal that work should be worthwhile was that the *worker* should be worthwhile. In the context of technological deterministic ideologies which fetishized machines, reified living labor, and resulted in spontaneous resistance to efficiency, this meant that resistance itself was worthwhile. *Technological ideologies created worker resistance to human efficiency; humanistic ideologies legitimated this resistance, which thus assumed the status of a political act.* In short, while the "loss of the work ethic" was inexplicable in totalistic terms except in the context of the conjuncture of worldwide resistance and struggles as mediated by mass communications, international relations, etc., it was also deeply rooted in the ideological practices of the regime of large-scale capital.

As we have seen, the social relationships of production within the capitalist enterprise developed within ideological forms of organization of managerial ideologies of control, namely the bureaucratic organization of ideologies and work. Individual workers, work groups, and unions also appropriated formal organizational rules developed within the enterprise to regulate and rationalize worker struggles, hence helped to define the rules and rule structures themselves. "Working to rule" typically lengthened the working period and turnover time of capital, which was evidence that the rules themselves were infused with forms of resistance. Rules were also ideologies in so far as they consisted of regulations pertaining to formal job definitions. Workers were typically expected to do more work and dif-

[98] Louis Davis and Richard Werling, "Job Design Factors," *Occupational Psychology*, 34, 1960.

[99] Clayton P. Alderfer, "Job Enlargement and the Organizational Context," *Personnel Psychology*, 22, 1969.

ferent kinds of work than those specified in particular rules governing concrete work tasks (rules and job definitions were created to keep formally defined skills low, hence wages minimized). In these cases, "working to rule" meant that functional tasks were done badly or not at all. This created ruptures or slowdowns in the labor process. More, "working to rule" was an important factor forcing capitalist management to experiment with job enrichment and worker self-management schemes.[100] Perhaps most importantly, bureaucratic control by formal rule structures created aspirations for enlarged democracy in the workplace.[101] Also, when the corporation established itself as a permanent bureaucracy, it assumed some of the attributes of a public institution, which legitimated turning workplace conflicts into political issues,[102] or, at the least, ideologically underwrote the workers' search for regulation and protection within political-administrative processes.

Roughly similar conclusions may be drawn with regard to the individualistic struggles of the salariat charged with making, enforcing, and changing rules and norms specifically, and ideological legitimations and organizational structures generally. Status-striving and attainment within the formal structure of the capitalist enterprise helped to shape salariat role adaptation, motivation, communication abilities, and other capacities essential to habituating individuals and groups to enterprise goals. Weakened status-striving and status-attainment activities within formal roles tended to subvert the valorization process. Given the salariat's well documented obsession with individual self-realization in a reified social context in which formal status was in effect a negation of self-worth,[103] salariat struggles for "individuality" may be regarded as *struggles against status through status*. This appeared to partly underlie the "rebellion of the middle class" which, although individualistic to the core, still had a negative impact on valorization. In "full capitalism" productivity depended on group and individual adaptability to reformed status hierarchies and goals, information, technique, and organizational capacity.[104] Hence, motivation deficits, distorted communications, and/or "polluted information" increased legitimation deficits within the enterprise, and impaired organizational capacities and adaptability. Salariat struggles for "individuality" may be construed as different kinds of appropriation of tech-

[100] Edwards, *Contested Terrain*, 154.

[101] Ibid., 153.

[102] Ibid., 160–2. See also Deena Weinstein, "Bureaucratic Opposition: The Challenge to Authoritarian Abuses at the Work Place," *Canadian Journal of Social and Political Theory*, 1, 2, Spring–Summer 1977.

[103] Jeff Livesay, "The Dialectics of Status Competition," Ph.D. dissertation, Univ. of California, Santa Cruz, 1978.

[104] Hirschorn, "Theory of Social Services," 299.

nological deterministic, humanistic, and bureaucratic legitimations for the advancement of individuals' life chances at the expense of the capital-value producing capacity of the enterprise specifically, and system reproduction generally.[105]

In these ways, *individualistic* struggles undermined the reproduction of human labor-power *as a commodity*. These struggles should not be interpreted ahistorically, but rather within the objective context of managerial ideological practices, i.e. as legitimate struggles opposing the concept of variable capital and the many-sided practices associated with this concept. "Full capitalism" in this sense described not only the conditions of capitalist cooperation between workers (i.e. "competitive cooperation") but also the conditions of workers' cooperation (i.e. "cooperative cooperation"), which consisted of practical-theoretical critiques of individualistic ideologies, especially those embodied in work structures and the structure of individualistic appropriation from the social product.[106] These attacks against capital's lines of defense within the labor process included shop floor movements against technical change and changes in the industrial division of labor; struggles against plant closures; demands for permanent employment; struggles for working-class rules governing the definition of jobs and wage structures; equalitarian wage demands; struggles against labor mobility, speedup, etc.; "counterplanning on the shop floor," especially when labor unions and management collaborated at the level of the labor process; and individual salariat struggles against status and worker struggles against salariat authority in the form of challenges to authority roles. Last, but not least, there occurred social and political struggles within the working class which assumed the form of affirmative action, anti-racism, anti-sexism, anti-imperialism, and so on, which "preinstitutionalized" working-class power. Especially important in the regime of modern industry in which women workers constituted a large and growing portion of the work force were struggles by women for unity at the factory level.[107]

We must also mention the well documented decline in job satisfaction and stress on "quality of life" issues which was linked to demands pertaining to the character and meaning of work, as well as to growing "motivations and incentives deficits" expressed in the hoarding of labor-

---

[105] In 1982, "Middle Management is Disenchanted Enough to Pose a Serious Threat to Productivity" (*S.F. Chronicle*, Dec. 13, 1982).

[106] Sennett writes that "the very nature of this new ideology of human relations contains a contradiction which may also be its undoing. It is a system based not on mutual respect but on pseudo-mutuality" ("Boss's New Clothes," 46).

[107] The key role of women in struggle for unity at the factory level is documented in Lucy Middleton's *Women in the Labour Movement* (Totowa, NJ, 1971).

power, growth of the "leisure industry," crime, underground economy, self-help, and so on. Finally, environmental and worker safety struggles had the effect of reducing productivity and raising the value content of the average consumption basket, meanwhile rendering labor-power less variable.

These and other practices reflected and created an industrial milieu in which workers were considered to be expensive to employ and lay off, hence in which capital was cautious about accumulating new labor-power, and hiring young workers in particular. These practices also exemplified the tendency for the working class to ossify the division of labor in the course of struggles against the various "divisions of laborers." Meanwhile shorter hours, longer vacations, and higher turnover were, in the last analysis, dysfunctional for capital in that they weakened the valorization process. They were also dysfunctional to the extent that they impaired the capacity of the system to correct itself through economic crises in the short and medium runs.[108]

In sum, the class struggle was to determine whether concrete labor services or abstract labor-power would in real practice exchange against wages and salaries, i.e. whether use or exchange value ruled production and social reproduction, whether conscious social laws established by the producing classes themselves or the law of value dominated the world of material production and distribution. These struggles within and against reified roles could not be adequately characterized in the full sense as "struggles against productivity." Still less could they be described as struggles for "economic democracy" or "workers' control of industry." Nor did these struggles originate in the "desire for more leisure" alone (early retirement, for example, was better explained in terms of the prevalence of unemployment and worker immobility).[109] Moreover, it remained generally true that individual self-esteem was still based on paid work,[110] indicating that labor-power was not and could not be merely a "factor of production."

Instead, worker struggles within and against status roles were struggles for a redefinition of self in terms of the "other," not over and against it, i.e., a rejection of the reified concept of self. They were struggles for "workers' work," that is, self-valorization or self-defined activity, or *forms and contents of labor which permitted workers to develop labor-power for*

[108] David Gordon, "Capital vs. Labor: The Current Crisis in the Sphere of Production," *URPE, Radical Perspectives on the Economic Crisis* (New York, 1975).

[109] See for example Jan Newton and John Young, *Capitalism and Human Obsolescence* (Boston, 1979), 28, 135.

[110] See for example Frank Field, ed., *The Conscript Army: A Study of Britain's Unemployed* (London, 1977).

fuller and creative utilization during free time, but which meantime remained paid work; not alienated work, but labor based on the premise that the worker was the subject of both exchange and labor, hence could not be reduced to the "status" of variable capital. John Goldthorpe, Richard Edwards, and others have summed up this issue with their stress on the importance of concepts of citizenship rights as legitimations for struggles within production. Perhaps we can go one step further and conclude that it was precisely in the course of legitimate struggles that the working class began to find its *social individuality*, which is the only kind of individuality possible in the context of the modern division of industrial and social labor. These struggles, of course, were not politically organised in the USA, and perhaps for this reason, with the breakdown of "systems of consistent expectations," they were bound to take populist and at times nihilistic forms. This was particularly true when "culture workers" and image-makers, whose imaginations were alienated and embodied in commodities themselves, rebelled against the wage form. Yet even within the salariat, there were demands for the decommodification of labor-power as well as for salaries based on new needs explicable only in terms of decommodified labor-power, product of labor, and labor processes based on the social development of the individual.

Struggles for Reproduction and the Law of Value

The significance of worker struggles in the production process was that they were at least implicit critiques of the fetishistic premises of capitalism as a whole, directed in particular against collaboration with a social order which works in such "natural" yet opaque and mysterious ways. Herein lies the meaning of struggles which made variable capital "less variable." They could be tempered but not eliminated by reformist measures because the working class/salariat's appropriation of managerial ideological practices erected barriers not only to the reduction of socially necessary labor-time, but also to the *formation* of necessary labor-time. Capitalist labor control mechanisms and worker struggles not only raised the cost of reproducing labor-power, but redefined its historical nature. Capitalist concentration, centralization, and conglomeration meant that "markets" potentially became mechanisms, less for establishing socially necessary labor-time than for the circulation of workers' struggles. The growth of a relatively highly paid salariat and managerial inflexibilities associated with capital concentration and conglomeration; struggles within the salariat for and against status; and struggles within the working class for "workers' work," especially women's struggles based on the explosive release of repressed anger produced within domestic life, introduced use value criteria into the productive circuit of capital. These features of modern capitalism helped to underwrite inflation; more important, they were so much "noise" interfering with the fateful workings of the law of value.

This was a crucially important issue because science and technology were systematically integrated into the production and circulation of capital-value; because socially necessary labor-time was determined by scientific and technological developments in a systematic sense not true in earlier stages of capitalism; and because the law of value itself was inseparable from the production and reproduction of science and technology. The integration of the so-called economic base and scientific-ideological "superstructure" meant that capitalism as a system required maximum flexibility, adaptability, and internal coherence with regard not only to new production processes, product innovation, new forms of credit, etc., but also to cultural and political change. Capitalism developed a big stake in flexible and consistent functional relationships and organizational links betwen the education system, the science establishment and its technical applications, financing and marketing, state planning organs, and directly productive labor itself. In this world of "aggregate social capital" it was essential that the working class and salariat adjust expectations, functional tasks, and ideologies to continual change, respond positively to constant demands for mobility and adaptability, and withstand "future shock." The capitalist enterprise and system as a whole needed not merely the passive consent but the *active* participation of the working class and salariat, not to speak of independent suppliers, the academic establishment, state agencies, etc. However, this consent and participation consisted precisely in the agreement to objectify oneself, i.e. to subject one's work group, union local, department, family, etc. to systematic powers enforced by contradictory ideological practices whose "complete totality" remained mysterious and inexplicable.

Independent of the particular forms which struggles assumed in large- and small-scale capital, in the branches of economy organizing the money and commodity circuits of capital, on the shop floor, etc., there were few if any ways that capital could legitimate its increasingly mysterious needs to workers, technicians, and managers. Hostility to alienated work, poor role adaptation, indifference to capitalist status attainment, motivation deficits, and system irrationalities within planning functions produced systemic inflexibilities *at precisely the time when capitalism required maximum flexibility*. Slowly but surely, struggles for self-reproduction within the production process threatened the edifice of the system – labor-power as variable capital. Competitive forms of cooperation increasingly "squeezed out" the substance of cooperation itself. Capital was forced to develop forms of cooperation which were not merely means to an end, but, in the popular mind, ends in and of themselves – traces of the dream of ancient political theory. Cultural trends which emphasized "process" and downgraded the product – a trend in which capital itself participated to solve the problem of valorization – undermined the accumulation process still more. "Politics of production" theories and practices, ranging from corporate dominated quality circles to left-wing worker and community control models, proliferated. Precisely because social labor was *the* productive force (because science wedded to social labor was the contemporary source of valorization) cooperative forms of cooperation were essential for the reconstitution and further development of material life. In their absence (and/or the failure of Reagan's neo-liberalism and neo-conservatism to pound the round pegs of working-class/salariat consciousness into the square holes of capitalist functional specializations), the division of labor would ossify; the system would become too rigid; cost reductions in particular branches of the economy could not work their way smoothly through the economy as a whole; the economy and society would become increasingly "Balkanized." Changes in relative market demand would be less likely to result in capital devaluation, hence reallocation of social labor and capital revaluation. Absolute surplus value would remain limited by constellations of forces beyond any organized center of power, e.g., bureaucratic inflexibilities, the refusal of youth to alienate its powers, the demand for part-time and temporary work, etc.[111] At the intersectoral level, integration between economic sectors and flexibility would be weakened thanks to bureaucratic organization capable of the efficient fulfillment of routine tasks only; vested interests in various industries and sectors; labor immobility;[112] incoherent state planning;[113] and the malfunctioning of the labor reserve army.

[111] See the provocative analysis in "The Underground Economy," *The American Owl*, 2, Nov. 1978; "An Aging Conflict: the Politics of Retirement and Pensions," *The American Owl*, 4, Jan.–Feb. 1979; "Off the Job: The Renewed Struggle to Shorten the Working Day," *The American Owl*, 5, March 1979; "On the Margin: Unemployment and the Crisis of Youth," *The American Owl*, 7, May 1979.

Monthly Labor Review surveys show that more workers seek early retirement and fewer workers want to work beyond the manadatory retirement age ("Economic Diary," *Business Week*, Aug. 17, 1981, 14).

[112] *Business Week* (Nov. 14, 1977, 142) refers to "a new layer of structural unemployment" arising from immobilities due to the unwillingness of workers to abandon friendship and family networks which are important, among other reasons, for the exchange of services (149). In another article, *Business Week* reports that the percentage of people changing addresses each year drops; sunbelt migration has been only a tiny percentage of the total US work force; and more workers refuse to relocate. "People are not nearly as flexible as they

"High corporate profits" presented merely the illusion of capital valorization; they owed their existence to permanent credit expansion, i.e., growing business, consumer, and public debt. In place of the law of value, there developed price structures unrepresentative of shortages and surpluses; structural unemployment; permanent minority and youth unemployment; excess capacity alongside limits on capacity; and new social rigidities associated with the rapid growth of the "underground" economy. These originated in the struggle against reification and the law of value; the nature of modern capitalist competition; the character of the organization of the division of industrial and social labor; and associated state policies. In particular, struggles fought out in ideological individualist forms within the workplace damaged the valorization process. The effects of social struggles in the "individualism form" conferred not "blame" and guilt, but rather potential responsibility and power, that is, "social individuality," precisely because they originated in objectively determined needs, consciousness, and ideological-material experiences within production, and the totality of the conditions of reproduction of labor-power, including and especially the sphere of "consumption."

---

used to be," states one personnel executive ("America's New Immobile Society," *Business Week*, July 27, 1981, 62).

[113] See Chapter 7.

6

The Process of Consumption

Introduction

As we have seen, the development of the modern capitalist division of social and industrial labor was a highly contradictory process. The growth of abstract social labor both required and permitted the variability of concrete labor within and between capitalist enterprises and, at the same time, created potentials for working-class unity and struggles, including the dereification of managerial ideological practices and the subversion of the concept and practice of labor-power as variable capital itself. Abstract social labor was thus not only a condition of the systemic production of relative surplus value via reductions in the value content of the average consumption basket. It was also the condition for the social destruction of relative surplus value via the struggle for workers' work.

The struggle for workers' work is fully explicable only in the context of economic struggles in the money and commodity circuits of capital and modern capitalist product competition (Chapter 4) and social life and politics outside of the workplace. Accordingly, this chapter examines the consumption process during the post-World War Two period. The next chapter takes up the problem of the state and the reproduction of the working class/salariat during the same period.

Consumption may be defined as two related social processes: first, the formation of working-class/salariat social needs, hence the social demand for means and objects of reproduction; second, the social activity of utilizing these means and objects, i.e. household and other forms of subsistence production which combine pre-wage, non-wage, and post-wage forms of labor.[1] The argument developed in this chapter is that

[1] The bourgeois concept of "consumption" does not distinguish between the activity of buying "consumer goods" and that of using them. The former, strictly defined, is "exchange labor." "Consumption" is defined empirically as the total quantity of commodities purchased less means and objects of production (commodities used to produce other commodities).

modern US reproduction conditions increased both the size and value content of the consumption basket, hence decreased relative surplus value production. It is also argued that the development of "workers' consumption," or non-commodified, social forms of need satisfaction, subverted dominant individualist ideologies and their practice as well as the concept and practice of the commodity form and relative surplus value production itself.

In orthodox Marxist theory, the significance of consumption defined as effective demand lies in its importance for the *realization* of values. Consumption is not regarded as a source of potential strength or weakness of capital or the working class in relation to the *production* of capital. While Marx included the circulation of wage goods in the reproduction of "aggregate social capital," he did not investigate the social conditions of reproduction of the working class, much less the relationship between struggles for reproduction within the labor and consumption processes. Until recent years, Marxists have more or less ignored the sphere of consumption, excepting various underconsumption models of economic crisis. Until the appearance of modern social history, the work on individual and collective consumption and the "social factory" by neo-Marxist sociologists such as André Gorz and Manuel Castells,[2] the studies of household production and the sex division of labor by Maria Dalla Costa and other feminists,[3] the work on Marx's theory of needs by Michael Lebowitz and others, and the investigation of the reproduction of labor-power in the world economy by Samir Amin and others, there was no way to evaluate the significance of struggles to determine reproduction conditions within the household and housing, health, education, transport, and other spheres for the central value relationships in Marxist theory.

In the Frankfurt School tradition (and in neo-Marxism, to the degree that it has been influenced by the former) mass consumption is regarded as a source of capital's domination of the working class. The argument is that the essence of modern labor is its relentless alienation from the working class's actual social condition. Salariat production relations are regarded as nothing more than organized status differentiations which confer merely the illusion of autonomy. Abstract social labor is seen as frustrating every social instinct and every need for freely chosen social relations and

[2] Manuel Castells, *City, Class and Power* (New York, 1978), especially chs 2, 5 and 8; André Gorz, *Strategy for Labor* (Boston, 1978), chs. 4 and 5.

[3] Recent examples include Susan Himmelweit and Simon Mohun, "Domestic Labor and Capital," *Cambridge Journal of Economics*, 1, 1, March 1977; Meg Luxton, *More Than a Labor of Love: Three Generations of Labor in the Home* (Toronto, 1980); Jean Gardiner, "Women's Domestic Labor," *New Left Review*, Jan.–Feb. 1975; Martha Gimenez, "Theories of Reproductive Behavior: A Marxist Critique," *Review of Radical Political Economics (RRPE)*, 9, 2, Summer 1977.

every impulse to develop physical, intellectual, and other human capacities through society rather than over and against society. The individual's need for wage labor is thus regarded as an alienated need; the worker's basic need outside of work is construed as the need to possess and consume.[4] The extreme view is that alienated labor abolishes any social connectedness within the labor process, hence that commodities are required to purchase a social self.[5] This line of argument also stresses the ideological and structural integration of leisure time into the technocratic and other needs of capital.[6] Capital's power resides (it is thought) "more in the control over and formation of a subject's needs, desires, and very identity ... than solely over the conditions of labor."[7] In sum, Marxist capital logic combined with the Frankfurt School tradition constitutes a powerful *theoretical* totalization. *It does not, however, constitute a historical-theoretical totalization; it is not an adequate account of reality.*

Class Struggle and the Value of Labor-Power

The theory of the "social factory" raises the possibility that the sphere of consumption (as well as the money, commodity, and productive circuits of capital) is another "contested terrain." Although the Frankfurt School tradition studies consumption from the perspective of capital's domination of the working class, "social factory" theorists regard consumption not only as another capitalist weapon in the class war, but also as another Achilles' heel of the capitalist system.[8] The premise is that capital-labor

---

[4] Agnes Heller, *The Theory of Need in Marx* (New York, 1976), 96. Therefore, for Heller, workers' struggles to fulfill material needs affirm rather than deny capital. "The exploited classes generally ask for no more than a better satisfaction of the needs assigned them" (97). (See Michael Lebowitz, "Heller on Marx's Concept of Needs," Simon Fraser University, unpublished MS.)

[5] Stewart Ewen, *Captains of Consciousness* (New York, 1976).

[6] Robert Goldmann and John Wilson, "The Rationalization of Leisure," *Politics and Society*, 7, 2, 1977.

[7] Robert D'Amico, "Desire and the Commodity Form," *Telos*, 35, Spring 1978, 88. "The factory is becoming generalized. The factory is tending to pervade, to permeate, the entire arena of civil society" (Raniero Panzieri, "Lotte operaie nello sviluppo capitalistico," *Quaderni piacentini*, 1967). Panzieri is the father of the theory of capitalism as a "social factory." See also, Dallas W. Smythe, "Communications: Blind Spot of Western Marxism," *Canadian Journal of Political and Social Theory*, 1, 3, Fall 1977.

[8] The *limits* of industrializing the household were discussed long ago by Wesley C. Mitchell, "The Backward Art of Spending Money," *American Economic Review*, 2, June 1912. Mitchell was also one of the first to point to "social factory" trends in the USA (J. Ron Stanfield and Jacqueline B. Stanfield, "Consumption in Contemporary Capitalism: The Backward Art of Living," *Journal of Economic Issues*, 14, 2, June 1980, 441).

antagonisms express themselves in social life when the latter is incorporated into the reproduction of capital, hence that capital is vulnerable not only to struggles within the labor process, but also social struggles generally. In the period of capitalist development, concrete labor and consumption patterns and family life were governed respectively by traditional work norms and social values. In modern capitalism, it is thought that variability of concrete labor and consumption comes to depend less on traditional norms and values and more on (highly mediated) class struggles.

Variability of consumption exists because the value of labor-power consists of two general variable elements: first, the total mass of wage goods consumed per worker; second, the socially necessary labor-time required to produce this mass of commodities, or the value content of the average consumption basket. Capital thus has at least two weapons in its struggle with the working class. The first is reductions in money wages (including transfer payments) and/or inflation and reductions in real wages which reduce the actual quantity of commodities consumed irrespective of the amount of socially necessary labor embodied in these commodities (today, this is accompanied by social policies which substitute unpaid domestic labor for paid wage labor and especially state service labor). The second is increases in productivity in wage good industries, which lower the value content of a given basket of consumer goods. Historical examples are the development of simplified metal shaping techniques; the replacement of casting processes by cutting and stamping; and elaborate product designs giving way to simplified forms (the best example today is the electronics revolution and automation, which cheapen the production of many if not all wage goods). A related capitalist weapon is the substitution of low-value for high-value wage goods (e.g., mobile homes for single-family suburban housing).

Mass consumption may be regarded as a capitalist weapon because, first, it increases chances of lowering absolute living standards by reducing consumption on a mass basis; second, it increases chances of cheapening the value of a given consumption basket and/or substituting low-value for high-value wage goods on a mass basis, or by restructuring working-class/salariat consumption on a broad front quickly and efficiently. The use of the first weapon (especially inflation and real wage reductions and also increasingly actual reductions in money wages in troubled industries) in the contemporary crisis is eloquent testimony to the failure of the system significantly to reduce socially necessary labor-time.

Mass consumption also may be regarded as an Achilles' heel of capitalism. This is so because of the irreducible autonomy of the process of social reproduction of labor-power. As we have seen, "labor power is consumed by the worker and exists for the worker,"[9] i.e. it is consumed outside capitalist relations of production. This means that in the model of full capitalism individual workers and their families utilize accumulated stocks of "means of subsistence production," e.g., housing, consumer durables. While this creates potentials for capital to shift the burden of reproduction costs of labor-power to the household and community, it also creates potentials for the working class to hoard labor-power or withdraw labor-power from capital on a mass basis.

More specifically, mass consumption may be unproductive of capital for two related reasons: first, in modern capitalism, the struggle to increase the mass of wage goods assumes mass dimensions with all the political "chain reactions" this suggests. As we saw in Chapter 4, vehicles of the struggle to expand the consumption basket include not only labor unions, occupational groups, and political organizations, but also emulation and invidious distinctions between unions and work groups, individual workers bargaining with individual capitals, and class alliances with merchant and bank capital eager to expand consumption demand and consumer credit. Familiar forms of this struggle include demands for annual increases in money wages, for cost-of-living wage and pension adjustments, and for expanding consumer credit; rent strikes; struggles against monopoly utility pricing; the fight against inflation, and so on. "The upsurge of consumer movements and of urban movements in most advanced capitalist societies creates yet another obstacle to capitalist exploitation in the consumption process.[10]

Second, the struggle for high-value wage goods also assumes mass dimensions, albeit through labor unions, occupational and interest groups, community organizations, and other "pluralistic" vehicles. Forms of this struggle include environmentalist struggles against nuclear power, stripmining of coal, etc.; women's struggles against dangerous albeit cheap contraception methods; struggles for qualitatively better medical care, housing and education.

Related to struggles for more and higher-value wage goods are struggles for workers' work which, as we have seen, counteract capital's drive to raise the rates of exploitation and profit by lowering the value of the

[9] Michael Lebowitz, "The One-sidedness of Capital" (*RRPE*), 14, 4, Winter 1982). Lebowitz adds that "the worker cannot be for capital and self simultaneously." However, this assumes that labor-power is subsumed under capital in production *in fact*, and also that the worker has little or no "fixed" means of consumption, i.e. means of subsistence production, and, finally, that the worker has no access to purchasing power except through the wage exchange. For an interesting discussion of the traditional "one-sided concept of the value of labor-power," see Michael Lebowitz, "Marx After Wage-Labour," *Economic Forum*, 13, 2, Autumn 1982, 19–17.

[10] Manuel Castells, *The Economic Crisis and American Society* (Princeton, 1980), 62.

average consumption basket. Workers seek security, stability, and pre-dictability, not only in the workplace, but also in domestic and community life, where social activity is not governed by the valorization process, in this way challenging the law of value at still another level. In sum, although mass consumption is often regarded as ideologically indispensable in late capitalist society, theoretically it may also be regarded as posing economic dangers for the capitalist system.

Marx argued that the value of any commodity consists of the socially necessary labor-time required for its production. However, capitalist pro-duction is not based on planned social need but rather on market demand. This means that the amount of socially necessary labor cannot be known until products are sold. In other words, because value is not determined by total labor-time but by socially necessary labor under average conditions of production, it is impossible to know the value of a commodity without knowing its price. This raises a fundamental problem for the theory of the value of labor-power. As we know, labor-power is not a commodity which is produced and reproduced for sale on the market, but rather consists of human attributes which cannot be separated from their owners, hence cannot circulate freely on the market. Precisely because labor-power is not produced and reproduced within capitalist enterprises subject to the law of value, the price of labor-power cannot be "explained" in terms of its value because, strictly defined, labor-power has no value.[11]

This line of reasoning compels us to reconceptualize the value of labor-power. It will be recalled that workers are both the subjects and objects of the exchange of labor-power against wages. If labor-power in fact is treated by workers as if it were a commodity, then it may be treated "as if" it has a value. By contrast, if workers do not permit their labor-power to be treated as a commodity, then it can no longer be treated as if it has a value. As we suggested, in this event, individual workers and groups of workers *value their own labor-power*. The "self-valorization" of labor-power is in this event explicable only in the context of the class struggle. No longer is it sensible to say that wages are above, below, or equal to the value of labor-power; only that wages are above, below, or equal to the value workers place on their own labor-power.[12] This is crucially important to

---

[11] There is no guarantee that labor-power in fact will be available in the commodity form, much less reproduced under conditions which permit capitalist production (i.e. profits). Orthodox Marxism thus underscores the importance of state policies which attempt both to guarantee the existence of labor-power in the commodity form and to insure that it is reproduced as such (see Chapter 7).

[12] "*The development of the class struggle*, and, in particular, the growth of the power of the workers' movement, has permitted an expansion of popular needs, both in terms of the aspirations of the workers and the *demands* which result" (Castells, *City, Class and Power*, 41).

the whole theory of capitalist accumulation and crisis precisely because the distinction between labor-power and labor is required to establish the existence and magnitude of exploitation, i.e. surplus value production, hence the rate of profit and potential rate of accumulation.

The reproduction of the "commodity" labor-power requires abstract labor contained in the means and objects of reproduction, or wage goods. How much abstract labor is contained in a given basket of wage goods depends on working-class struggles within the productive, money, and commodity circuits of capital. However, the reproduction of labor-power also requires self-organized living labor utilizing these means and objects of reproduction or "domestic labor." How much domestic labor is "required" depends on family and community relationshps and the many-sided social struggles therein. Further, the reproduction of labor-power also requires living labor organized administratively and politically by state agencies and elected bodies. How much living labor within the sphere of collective reproduction is "required" to reproduce labor-power depends on the nature of the political system, its capacity to channel and neutralize or resolve social struggles fought out in the political sphere, and many related factors. In short, the value of labor-power is determined socially and politically in the broadest sense, i.e. by relationships within the factory, labor market, commodity markets, family-kinship structures, political relationships, state and election systems, and cultural processes, as well as within the process of valorization of wage goods described by Marx. This is doubtless why economists generally have followed Marx's method, which is to assume a certan "consumption basket" and focus theoretical analysis on the value of the elements it contains.[13] It also

---

[13] "The precise theoretical determination of the value of laborpower is problematical. Marx took it as 'given' . . . " (Donald J. Harris, "Capitalist Exploitation and Black Labor: Some Conceptual Issues," *Review of Black Political Economy*, 8, 2, Winter 1978, 149, note 6).

In *Capital*, Marx reasoned that the "value of labour-power is determined, as in the case of every other commodity, by the labour-time necessary for the production, and consequently the reproduction, of this special article. So far as it has value, it represents no more than a definite quantity of the average labour of society incorporated in it" (*Capital* I, Kerr edn, New York, The Modern Library, 1906, 189). Marx then states that for the worker's "maintenance, he requires a given quantity of the means of existence. Therefore the labour-time requisite for the production of labour-power reduces itself to that necessary for the production of these means of subsistence; in other words, the value of labour-power is the value of the means of subsistence necessary for the maintenance of the labourer" (190). But why does the worker require a "given quantity" of wage goods? Here Marx falls back on historical analysis. "So-called necessary wants" depend on "the conditions under which, and consequently on the habits and degree of comfort in which, the class of free labourers has been formed." But, so-called necessary wants defined this way do not exemplify *capitalist* needs at all, rather pre-capitalist needs. At times, Marx abandons altogether any social analysis of needs, e.g.,

explains why the economists have failed to say much that is useful about the value of labor-power and its relation to total value/surplus value and the rates of profit and accumulation.

If we ignore the living domestic and state-organized labor entering into the reproduction of labor-power, the value of labor-power varies directly with the amount of socially necessary labor-time embodied in the consumption basket. Everything else being equal, the more socially necessary labor that is required for a given quantity of wage goods, the less surplus value is produced. Therefore, if labor-time expended in wage good industries increases faster than labor-time in capital goods industries (everything else being the same), the value of labor-power increases at the expense of surplus value. The extreme case is the expenditure of all labor-time in the wage good industries, hence the impossiblity of producing any relative surplus value.

Capital goods are "pure commodities" in the sense that they remain within the circulation of capital, strictly defined. "Surplus value . . . is the difference between two homogeneous quantities: on the one hand, the value produced at the social level by the collective labourer; on the other hand, the quantity of value that leaves capitalist circulation . . ."[14] Capital goods have no other use than to augment the productivity of labor, and they are desired only in so far as they reduce socially necessary labor, or cheapen consumer good and/or other capital good products. The social demand for capital goods is thus governed strictly by the capitalist demand for profits, excepting new capital goods designed to produce new and different wage goods.[15] Within the capital goods sector, *ceteris paribus*, living labor is continually expelled, the value composition of capital increased, and socially necessary labor-time reduced.

By contrast, social demand for consumer goods is formed within the context of working-class needs, class struggles, domestic relations, politics, and culture generally. Consumer goods are not used to expel living labor from production but rather to meet working-class needs in the commodity

when he speaks of the "minimum limit of the value of labour-power" which is determined "by the value of those means of subsistence that are physically indispensable" (192).

In the *Grundrisse*, Marx states that needs are historically variable. The creation of new needs, in fact, is considered to distinguish human beings from other species. Human "production not only creates the objects which satisfy needs, but also the needs which the objects satisfy." This paraphrases many passages from the *Grundrisse* and other writings. A fine summary of Marx's theory of needs is Michael Lebowitz, "Capital and the Production of Needs," *Science and Society*, 41, 4, Winter 1977–78. As Lebowitz shows, Marx supposes that three levels of need exist: physiological needs; necessary needs; and " 'social needs'." Physiological needs must be satisfied for the physical reproduction of the worker. The problem with this concept is that science and cultural labor are materialized in all "physio-

form, that is, as means and objects of reproduction utilized outside of the three circuits of capital. An increase in social demand for capital goods means that there is a given capitalist demand to *reduce* socially necessary labor-time, hence raise surplus value a process intensified by economic crisis. An increase in social demand for consumer goods means that there is a given working-class demand to *expand* socially necessary labor, or to increase the consumption basket and/or its value composition.

The social demand for wage goods thus pushes up socially necessary labor (everything else being the same) while the social demand for capital goods pulls in the opposite direction. The composition of total value between the capital and wage good sectors therefore reflects the class struggle. An increase in the share of total value produced in the consumer good sector in relation to the capital good sector means that the working class has strengthened itself in relation to capital.[16] To complicate matters, the social demand for capital goods may also derive indirectly from the social demand for consumer goods. The less the demand for consumer goods, the less may be the demand for capital goods to reduce socially necessary labor in the consumer goods sector. Social demand for capital goods thus derives not only from struggles within production, but also

---

logically necessary" commodities' e.g., there is no way to buy flour without buying packaging art. Necessary needs are needs based on custom and habit, i.e. needs which make up the consumption norm. The problem with this concept is that capitalism is always revolutionizing the consumption norm; i.e. there is no such thing as normal or habitual needs in full capitalism. " 'Social needs' " are needs which are typically frustrated owing to the low level of real wages.

As Lebowitz points out in his critique of Agnes Heller, Marx believed that there exists a specifically capitalist need, i.e. the need to accumulate, depress the wages of the working class, suffer economic crises, etc., which frustrates the realization of " 'social needs'." Lebowitz shows that the growth of " 'social needs' " thus does not (everything else being the same) increase the value of labor-power, but rather only the degree of immiseration. The problem with the concept of " 'social needs' " as defined by Marx is (as we will see in more detail) that it neglects the reality that all needs construed as the need for commodities strictly defined and fulfilled in the commodity form are alienated needs, i.e. that *use values themselves* are fetishized and embody alienated social relationships. " 'Social needs' " as Marx defines them are so many more alienated commodity needs. In our view, social needs are negations of commodity needs, i.e. needs for different kinds of social relationships unmediated by the commodity form, as will be seen.

[14] Aboo T. Aumeeruddy, Bruno Lautier, and Ramon G. Tortajada, "Labour-Power and the State," *Capital and Class*, 6, Autumn 1978, 58.

[15] See Chapter 4, 79–88.

[16] This assumes that the value composition of capital in Departments I and II remains the same. If the value composition of Department II products fall while that of Department I products remains unchanged, an expansion of Department II relative to Department I is, of course, consistent with a constant or even expanding rate of exploitation.

from struggles to expand the size and/or value content of the consumption basket. In sum, the demand for capital goods is not determined by the demand for consumer goods (as bourgeois economics claims) but rather by the demand for profit (or, more strictly speaking, "technological rent") in both the capital and consumer goods sector.

To the degree that the expansion of wage good demand presses on surplus value and profits, capitalists in the wage goods sector demand more (or more productive) capital goods. In this way, a potential increase in the social demand for capital goods is formed. The contradiction arises, however, that the means of making the demand for capital goods effective are impaired to the degree that the working-class demand for wage goods is effective; hence the importance of the role of capitalist concentration and centralization, monopoly, and capitalist credit in the class struggle; hence also the importance of the counter-role of working-class cooperation, wage struggles, the struggle against prices, and consumer credit in this struggle. As we know, consumer credit overcomes the disjuncture between the amount of commodities workers and salariat are able to appropriate through wages and salaries, on the one hand, and the amount of total values produced, on the other; i.e., consumer credit (like government transfers and public credit) permits workers to appropriate a larger amount of total values produced than wage and salary payments would otherwise allow. The traditional Marxist view is that capital *supplies* consumer credit to sell goods which would otherwise remain in inventory. As we have seen, Marx himself stressed the need to expand the means of realizing capital to expand capital itself, i.e. the need for "the production of a constantly widening sphere of circulation."[17] However, workers and salariat *demand* credit to buy goods which would otherwise either not be produced or would be produced in the form of capital goods, i.e. goods which would not otherwise appear as wage goods. The collateral offered by workers and salariat is, in effect, their jobs, which partly underwrites high levels of employment and partly counteracts the basic capitalist tendency towards maximum production per unit of labor-time. In the 1970s, for example, the growth of workers' wealth in the form of inflated home equities underwrote huge amounts of borrowing by workers and the salariat, the effect of which was to redistribute credit from capital to labor. At the end of the 1970s, consumer borrowing remained high, despite the fact that interest rates were at all-time highs. "As long as there is a supply of credit, people will use it."[18]

This line of argument may be summarized thus: there exists a permanent antagonism between capitalist credit and working-class/salariat credit;

[17] *Grundrisse* (Baltimore, 1973), 407.
[18] "A Tighter Clamp on Consumer Credit," *Business Week*, Nov. 26, 1979, 33.

state credit for social constant capital and state credit for social consumption and social expenses; tax reductions on capital versus tax reductions on labor; fictitious capital versus fictitious advanced variable capital. These kinds of antagonisms, expressed empirically in highly complex ways, appeared to highlight the essence of the economistic struggle between capitalist profits and working-class/salariat needs in the over-heated credit regime of "full capitalism."

Working-Class Needs and the Value of Labor-Power

In his theory of capitalist development, Marx assumed that the working class consumes a given basket of wage goods, the average value of which falls because of the expansion of the social productive forces, or the rise in the technical composition of capital. Marx them demonstrated that the fall in the value of the average consumption basket means that the quantity of wage goods consumed per worker may increase over time. However, he argues that, despite any quantitative expansion of the consumption basket, the rate of exploitation typically increases, which up to a certain point counteracts the tendency of the rate of profit to fall.

It needs to be stressed that systematic *reductions* in the rate of exploitation are flatly impossible within the framework of Marx's theory of valorization, although the same thing cannot be said about the existence of *limits* on the rate of exploitation. The reason is that Marx abstracted from product competition, consumer credit and the modern wage struggle, struggles within the productive circuit of capital, the social wage and state transfer payments, and other modern conditions of social reproduction which were undeveloped or did not exist in his own time. As we have argued, this is no longer a valid method of study in the model of full capitalism, which means that the social determinations of the quality and quantity of use values which entered into the consumption basket (as well as their average value) in post-World War Two US capitalism need to be investigated. This requires a general study of the determination and social and economic significance of needs in "full capitalist" America, that is, needs construed as the need for commodities and satisfied in the commodity form.

The basic premise of the theory of needs is that the working class and salariat established their own reproduction conditions or ways of living,[19]

---

[19] Even the most extreme "working-class victimization" Frankfurt School theorists admit that the working class to one degree or another establishes its own autonomous life. For example, Adorno refers to "products which are tailored for consumption by masses, and which to *a great degree* determine the nature of consumption. . . . the culture industry

i.e. they were free to determine the character and extent of their own needs. This irreducible autonomy, however, originated within the world of commodities generally and "object fetishism" and "commodity fetishism" in particular. Object fetishism included invidious distinction, emulation, symbolic determinations, and the "ceremonial character of utility."[20] Commodity fetishism meant not only that utility had a "ceremonial character," but also that specialized "ceremonial needs" were "naturally" construed in terms of *their capacity to be satisfied in the form of commodities*. Needs acquired a "naturalness," which belied their social origins in capitalist accumulation, uneven and combined development, and, above all, class and social struggles.

If, for the moment, we abstract from the class struggle, it can be said that working-class consumption and the needs determined therein in postwar USA had no status unless they could be satisfied through commodity ownership and use.[21] The need for social identity, for example, was construed as the need for new fashion; the need to move as the need for a car; the need for security as the need for "savings." The need for good health was interpreted as the need for medicines, drugs, "medical services."[22] "The need for air . . . is immediately apprehended as the need for vacation, for public gardens, for city planning, for escape from the city . . . the need for nightly rest, for physical and mental relaxation . . . becomes the need for tasteful, comfortable housing protected against noise . . . the need to eat . . . becomes the need for food which can be consumed immediately after a day of work . . . "[23] As Hans Enzensberger writes, "hunger for com-

---

undeniably *speculates* on the conscious and unconscious state of the millions towards which it is directed. . . . the culture industry itself could scarcely exist without *adapting to the masses*" (Theodor Adorno, "Culture Industry Reconsidered," *New German Critique*, 6, Fall 1975, 17, italics added).

On the other hand, even the most extreme Marxist "voluntarists" can be excessively structuralist and "productionist." "Only one way of life, more or less rigidly determined, is open to him, and this way of life is conditioned by the structure of production and techniques" (André Gorz, *Strategy for Labor: A Radical Proposal*, Boston, 1964, 77).

[20] This is Veblen's phrase. See William Leiss, "Needs, Exchanges, and the Fetishism of Objects," *Canadian Journal of Political and Social Theory*, 2, 3, Fall 1979, for a review of object fetishism. See also, Robert D'Amico, "Desire and the Commodity Form," *Telos*, 35, Spring 1978.

[21] The modern world is defined as "a world in which it increasingly *makes sense* that if there are solutions to be had, they can be bought" (Stuart and Elizabeth Ewen, "Americanization and Consumption," *Telos*, 37, Fall 1978, 42).

[22] "Medicalization . . . involves convincing people they are sick and results in the treatment of social problems as if they were asocial pathologies residing inside individual bodies" (Michael Radlett, Review of *Disabling Professions*, Ivan Illich et al., eds. (London, 1977), in *Contemporary Sociology*, 7, 3, May 1978, 370).

[23] Gorz, *Strategy for Labor*, 89.

modities, in all its blindness, is a product of the production of commodities."[24]

This became all the more true in the sphere of services. In modern capitalist society, "people become so indifferent to one another that they themselves no longer produce a 'neutral understanding' of others' problems necessary for a minimum psychic survival. Thus a special, and therefore expensive, service organization is required which approaches the 'individualized individual' . . . ."[25] In these typically professionally organized services, the identity between work process and product enabled the "professions to translate their needs into client demands through a dominant cultural power that convinces citizens they possess a series of individual deficiencies which can be resolved only through professional intervention."[26] In mental health, therapy "is confined to such practices as can be stipulated through an individual social contract. . . . the categories of therapy are individualistic and so reproduce the individual structures of capitalist domination . . ."[27] In the field of law, the weakness of processes of *community* self-determination in the USA meant that the cost of resolving civil disputes was exceptionally high. (There are more lawyers per capita in the USA than probably any other country in the world.) In sum, when every activity became potentially exchangeable, "needs and desires come to be objectified in a specific form."[28]

Working-class/salariat autonomy and needs originated not only within the world of commodity fetishism, but also within the totality of relationships of social reproduction (e.g., family, community, labor union, etc.).[29] These included material needs strictly defined, or needs which originated in material production within given social relationships and forces of production. Some kind of protective clothing, transportation to work, etc.

---

[24] Hans Enzensberger, "A Critique of Political Ecology," Delores LaChapelle, ed., *Earth Wisdom* (Los Angeles, 1978).

[25] Michael Schneider, *Neurosis and Civilization* (New York, 1975), 112.

[26] Ibid., 369.

[27] Richard Lichtman, *The Production of Desire: The Integration of Psychoanalysis into Marxist Theory* (New York, 1982), 265.

[28] J. J. Goux, cited in D'Amico, "Desire and the Commodity Form," 96.

[29] Of course the subject of human needs is immense and has been explored from seemingly every conceivable perspective. Psychologists refer to "basic needs" such as safety, love, esteem, and self-actualization. Other needs examined in the social psychology literature are abasement, exhibition, play, sex, and understanding. The list is apparently endless. Theories of consumption are similarly many and varied. The "process of socialization," "symbolic interaction between people," "social differentiation," "developmental needs," "tastes," "income and prices," etc. are a handful of the concepts introduced by bourgeois social scientists with the aim of understanding and in many cases controlling "consumer behavior" (Marguerite C. Burk, "Survey of Interpretations of Consumer Behavior by Social Scientists in the Postwar Period," *Journal of Farm Economics*, 49, Feb. 1967).

was needed. More important theoretically, needs also consisted of material objects and services required by capitalist production relationships. Under the sign of "company policy," "community standards," "peer group pressure," etc., needs originated in the process whereby divisions within the working class were reproduced; for example, differentiated living conditions based on hierarchical wage and salary structures. Social relationships originating outside capitalist production relationships narrowly defined and the needs formed within these relationships were, of course, variable: "community standards" were less clearly defined than "company policy"; building codes were more confining than local aesthetic norms.

In any and all cases, reproduction conditions were established within the prevailing structure of labor, marriage, divorce, child-raising, and friendship which is infused with classism, sexism, racism, national chauvinism, and so on. *Total* social labor mediated in a thousand different ways was the well-spring of cosciousness and social needs. In sum, the amount of variable capital required to reproduce social labor-power, thus how much surplus labor-time was expended, was inexplicable unless commodity production was grasped both as a productive force and production relationship, or in Marx's words, "the whole social organization."[30] "The level and nature of workers' needs are . . . not to be found in the intrinsic qualities of things, but in the nature and level of capitalist society itself."[31] Capitalist production relationships, however, were fundamentally contradictory; the working class was simultaneously dependent upon and antagonistic to capital. Reproduction conditions developed within this framework of dependence and antagonism.[32]

The premise that needs were construed as the need for commodities, hence that all needs were fulfilled in the commodity form, means that the reproduction costs of labor-power and the cost of wages and salaries, which were at one time historically distinct, became identical. "As capitalism develops . . . an increasing proportion of the necessary use values must be purchased at their value; and, therefore, the wage must cover a growing mass of use values, even if the standard of living of the working class does not change."[33] Child and health care, cooking, cleaning, play, education,

[30] The consumer's judgement depend on his means and ends. Both of these are determined by his social position, which itself depends on the whole social organization": (Karl Marx, *The Poverty of Philosophy*, New York, International Publishers, undated, 37).

[31] Lebowitz, "Capital and the Production of Needs," 437.

[32] "The use of products is determined by the social conditions in which the consumers find themselves placed, and these conditions themselves are based on class antagonisms" (Marx, *Poverty of Philosophy*, 54).

[33] Elizabeth Dore and John Weeks, "Capital, Class Struggle and Wages in the Context of Backwardness," Paper for Seminar on Third World Strikes, Institute of Social Studies, The Hague, Sept. 12–16, 1977, 7.

etc. ceased to be more or less exclusively organized by kinship or community. Although variable capital advances were contingent upon the location of workers in production, custom, etc.,[34] from a historical perspective one meaning of capital accumulation was that average variable capital outlays increased (everything else being the same). *In this sense, capital accumulation itself intensified the struggle between capital and labor.* The view that "commodities can only form part of the consumption norm if their unit exchange value is on the decline and is already sufficiently low"[35] exemplified one *condition* of capital accumulation; this was not necessarily true in any particular economic and political conjuncture. More important, as will be seen, the commodification of needs tended to *create* economic crisis, meanwhile undermining society's capacity to *absorb* crisis because of the subversion of traditional social infrastructures which at one time functioned as "crisis cushions."

In "full capitalism," even "luxuries" became necessities when they were incorporated into working-class/salariat ways of life, whether through conspicuous consumption, or other social processes.[36] The more or less full commodification of needs means that art, science, and culture labor became incorporated into commodities. The size and average value of the consumption basket (the value of labor-power) thus tended to rise. Culture production ceased to be a luxury because most if not all commodities embodied the labor of culture workers, e.g., commodity design, packaging, display, advertisement. The same argument is applicable to scientific and technical labor organized with the purpose of discovering and developing new wage goods, as well as social-psychological labor organized to commodify self-help and personal development in which real learning disappears when "standards for efficient health care, sex, play, learning and creativity are built into the products we consume as 'basic necessities.' "[37] When social and psychological as well as material gratifications were satisfied through commodities, these needs (however they are otherwise interpreted – for example, as Maslowian "higher needs")

---

[34] Harris, "Capitalist Exploitation and Black Labor," 143.

[35] "This requires that the conditions in which these commodities are produced are those of the standardized labor process of mass production. And for this to be the case, the social demand directed toward these branches must be sufficiently large and rising" (Michel Aglietta, "Phases of US Capitalist Expansion," *New Left Review*, 110, July–Aug. 1978, 26). The argument throughout the present work is that historical conditions of accumulation and historical reality are two different things.

[36] Strictly defined, luxuries are not socially necessary for economic reproduction, because such consumption is destined exclusively for the capitalist class. Luxuries defined this way are commodities which exchange against capitalist revenues rather than against capital itself.

[37] Evan Stark, "Recreation in Everyday Life," unpublished MS, undated, 86.

entered into the costs of reproducing labor-power.[38] Gratifications once discharged outside of and against the framework of commodity exchange entered into the costs of wages and capital (and/or "social wages" expended by the state).

Similarly, social control mechanisms which hitherto assumed non-commodified forms became embodied in commodities, transforming discretionary expenditures into necessities. (This is more true in the USA than in Europe or especially Japan, where more traditional elements remain in the social structure.) When traditional legitimizations and ideologies of class and status disappeared, they were replaced by egoism and cynicism. The reproduction of social control became indistinguishable from the reproduction of labor-power. The absence of traditional social order organized by the working class itself in forms which expressed "individuality" as "indivisibility" created the need for concepts and practices of social order which were organized by job stratification systems and other ideologies which "built" social control into the costs of wages and salaries, and which outside of the workplace were organized by the "culture industry."[39] Hence the systematic production of fantasy values which were "the sponge for the free-floating energy of the millions who must be 'kept on ice' all or part of the time."[40] Sports and spectacles thus became embedded in social life and consciousness and entered into the cost of wages.[41] Also entering into capital outlays were the costs of disposing of waste of all kinds which (everything else being equal) increased with the expansion of material consumption.[42]

These lines of analysis may be summarized thus: the construction of all needs as the need for commodities meant that the basic need in "full capitalism" was the need for wage labor, i.e. alienated labor. *This meant that all needs construed as the need for commodities were in effect*

[38] "The general tendency of the present-day market economy . . . is to embed the network of symbolic mediations that shape the character of human needing exclusively into material objects (or more precisely, to orient needs entirely towards commodities)" (William Leiss, *Limits of Satisfaction*, Toronto, 1976, 67). "The American way of life may well have been founded on the notion that obtaining products is the main route to obtaining greater affection . . . higher prestige . . . and even self-actualization" (Amitai Etzione, "A Creative Adaption to a World of Rising Shortages," *Annals*, AAPSS, 420, July 1975, 104).

[39] Adorno, "Culture Industry Reconsidered," 17; D'Amico, "Desire and the Commodity Form," 104.

[40] Stark, "Recreation in Everyday Life."

[41] Ike Balbus writes that "the inevitable consequence of the transformation of play into organized sports is that sports increasingly assume the character of *spectacles*, produced by a relative handful of experts, which are designed for the consumption of the majority of non-experts, i.e. the rest of the population" ("Politics as Sports," *Monthly Review*, March 1975, 32).

[42] Leiss, *Limits of Satisfaction*, 32–6.

alienated needs, i.e. needs which alienated individuals from one another. The commodity form of need satisfaction in this sense was expressive of the ways in which individuals were *separated* from others. Commodities were "fences";[43] e.g., private home ownership.[44]

However, the commodity form of need satisfaction did not only *objectify* needs in the sense that they were fulfilled by "technique." It also *subjectified* needs in the sense that it contained an irreducible individualistic humanism, e.g., goods were advertised as designed "to bring family or friends together." It is within this contradiction that we may grasp the individual's autonomy to determine the character of his or her needs originating within the structural dependencies and antagonisms between capital and labor, i.e., exploitation, alienation, and reification exemplifying *social class relationships* rather than merely market relationships. This was the reason that there existed the possibility that individuals might construe their needs as social and collective, i.e. use goods as "bridges." *Needs therefore were inherently conflicted.* Precisely because commodified needs were alienated, the potential existed that needs could be reinterpreted as the need for liberation from the objectification of labor-power, alienation of labor, ideologies of labor control, and the commodity form of need fulfillment generally. The need for social identity could be reinterpreted as the need to find individuality within and not over and against society; the need to satisfy hunger as the need to regulate the ecology of the body; the need for security as the need for secure social relationships; the need for good health as the need for ecological balance; the need for transportation to work as the need to soften the hard lines between work, residence, and leisure; the need for recreation as the need for spontaneous play; and so on. These are all examples of "workers' consumption."

Limitless Needs and the Value of Labor-Power

Alienated needs were inherently conflicted, hence could never be satisfied in the strict sense of "being pleased, contented." If they were satisfied in one form, they were frustrated in another, the extreme example being an obsessive compulsion. One reason was that alienated needs were construed as the need not merely for particular commodities, but rather for commodities in general, or as the "need for needs" exemplified by the demand for "more," i.e. "the one idea of the modern worker . . . to 'grab all

---

[43] Mark Douglas and Baron Isherwood, *The World of Goods* (New York, 1979), 12.

[44] The most detailed review of the literature is Jim Kemeny, "Home Ownership and Privatization," *International Journal of Urban and Regional Research*, 4, 3, Sept. 1980.

you can get hold of.' "[45] This was one form of the abstract formula, "the self-expansion of capital requires the self-expansion of needs." Limitless need production presupposed not only limitless commodification but also limitless human dissatisfaction, which in turn created more possibilities for the reconstruction of need to mean social or collective needs. Nixon said in his 1970 State of the Union message: "Never has a people had so much and enjoyed so little." The leading consumer economist more cautiously wrote that "the desire to save is frequently pushed into the background and discretionary saving becomes residual because of the perceived urgency of numerous wants for consumer goods. . . . The population groups which make the largest discretionary purchases also have the largest number of unfulfilled desires."[46]

The question arises, what exactly was the process whereby alienated needs expanded without limit, thus representing for the workers an increase in the value of labor-power?[47] First, the sense of limitless needs can be traced at least as far back as the Romantic movement, with its sense of infinity of individual human longing; its supreme concern with the self and the self's overflow of feelings; its disregard for status or rules; and its credo of endless excitement and adventure. In the USA, these themes were developed into highly articulated ideologies of individual "self-development," which finally degenerated into modern consumerism. Second, limitless need production presupposed that the working class and salariat were materially freed from all habitual ways of living, including precapitalist and semicapitalist ways of working, i.e. that there was a rupture with the fixed consumption patterns associated with the epoch of manufacture, craft labor, ethnic community, kinship, and social "indivisibility."[48] Third, there was required a break with the natural-economic world and the sensuality or "feudal pleasure" therein.[49] All three conditions were established with the development of abstract social labor, the

[45]   J. P. Mayer, ed., *The Young Workers of Today: A New Type* (Glencoe, Illinois, 1955), 56.

[46]   George Katona, *The Mass Consumption Society* (New York, 1964), 179, 257.

[47]   Some writers have attempted to explain the expansion of commodity needs by arguing that commodities are cheaper than "free time." Hence non-commodity intensive activities are neglected in favor of commodity-intensive activities (Staffen Linder, *The Harried Leisure Class*, New York, 1970, 77–109). This is mistaken because activities in which needs are satisfied in the commodity form are not comparable with activities satisfying needs in the non-commodity form. The first is at root an anti-social or asocial activity; the second is a social activity.

[48]   In England during the industrial revolution workers sought to pay the lowest rents possible for traditional housing, and also to purchase familiar and traditional clothing (Sidney Checkland, *The Rise of Industrial Society in England,1815–1880*, London, 1964, 326).

[49]   Schneider, *Neurosis and Civilization*, 220.

world market, capital and labor moblity, the incorporation of science into capital and the domination of nature. Finally, there was required a rupture in capitalist *economic thought* which, beginning as early as the mid-eighteenth century and culminating in the twentieth, stressed the importance of awakening new needs as the basis for expanding markets.[50]

While capital was fully implicated in the process of need production (e.g. modern product competition), limitless accumulation could not be based merely on capitalist *conceptions* of individual needs. Despite the merger between the "consciousness industry" and wage good industries, the primary impulses for unlimited need expansion were the processes whereby commodities were *produced*; working class/salariat conceptions of needs; and the economic and social struggles to fulfill them.

Needs therefore may be explained in terms of the exploitative and alienated conditions of wage labor and institutionalized domination. "Torn between compulsive instinctual repression in the sphere of production and compulsive instinctual unshackling in consumption, the working consumers enter into a kind of unending 'double-bind' situation."[51] This found one reflection in bourgeois sociology's distinction between "culture" and the "technocratic economic order."[52] "Culture" celebrated Romantic values such as self-realization, self-gratification, and an obsessive search for novelty. These "cultural processes," especially escapism, were the results of the production and reproduction of alienated labor-power and its negations.[53] Self-actualization through commodity ownership was explicable in terms of capitalist domination of production. The worker daydreamed that he could find his individuality within society outside of class struggle; his nightmare was the fear of losing the illusion of individuality which commodified social life conferred. Self-gratification was sought because of the deprivations suffered by the worker within the production process and the absence of real autonomy of the role-defined salariat. The daydream was the illusion that individuals could find an authentic sense of self-worth outside of social struggle, or freely organized social production, i.e. "social individuality." The nightmare was that the illusion of identity afforded by the normed roles within production and the

[50] For example, see Ewen and Ewen, "Americanization and Consumption," 49.

[51] Schneider, *Neurosis and Civilization*, 232.

[52] Daniel Bell, *The Cultural Contradictions of Capitalism* (New York, 1975).

[53] Sidney Checkland relates the way in which English workers assimilated themselves to city life and first developed escapist values in "sport . . . the public house, the music hall, oratorios and brass bands, cheap fiction. . . " (*Rise of Industrial Society*, 326). Gareth Stedman Jones analyzes the relation between the decay of London artisan culture and the rise of industry and growth of escapist culture in "Working-Class Culture and Working-Class Politics, 1870–1900: Notes on the Remaking of a Working Class," *Journal of Social History*, 7, 4, Summer 1974, 478–9.

ideologies of individualism established in social life would be shattered by sudden comprehension of the reified conditions of life. Novelty and instant gratification were sought because of the deprivations, monotony, humiliation, and meaninglessness of alienated labor. The daydream was that novelty, love junk, constant physical mobility, and spectacles actually compensated for the physical and psychic damage of alienated work. The nightmare was that the individual would no longer be able to be "taken care of" or experience the fleeting power of "taking care of," but rather would need to "take care with," that is, establish principles and practices of working-class unity, organization, and struggle. These daydreams and nightmares were elements in the fantasy system of "modern society" which flourished because of the alienated conditions of capitalist production.

Within the production process there originated boredom, aging, fear, sickness, insecurity, and loss of privacy which constituted the subjective moment of alienated labor. Also in production originated the commodities designed to alleviate boredom, aging, etc., and restore privacy. Illusory promises to alleviate bordeom, slow down aging, etc. were sold with the commodity. The existence of these promises, however, did not make the needs themselves any less real. Advertising was primarily a way of making individuals aware of needs which they had already produced within themselves, rather than of creating new needs. Capitalism required healthy young workers. Hence the need for "eternal youth" was a real albeit alienated need,[54] although commodities could not actually be fountains of youth, but rather merely kept up the illusion of youthfulness. In sum, "cultural values" of the modern working class/salariat were liberated from customary senses of respectability, thrift, moderation, practicality, i.e. bourgeois, petty bourgeois, and craft worker norms. Hard work, education, self-improvement, defined by bourgeois success criteria, were replaced by "deviance," "extremism," "zerowork," credit spending, compulsive craving, and wasting time. Discipline turned into rebelliousness which expressed itself first and least critically as the limitless need for commodities, the social demand for "more."

The second process whereby needs expanded without limit pertained to the construction of needs in ways in which they were satisfied and frustrated at the same time. *Needs were understood as the need for commodities, or individually owned private property. Hence they were construed as individual needs, individually satisfiable.* These presupposed that every individual appropriated values from the social product individually, i.e. exchanged individual labor-power for wages and salaries. In a fully com-

---

[54] "The continual promise of youth . . . . is an offer of that which was increasingly demanded by the industrial process, and that was sorely felt among the older (twenty-five plus) working population of *Middletown*" (Ewen, *Captains of Consciousness*, 148).

modified world no alternative source of need fulfillment existed, excepting the need for liberation from commodified need. *It follows that needs were viewed as individually rather than socially produced.* "Illness is . . . regarded as a natural process to be treated independently of its social causes by a vast array of experts utilizing the most complex technologies."[55] Malnutrition, illiteracy, mental disorder, substandard housing, etc. were regarded as individual "problems." Needs construed as individually created and discharged under these conditious could not possibly be satisfied directly within social relationships unmediated by commodities (hence the elusiveness of comradely love, parental love, sexual love, etc.). On the contrary, the satisfaction of needs in the commodity form isolated individuals from social relationships of reproduction generally. It reproduced the social separation which was originally produced within the capitalist production process. The individual's need for freely organized social production and reproduction was thereby frustrated. Capitalist production also meant that individuals could not decide before production began what needs they wanted to have. Needs were formed behind one's back, hence the need to decide what needs were desirable (i.e. need priorities) was also frustrated. Finally, commodities were acquired not only for what they did, but also for what they meant, hence any "deficit" in acceptable culture symbols created the experience of meaninglessness, hence frustration.

In short, *neds which were actually satisfied in the commodity form were necessarily frustrated in the social form.* Every need fulfilled through commodities isolated the individual from society defined in the sense of social individuality, i.e. "fellowship" or "common doing." The construction of needs in the commodity form diminished the sense of self; it was a form of "absolute impoverishment" frustrating all social needs formed and satisfied within cooperative activity with others. The compulsive need for status striving and identity through commodity ownership thus resulted in social separation. The need for shelter construed as the need for individually owned differentiated space satisfied the individual need and simultaneously frustrated the social need. The home buyer individually established himself in society in the terms of his relationships with things, and at the same time socially isolated himself in the terms of his relationships with other people. The need for personal integration construed as the need for psychotherapy satisfied this need within the individual relationship with the therapist and for this reason frustrated it within social relationships generally, and class relationships in specific. The meaninglessness of alienated labor and absence of autonomy and self-understanding

---

[55] Marc Renaud, "On the Structural Constraints to State Intervention in Health," *International Journal of Health Services*, 5, 4, 1975, 560.

compelled the individual to purchase understanding in the marketplace, or to buy an ego and superego as commodities (frustrated real ego and superego development was a process directly social in nature). In short, production produced not only the objects that satisfied alien needs, but also the alien needs that the objects satisfied. The circle was closed in a "spectacle system" in which "all goods selected . . . are . . . weapons for a constant reinforcement of the conditions of isolation of 'lonely crowds'."[56]

It was an apparent paradox that while needs were satisfied in the commodity form, hence interpreted as individual needs, in "full capitalist" America individual needs, strictly defined, no longer existed. Abstract social labor stripped workers of all traditional individuality and at the same time defined individualism within the salariat in terms of organizational requirements and institutionalized role definitions. Within the salariat, role status replaced an authentic or trustworthy sense of self-worth and invididual identity. The "individuality" prevalent within the salariat was thus ironically *institutionally* defined. The "individual needs" of the salariat consisted of institutional needs. Within the working class, as we have seen, in place of traditional individuality there were erected management ideologies of labor control which manufactured the illusion of worker individuality, which became the basis for competition within the working class.

The failure to criticize these ideologies and create the conditions for the development of social individuality and self-worth ("workers' work" and "workers' consumption") in the struggle against alienated labor and the commodity form of need fulfillment had important material consequences. Ideological needs for individual pay scales, career ladders, promotions, etc. meant that capital had to be advanced for fabricated status differentiations and prestige scales defined as the "organization of illusion." The ideology that workers were individually important and that concrete labor tasks within production actually were significantly different (together with the real differences when these ideologies were actually embeddded in the labor process) had to be reinforced with differential wage scales, individual attention to workers' problems, etc. Although it was always problematic whether or not these individualistic ideologies actually created internal labor markets and status competition or otherwise created divisions within the working class (and we cannot be certain in the absence of empirical studies of the quantitative effects of these ideologies), in principle they expanded the cost of wages and salaries and social expenses of production.

The absence of individuality (excepting social individuality established

[56] Guy Debord, *Society of the Spectacle* (Detroit, 1970), 28.

through struggle by workers themselves) meant that "individual" needs were, in reality, social needs generally and class needs in particular. *The contradiction arose that at the same time that individual needs were increasingly social in the sense of being universal, these same needs were increasingly satisfied in the commodity form. Needs construed as the need for commodities satisfiable as such were in reality social needs frustrated as such.* The individuation of health needs obscured the systemic origin of disease, which functioned to legitimate capitalism (at the cost, however, of higher reproduction costs). Similarly, needs for transportation, housing, nutrition, etc. fulfilled in the commodity form were necessarily frustrated in the social form. The result was generalized dissatisfaction and compulsive acquisitiveness. The compulsive nature of alienated work, and role definition within production, were internalized and projected in the form of compulsive consumption, which may be interpreted as the systemic frustration of social needs construed as individual needs satisfiable through commodities. The satisfaction of needs in the individual form negated their fulfillment in the social form.

The third process whereby needs expanded beyond limit was their construction such that they could never be satisfied within the commodity form but rather were *always* frustrated, whether construed as individual or social needs. This line of reasoning begins with the observation that individual judgments of particular commodities were more or less arbitrary because in the "jungle of commodities" there was "very little basis for an independent assessment of their qualities."[57] Needs interpreted as the need for commodities were necessarily fragmented, reflecting the "fragmentation of the personality."[58] Bereft of any "craft skill of knowledge" about particular use values, hence perpetually confused about the concrete nature of the means available to satisfy needs, "the fragmentation of need requires on the individual's part a steadily more intensive effort to hold together his identity and personal integrity. In concrete terms this amounts to spending more and more time in consumption activities."[59] The gist of this argument is that *individuals could not really be aware when their needs were in fact satisifed* because of the fragmentation of needs and "the regular reshuffling of these components into momentary desires or states of feelings."[60] Various authors have also referred to a "psychology of scarcity" associated with the increase in the number of kinds of available commodities. This "arises from the kinds of social interaction whereby

[57] Leiss, *Limits of Satisfaction*, 15. This seems, however, to be an empirical question. The home craftsman may be familiar with the qualities of his bandsaw.

[58] Ibid., 18.

[59] Ibid., 20.

[60] Ibid., 27.

individuals encourage each other to believe that failure to procure the means of purchasing certain goods will exclude them from all hope of satisfying the needs which have come to be associated with these goods."[61] The frustration of needs, hence their theoretically limitless character, occurred because the "sources of satisfaction for any need will be as scarce as the particular commodities in question."[62]

Ultra-Individualism and the Reproduction of the Working Class/Salariat

In the nineteenth and early twentieth centuries, the standard of life in the USA was relatively high and the costs of wages relatively low. The reasons included the cheapness of land, water, building materials, minerals, etc.; the advanced physical productivity of labor; the ceiling on other costs of elements entering into constant and variable capital because of slave labor; immigration and the persistence of kinship subsistence economies; "familist values," hence the availability of entire families for wage labor;[63] and last but not least, capital's direct control of reproduction costs through the system of "welfare capitalism" which flourished between 1880 and the 1920s.[64] The latter permitted individual capitals to control the cost of wages by laying out variable capital on company housing, stores, recreational, and other facilities in quantities required to attract skilled labor-power and also to minimize the cost of wages for unskilled workers.

The development of the working class/salariat in the context of a "corporate liberalism" which stressed gratification of personal desires as

[61] Ibid., 31.
[62] Ibid., 31.

A different but related analysis of need frustration based on scarcity is Fred Hirsch's thesis that "positional goods" such as houses with a view had use value only when owned and used by a minority, and that satisfaction decreased when their use was democratized (Fred Hirsch, *Social Limits to Growth*, Cambridge, Mass., 1977; see also Tibor Scitovsky, *The Joyless Economy*, New York, 1977). This line of reasoning seems to be excessively based on the relation between individuals and things (e.g., freeway space; views; clean air; etc.) rather than between one individual, group, etc. and another.

[63] Louise A. Tilly, "Comments on the Yans-McLaughlin and Davidoff Papers," *Journal of Social History*, 7, 4, Summer 1974, 458. The survival of familist values in the form of extended kinship networks within the reserve army of labor is described in Carol Stack's *All My Kin* (New York, 1974).

[64] Stuart D. Brandes, *American Welfare Capitalism, 1880–1940* (Chicago, 1976), passim; J. O'Connor, Review of *American Welfare Capitalism*, in *American Journal of Sociology*, 82, 5, March 1977, passim.

opposed to moral duties and the "social interest" ruptured the equation between low reproduction costs and relatively high living standards. The basic reasons were the commodification of everyday life, the destruction of traditional communities and reproduction processes directly organized by capitalist enterprises, the replacement of familist with individualistic values, and growing scarcities of natural resources. Moreover, the decline of immigration required capital to develop available labor-power more intensively.[65] This "law of rising requirements," which Lenin used to explain the growth of real wages in terms of growing education and skill levels, finally came to include "social training" and ideological differentiation used to divide workers against one another. The cost of wages increased not only because of the expansion of labor-time needed to train and socialize workers, but also because of labor-time needed to train the salariat to specialize and divide both labor and laborers.

One key change was the development of the mass market for wage goods, or capital's loss of control of reproduction conditions within company towns and mill towns and in mining and agricultural communities. "The fact is that a society making heavy investments in capital goods cannot at once afford good housing, good schools, good medicine, and generous pensions for all its workers."[66] The development of the wage form and the mass market for housing, automobiles, and other "consumer durables" dislodged capital's control of reproduction conditions and at the same time destroyed traditional self-regulation within working-class communities. Needs finally came to be determined by social and systemic forces "working behind people's backs." Anarchic location patterns, especially the separation of work, living, and recreation and increased transportation and communication needs expanded the variety and scale of social reproduction processes.[67] "The hierarchical organization of capitalist production requires an equally complex system of rewards and deprivations which by a variety of mechanisms lead to a spatial segregation that must be overcome by capitalist transit."[68] Suburbanization and Manhattanization of the cities increased congestion and expanded the costs of wages and salaries by raising rents, insurance premiums, and commuting costs, undermining subsistence production, creating inflexibilities in the built

[65] "The restrictions on immigration . . . have led employers to conserve the skill and strength of their labor and to put considerable investment into training and improving it" (William M. Leiserson, *Adjusting Immigrant to Industry*, New York, 1924, 10).

[66] Brandes, *American Welfare Capitalism*, 147. Welfare capitalism also permitted capitalists to vary labor-power costs in accordance with the phase of the capitalist cycle.

[67] James O'Connor, *The Fiscal Crisis of the State* (New York, 1973), chs 4–5.

[68] Marshall Feldman, "The Political Economy of Class and the Journey-to-Work: The Case of San Fransisco," unpublished MS, Dec. 21, 1976, 16.

environment, duplicating facilities, and making waste.[69] "Sprawl is the most expensive form of residential development in terms of economic costs, environmental and natural resources consumption and many types of personal costs."[70] Urbanization also increased the scope and complexity, and hence the cost, of producing and distributing a given volume and quality of services. Closely related to suburbanization was the mass production of specialized household goods and services, or individualized, socially expensive labor-saving devices.

These and related changes associated with the emergence of the modern working class/salariat raised reproduction costs as well as forging new markets to combat realization crisis tendencies. They also "freed" women from the home for wage labor, meanwhile creating new needs requiring two or more wage earners to fulfill, costly new ideologies of "motherhood as a profession" and "scientific housework" in the 1920s,[71] and ideologies of "togetherness" in the post-World War Two period.[72]

The process of incorporating use values and services which were once provided in the home into variable capital outlays and social expenses was associated with the individualistic character of working-class/salariat needs. The "full" commodification of labor-power, production, and need fulfillment presupposed the subversion of the family, and the separation of men from women, young from old, healthy from sick, etc. The material dependence of women on men, the elderly on youth, and the young on the family, progressively weakened. An increasing share of the total costs and expenses of reproducing society fell on capital and the state. "The need for new forms of social and health services as well as for social control grew due to the increased proletarianization and urbanization of the population, the increased numbers of elderly and dependent people, and a general increase in alienation. . . . there was an increasingly individualized, atomized populace containing rapidly rising numbers of displaced persons."[73] A

[69] As Mathew Edel has shown ("Rent Theory and Labor Strategy: Marx, George and the Urban Crisis," *RRPE*, 9, 4, Winter 1977), suburbanization in the USA was in part the result of the working-class demand for suburban housing in the context of a severe urban crisis.

[70] *The Costs of Urban Sprawl* (Washington, DC, 1974), quoted in *The San Francisco Chronicle and Examiner*, Dec. 8, 1974. This study was made by HUD, the Environmental Protection Agency, and the Council of Environmental Quality.

[71] Barbara Ehrenreich and Deirdre English, "The Manufacture of Housework," *Socialist Review*, 26 (5, 4), Oct.–Dec. 1975.

[72] "Our goal is to put the burden of operation into the design of the machines . . . in order to have more time for each other, the working couple has to spend less time on the rote chores of the household" ("How Changing Age Mix Changes Markets," *Business Week*, Jan. 12, 1976, 74, quoting a spokesman for Whirlpool Corporation).

[73] Gelvin Stevenson, "Social Relations of Production and Consumption in Human Service Occupations," *Monthly Review*, July–Aug. 1976, 79.

shared way of life or traditional "indivisibility" became increasingly impossible – excepting in the act of resistance against alienated labor and needs.

In "full capitalism" the number of separate households was limited only by the absolute size of the adult population. In the USA, in recent years, the fastest-growing housing markets were single households at both ends of the age scale.[74] The concentration and centralization of finance capital and land and housing speculation increasingly raised housing costs and rents. These were "earned at the expense of . . . other capitals . . . indirectly raising the cost of reproducing labor-power."[75] The pursuit of "self" meant in the most extreme cases that every adult required not only individual shelter but also transport, communications, medical services, restaurant meals, recreational equipment, etc. America more than any other country exemplified "full capitalist" trends in the form of more single women and men, divorced persons, women bringing up children alone, youth and retired people living alone, and more two-house families; hence the need for more car insurance and repairs, home insurance and home maintenance per capita. Automobiles were needed not merely to get to work, but also to escape from work on weekends and vacations. "The automobile . . . is . . . one of the strongest social demands as a mythical means for individual autonomy."[76] While labor-time required to purchase an auto remained more or less unchanged during the postwar period, more labor-time was required to pay for gas and oil, insurance, fees, parts and components, repairs, parking, public road construction and maintenance, and pollution control.

As we have noted, needs construed as individual needs satisfied by commodities in fact frustrated needs for sociability, emotional intimacy, and personal integration, which, in turn, became the source of the need to escape from single living. This need was also construed as the need for commodities (e.g., EST, discos, salvationist religions) which entered into costs of wages and salaries. In US "full capitalism," the mass identity crisis and "age of anxiety" associated with ultra-individualistic ways of life

[74] Carolyn Shaw Bell, "Another Look at the Distribution of Income," *Wall Street Journal*, Nov. 12, 1976. In 1960, for example, 75 per cent of households consisted of "families"; in 1976 only 66 per cent. In the late 1940s, 15 per cent of 20–24-year-olds headed households; today the figure is 25 per cent. The figures for people over 65 years old are 55 per cent and 63 per cent, respectively. While the US population grew by only 11.5 per cent from 1970 to 1980, the number of households increased by 24.8 per cent. Meanwhile, the number of people in the average household declined from 3.14 to 2.75 (Andrew Hacker, "Farewell to the Family?" *New York Review*, March 18, 1982, 37).
[75] Simon Clark and Norman Ginsberg, "The Political Economy of Housing," *Kapitalistate*, 4/5, 1976, 88.
[76] Castells, *City, Class and Power*, 31.

created new needs for "leisure goods," "health care," "entertainment," "therapy," etc.[77] The explosion of medical and recreational outlays reflected the stresses and strains within a society in which production was social, whereas ideologies of reproduction were individualistic and narcissistic.[78]

Ultra-individualism in the USA meant that needs were defined and satisfied in ways which created peculiarly American illusions of good health, food, recreation, and states of mind in general because of the persistence of ideologies of rugged individualism, dreams of individual beauty, success and fame, etc. In the USA more than anywhere else, illusions, not needs defined in social terms, were satisfied through commodities. Real social identity, personality integration, self-worth, autonomy, adventure, and privacy were systematically replaced by "alienated socialization" with its costly economic and psychological consequences. "The entire process of economic production . . . has produced increasingly socialized human beings. Socialization itself has become a fundamental human need. . . . On the other hand, under alienated conditions this socialization is always combined with a simultaneous need to free oneself from it and retreat to private forms of existence."[79] This is one reason for the ultra-individualistic fragmentation of the mass market based on age, occupation, ethnicity, etc. The proliferation of segmented markets, product differentiation, style changes, and packaging "revolutions" were ideologies of social control in the same measure that occupational status, job ladders, professionalism, and so on functioned to control the working class/salariat within production.

All-pervasive individualist ideologies and practices had profound material and psychological consequences. Variable capital outlays covered not only food, clothing, etc. but also the daydreams and fantasies and their nightmarish consequences upon which modern reproduction processes were based. Privacy was impossible with noise pollution, traffic jams, high-rises, and recreational slums. Adventure became the monopoly of the Jacques Cousteaus. Social deceptions and self-deceptions created endless difficulties between the sexes, within youth cultures, and between young and old. They created expectations in the public sphere which were

[77] Health and recreational expenses have increased from 11.7 to 19.7 per cent in the most recent BLS index. The works of Illich, Navarro, Eyer and Sterling and others show not only how capitalist production and social life generally produce disease, but also how disease is produced in the process of "curing" individuals.

[78] Recent books on this subject are Richard Sennett, *The Fall of Public Man: Social Psychology of Capitalism* (New York, 1978); Christopher Lasch, *The Culture of Narcissism* (New York, 1979).

[79] Eberhard Knodler-Bunte, "The Proletarian Public Sphere and Political Organization," *New German Critique*, 4, Winter 1974, quoting Oskar Negt and Alexander Kluge.

frustrated and discharged in distorted ways; they diverted human energy away from the expression of anger, fear, pain, and pleasure which instead "leaked out" in the form of hostility, helplessness, seduction, etc. Herein lay the source of demand for drugs, divorce lawyers, psychologists, as well as for new illusions themselves. When illusions of individuality, independence, and autonomy were shattered, more labor-time was required to "reconstruct" the individual personality to "cope with modern life." The illusion that social distress, for example, was caused by disruptions in family life meant that more labor-time had to be employed to "maintain the family," e.g., home magazines, family counseling, home ownership market organization. Drug counseling became big business; more police were required in the schools; hence mounting costs of social reproduction when the nightmares overtook the daydreams, especially in the sphere of security and law and order.

More refined analyses of alienated needs should take into account the different values, self-perceptions, and conditions of daily life within the working class and salariat. In the first place, people with the same income working and living in different class relations spent their money in different ways.[80] Sociological analysis of class differentiation has stressed the differences between the "upper lower blue-collar" class in which needs were supposedly gratified or discharged immediately; the "lower middle white-collar" class which supposedly deferred gratification because of the prevailing anxiety about achieving respectability and success through performance; and the "upper middle" class which (it was claimed) utilized more integrated and varied means of satisfying needs.[81]

These distinctions, however, lack one crucial dimension. Within the working class, individualism was constrained by the absence of upward mobility, relatively narrow income differentials, and traces of collective sentiments established in the common struggle for survival. Ultra-individualism and its illusions were most prevalent in the salariat precisely because it did not constitute an "economic class" but rather a "heap" of individuals whose "socially established standards of an acceptable income level" were relatively high.[82]

The salariat engaged itself on many fronts in the defense of the production and distribution of illusions and daydreams. Their responsibility for

---

[80] Richard Coleman, "The Significance of Social Stratification in Selling," *Proceedings*, American Management Association, Dec. 1960.

[81] Sidney Fine, "Social Class and Consumer Behavior," in Harold H. Kassarijian and Thomas A. Robertson, eds, *Perspectives in Consumer Behavior* (Glencoe, Illinois, 1968).

[82] Standards seemed to rise as average income increased (James N. Morgan, "The Supply of Effort, the Measurement of Well-Being, and the Dynamics of Improvement," *American Economic Review*, May 1968, 32).

producing illusions and ideologies of social control (together with the absence of authentic social class referents) meant that individual salariat needs were especially alienated, fragmented, and abundant. It was no longer the bourgeoisie but rather the salariat which was living testimony to possibilities for individual success and upward mobility – possibilities which had to be kept alive for capitalist ideologies of individualism to withstand the pressures and strains created within the working class. Income differentials were essential to the maintenance of a loyal salariat because it was skilled in planning and controlling production in the material sense and the direct producers in the social sense. This labor of specialization and division of workers was the salariat's sacred duty and presupposed the "middle-class standard of life." In this sense, social control was commodified.

The salariat was rewarded to the degree that it successfully engineered capitalist productive forces and production relationships. In the enterprise, permanent status distinctions and income differentials within the salaried ranks became essential. High salaries or "skilled worker" wages were required. Management bonuses, commissions, fees, stock option plans, and other prerogatives of middle and higher salariat personnel may also be mentioned in this context. While status was "produced" within production, like commodity values, it was "realized" in the market. Statuses within salariat occupations thus became real only with the achievement of definite consumption norms associated with particular statuses. Reproduction standards were costly because a functional salariat had to internalize the authority of capital and assume responsibility for social control, which was essential for value production and realization.

The salariat's way of life was a vulgarized version of that of the capitalist class. It was what the worker was taught to aspire to and what the salariat sought at all costs to retain. It included the house in the suburbs surrounded by clean air, space, light, silence; good schools which reproduced inequalities of training, status and income; stable employment in large-scale enterprises; unhurried family vacations; pluralistic government responsive to salariat needs; individual feelings of self-worth; close and warm family bonds; the consumption of "culture." This description, of course, is a parody because it leaves out at least as much as it includes. The individualistic way of life was also repressed and "one-dimensional." It was not a critical and self-examined life and required little courage beyond a certain persistence in trying harder and pleasing others.

The exclusive suburbs, privileged education, and status striving associated with the production of more expensive brands, costly consumer goods, new fashions, and so on were very expensive for capital (and the state). The suburban way of life based on the objective position of the salariat in production and circulation expanded the costs of reproducing labor-power.[83] Precisely because status in the community and capitalist work hierarchy was defined more in terms of consumption patterns than of kinds of concrete labor,[84] status striving further increased the cost of reproducing salariat labor-power. The reproduction of false consciousness in this sense entered into variable capital outlays. Capital's excessive concern for its salariat/management personnel extended, of course, to production as well as reproduction conditions. Job performance was in effect measured by the degree to which corporate personnel were able to maintain the regime of wage labor. Outside of production, "owner-occupation of housing is of ideological importance to the white-collar workers,"[85] exemplifying another way that capital's managing and controlling arms were wedded to private property.

In sum, large-scale capital "created" the salariat in part to manage the production relations and productive forces and in part to solve the realization crisis tendencies which in an earlier time haunted US capitalism. However, this solution to the problem of realization crisis unintentionally resulted in the new problem of surplus value production and unproductive utilization of surplus value produced, i.e. working-class and especially salariat satisfaction of needs in the commodity form increased the value of labour-power. In turn, the growth of reproduction costs lowered the rate of exploitation and the real rate of profit. In this process *and also its negation* (the struggle for workers' work and workers' consumption – see below) we may find some underlying causes of the accumulation crisis. The contradictions within modern reproduction processes, in particular the systemic inability to maintain the daydreams and pay for the nightmares, may be regarded as central elements in modern economic crisis tendencies. A vast private and public credit structure and inflation were needed to make the system "work."

Struggles for Social Reproduction and the Law of Value

As we know, alienated labor may be defined in terms of the *systemic* domination of the law of value (which regulated the valorization process) and managerial *social* domination (which governed the labor process). The concept of the production process (valorization plus labor process)

[83] See, for example, Ann Markusen, "Class and Urban Social Expenditure," *Kapitalistate*, 4–5, 1977, 59–60.

[84] Pierre Martineau, "Social Classes and Spending Behavior," *Journal of Marketing*, 23, Oct. 1958.

[85] Clark and Ginsberg, "Political Economy of Housing," 88. See also Jim Kemeny, "The Ideology of Home Ownership," *Arena*, 46, 1977.

thus *combines* the concepts of system domination and social domination. As we also know, workers' work may be defined in terms of struggles within and against both systemic and social domination, including struggles against managerial ideologies of control; the uncertainties and insecurities of crisis; mindless accumulation without limit; repression of affect; and so on. Workers' work, in this sense, may be regarded as the historical negation of alienated labor; it combines the concepts of self-organized system *and* social relationships; it opposes capital fetishism on the global level and individual ideologies and their practices in the workplace. Finally, workers' work presupposes collective means, i.e. the labor of unity, or "social individuality."

Alienated needs may be defined in terms of the *systemic* domination of commodity fetishism and the *social* domination of object fetishism. The concept of alienated needs therefore also combines the concepts of system domination and social domination.

"Workers' consumption" is the historical negation of alienated needs. It may be defined in terms of struggles within and against processes of system and social domination. The critique of commodity fetishism consists of the construction of needs as the need for expressive and moral-normative relationships. The critique of object fetishism consists of the construction of needs as the need for use values to mediate (rather than substitute for) expressive, moral-social relationships. The concept of noncommodified needs thus theoretically parallels the concept of workers' work; i.e. needs in direct social forms rather than the commodity form parallel work in direct social forms rather than the wage form.

In the Frankfurt School tradition, alienated labor and alienated needs constitute a determinate *theoretical* totality. "A man who is alienated in his work cannot rediscover himself in his leisure time. He does not know how to live in the present, to mediate, or to create."[86] No such thing as part-time freedom outside of work can exist.

However, neither labor nor needs alone or together can be theoretically understood outside of the context of the class struggle. The wage and commodity forms of work and life exemplify the *conditions* of reproduction of labor-power as a form of capital, not social reproduction *historically* understood. Put another way, it is essential to distinguish between the concept of alienated labor and historical labor, and the concept of alienated needs and historical needs. In historical fact, labor-power is never purely a form of capital; consumption never merely reproduces alienation alone. The historical production process exemplifies capital and class struggle (or

[86] Mathilde Niel, "The Phenomenon of Technology: Liberation or Alienation of Man," Erich Fromm, ed., *Socialist Humanism* (New York, 1965), 341.

capital as class struggle) simultaneously, e.g. expressivity and its repression, moral-normative rules and their repression, reason and its negation. Similarly, the historical process of consumption exemplifies commodity and object fetishism and at the same time struggles against fetishism. In sum, in the model of full capitalism, the struggle for workers' work and workers' consumption combined with alienated labor and the alienated commodity form of need satisfaction to make up a determinate *historical* totality – one filled with contingency and ambiguity of meaning and practice.

The struggle for workers' work and workers' consumption (which by themselves constitute merely a determinate theoretical totality within the Marxist "class struggle logic" tradition) was invisible to both orthodox Marxism and the Frankfurt School tradition.[87] Orthodox "capital logic" methods could not grasp the connections between struggles for workers' work and workers' consumption because these methods were rooted in the concept of "structural determinations" as well as that of individuals as personifications of capitalist categories. Orthodox Marxism assumes that the value of labor-power is merely its capacity to produce exchange value; hence it sidesteps the problem of the determination of needs, concrete labor, and use value. However, it is obvious that real people with real social needs make up society, and their real practice to realize these needs in directly social forms demands some kind of theoretical expression.[88]

In other words, orthodox Marxism ignored individuals and their motivations and meanings. "Treating human beings as the congeries of their relations," Richard Lichtman writes, "will always appear to reduce them to those relations understood as an abstract pattern of merely conceptual determinations."[89] Lichtman deploys Freud's basic premise that individuals disguise their own selves to themselves, but makes the crucial disclaimer that what is disguised is not an "essential self" but the phenomenal forms which hide the social relationships of capitalist production, distribution, exchange, and consumption. Two levels of mystification exist: first, "the masking of underlying essential social structures through

---

[87] Or critical theory interpreted workers' work/workers' consumption in terms of the thesis of "artificial negativity," e.g., "the aversion to work ... does not stem so much from the failures of capitalism and the discontent of the workers so much as it flows from the successes of capitalist integration and the privatistic withdrawal of the workers to take fullest advantage of their integration" (Tim Luke, "Anti-Work?" *Telos*, 50, Winter 1981/1982, 193).

[88] Agnes Heller argues that radical needs are based on the "consciousness of alienation" which is associated with a "collective Ought" (*Theory of Need in Marx*, 94). As Lebowitz shows, Heller ignores the capitalist labor process and production relations and their relation to need production; thus, her "Ought" is not grounded materially ("Heller on Marx's Concept of Needs").

[89] Lichtman, *Production of Desire*, 259.

the phenomenal forms of individual life, and second, the further distorting of that individual psychic existence itself through the mechanisms of defense against threatening unconscious forces." In sum, "the traditional Marxist account never distinguished among *levels of reality within the realm of phenomenal forms*, for it mistakenly identified 'phenomenal' with 'conscious,' a common misconception which it took Freud's discovery to destroy."[90] In relation to the present argument, this means that the discovery of the "social unconscious," i.e. the law of value and individualism ideologies and practices, depended on a certain praxis within every level of existence in the workplace and consumption process. Every level of reality including the individual unconscious thus became "contested terrain."

The meaning of particular social activities therefore cannot be grasped categorically or through "conceptual determinations" except in the general sense that the only authentically *social* activity possible in a universe of wage labor and the commodity form of need satisfaction was *social struggle for "social individuality."* "New social movements" based on ascriptive identities and the politics of the body exemplified this general rule.

Freudian Marxists have argued that in modern capitalism desire is "robbed of its radical impact by continually being sublimated into socially available objects," i.e. commodities. "Its ideological appearance of fulfillment is simply the fact that desire is made to coincide with a pre-formed object. This is how needs and their satisfaction have an ideological effect, how the very act of consumption integrates and disarms the possibility of a demand that cannot be socially met."[91] However, precisely because love, creativity, sexuality, and so on were satisfied in the commodity form, the desublimation of desire necessarily emerged as struggles to redefine labor and life against and within the wage and commodity forms. One major battleground between capital and labor thus became the "personality." The stake was the personality structure itself, particularly the capacity of the ego to regulate new balances between id and superego, which, in turn, required not only new system functions but also new forms of self-organized social integration. In this psychopolitical economy, which emerged with the new left revolts of the 1960s, there appeared to be no middle ground between the commodity form of need satisfaction and social forms of need fulfillment based on materially and politically grounded moral-normative and expressive behavior. Similarly, there appeared to be no middle ground between alienated labor and struggles for workers' work within the divisions of social and industrial labor. Precisely because capital's basic need was to dominate labor and social

[90] Ibid., 262–3.
[91] D'Amico, "Desire and the Commodity Form," 107.

reproduction, workers' work and workers' consumption were in effect struggles against the basic capitalist wage and commodity forms.

As we saw in the last chapter, struggles for workers' work reduced surplus value absolutely and relatively, meanwhile undermining the status of labor-power as variable capital. The present argument is that struggles within the process of consumption had similar effects. At the level of the economic struggle, the commodification of needs united individuals as commodity owners and at the same time separated them as social individuals. This reproduction of the separation between individuals created physical and psychological "negative spaces" which were costly both economically and psychologically. "Consumerism" and the struggle for more commodities, i.e. more social separation, increased the size and/or the value content of the consumption basket. Total consumpton became less variable in the downward direction. Labor-power thus lost more of its status as variable capital. These tendencies were reinforced by consumer movements, service-sector unionism, and other modern economistic struggles. In addition, consumption-oriented growth increasingly fueled economic growth as a whole; cyclical upturns in the economy increasingly depended on the expansion of consumption spending. As we know, the result was that more labor-time was allocated to wage good and service industries with the effect (*ceteris paribus*) that surplus value was reduced. Finally, consumer debt increased much faster than capitalist debt,[92] which reinforced the strong tendency for more labor-time to be channeled into wage good industries. The result was the slow growth rate of capital and modern "stagflation" tendencies.

More significant socially and politically, in the same way that the struggle for workers' work was immanent in the production process, the struggle for social forms of need satisfaction was inherent in the consumption process. The struggle for workers' consumption or "more social relations and unity" originated within the contradictions of both the production and consumption processes. The struggle for workers' work meant that individuals construed needs less as the need for commodities and more as the need for social unity unmediated by commodities. Individualist ideologies thus became more problematic in relation to social integration and political legitimation. Social separateness, armor-plating, "sensuous waste and impoverishment," and the compulsive accumulation of commodities produced mass psychological stress. The growing shortage of acceptable cultural symbols produced and marketed commercially and

[92] In the USA, between 1946 and 1979, household debt grew from 16 to 54 per cent of GNP; business debt increased from 30 to 52.2 per cent. Between 1973 and 1979, government debt (all levels) grew by 100 per cent, consumer debt almost doubled, business debt increased by less than 30 per cent (*Federal Reserve Bulletin*, July 1979, Chart 1.59).

the discounting of status symbols in the commodity form undermined capitalist motivations and incentives and created the need for new counter-cultures.[93] At the same time, the accumulation of stocks of means and objects of reproduction within the household and community took the edge off the need for alienated labor.[94] In the household economy, workers employed mass-produced albeit differentiated products which were as homogeneous and "abstract" as the production process in which they were produced. Thus, while the form in which means of reproduction were employed in the home was individual, the content was social. Workers who were robbed of forms and contents of traditional individuality at work, i.e. who produced commodities which bore the stamp of social abstract labor alone, utilized these commodities outside of work "individually" only in the ideological sense of the word. Everyone drove their cars more or less in the same way; everyone used the same medicines, communications services, and so on; everyone watched the same television spectacles. In sum, alienated labor objectively as well as subjectively created both needs and possibilities for more "living time" and workers' consumption. Capital's strategies to make the working class work less for itself and more for capital were negated by the accumulation of means of reproduction and new forms of intersubjectivity which made it possible for workers to work less for capital and more for themselves.

As we have argued, the struggle for workers' work undermined modern US capitalism's capacity to produce surplus value. The struggle for workers' consumption further subverted capital's capacities for self-reproduction. The demand for more living time reduced absolute surplus value. The demand for high-value wage goods reduced relative surplus value. Consumerist action typically focused on the nature of wage goods as use values; environmental action as a form of consumerism effectively inhibited capital from reducing the value of the average wage good; feminist action threw into question the entire range of "male-defined" objects which functioned in ways which reinforced structures of male domination. Not only the individualistic nature of consumption and need fulfillment, therefore, but also its negation in the form of workers' consumption interfered with classical mechanisms of capitalist accumulation. Both

[93] Jürgen Habermas, *Legitimation Crisis* (Boston, 1975), ch. 7; Hans Peter Dreitzel, "On the Political Meaning of Culture," in Norman Birnbaum, *Beyond the Crisis* (New York, 1978), 89–90; Paul Blumberg, "The Decline and Fall of the Status Symbol," *Social Problems*, 21, 4, April 1974, 492–3; John Keane, "The Legacy of Political Economy: Thinking with and Against Claus Offe," *Canadian Journal of Political and Social Theory*, 2, 3, Fall 1978, 74.

[94] R. E. Pahl, "Employment, Work, and the Domestic Division of Labor," *International Journal of Urban and Regional Research (IJURR)*, 4, 1, March 1980, 16; Scott Burns, *The Household Economy* (Boston, 1977); S. Henry, *The Hidden Economy* (London, 1978); J. I. Gershuny, "Post-Industrial Society: The Myth of the Service Economy," *Futures*, 10, 2, 1978.

wage demands and the demand for private and public credit, based on needs which were systematically frustrated in the social form, *and* "quality of life" demands undermined the law of value. As we suggested, the result was modern stagflation/depression tendencies, which reduced possiblities of meeting wage and other economic demands. Economic hard times, in turn, created possibilities for the further redefinition of needs and work.

It is important to stress that workers' consumption as a critique of alienated needs was implicitly a critique of alienated wage labor, i.e. worked its way back into the production process via consumer, environmental, feminist, and other demands raised to the level of political struggle. This resulted in legislation and administrative rulings modifying the process and product of capitalist production, which was in this sense stripped of its "naturalistic" cover. The production process in effect became the germ of a production system based on need, consciously decided upon within and through social struggles. At the same time, workers' work as a critique of alienated labor was implicitly a critique of alienated needs, i.e. worked its way forward into the consumption process via, e.g., occupational health and safety movements. This resulted in new legislative and administrative law modifying the process and product of capitalist reproduction. The most dramatic example was the worker struggle against workplace hazards in the nuclear power industry combined with consumerist and community struggles against nuclear power. Other examples pertained to production processes and products ranging from petrochemical and other chemical products; food processing and food products; medical, transport, and other services.

In sum, the relationship between the various forms of class struggle in "full capitalism" appeared to be that workers demanded "job rights," meanwhle hoarding labor-power in production, in this way creating workers' work with the aim of seizing more living time and also wages, credit, and other moneys required to accumulate means and objects of reproduction. Labor-power was hoarded through absenteeism, sick leaves, early retirement, the struggle to reduce days worked per year, among other ways. Conserved labor-power was then expended in subsistence production, i.e. workers' consumption. *The capitalist process of "working for money" began to change to the working-class process of "moneying for work."* The living economy based on non- and anti-capitalist concepts of time and space went underground: in the reconstituted household; the commune; cooperatives; the single-issue organization; the self-help clinic; the solidarity group.[95] Hurrying along the development of the alternative

---

[95] See, John Case and Rosemary C. Taylor, *Co-ops, Communes and Collectives* (New York, 1979); Harry C. Boyte, *The Backyard Revolution* (Philadelphia, 1980); Ivan Ilich, *Shadow Work* (New York, 1981).

and underground economies was the growth of underemployment (full employment at less than a living wage), which originated in the expulsion of living labor from large-scale capitalist enterprise, and mass unemployment associated with the crisis of the 1980s. "Regular" employment and union-scale work contracted, which became an incentive to develop alternative, localized modes of production. This was a crucial aspect of the relationship between struggles *against* abstract social labor and *for* the reorganization of the social relationships of production. This relationship between the class struggle within production and reproduction processes was reinforced by the increase in health and safety risks at work associated with product competition and product innovation, as well as with traditional process innovation (excepting the traditional extractive industries, the workers' struggle against unhealthy and dangerous conditions was located in manufacturing generally, and the product-innovating industries in particular, e.g., chemicals). The relationship between struggles for workers' work and workers' consumption was reinforced by the effect of model changes, forced obsolescence, and the like, i.e., systemic waste, including waste of labor-power, on worker and salariat consciousness, which was reflected in the refusal of many to fully participate in an economic system in which workers worked only in order to work more in the future.

During the 1970s, localized, fragmented anarchic, and half-formed struggles squeezed capital from all sides. New social relationships of reproduction and alternative employment, including the informal and underground economies, threatened not only labor discipline, but also capitalist markets. Demands to employ local savings in credit unions and local cooperatives threatened capital's control of money and credit. Alternative technologies threatened capital's monopoly on technological development.[96] Environmental movements which fought to prevent resources from becoming commodities (or to decommodify resources) threatened capital's control of land, natural resources, and energy sources. Hoarding of labor-power threatened capital's domination of production. Withdrawal of labor-power undermined basic social disciplinary mechanisms and capital's control of the supply of labor. In general, redefinition of needs and reorganization of the social relationships of reproduction functioned as a double critique of US capitalism: first, as a critique of wage labor itself; second, as a critique of the ways in which the working class construed needs as individual needs satisfiable in the commodity form; in short, as a critique of commodity fetishism. Hence, precisely in a period when competing capitals required more product and process innovation,

[96] Richard C. Dorf and Yvonne C. Hunter (eds), *Appropriate Visions: Technology, The Environment and The Individual* (San Fransisco, 1978).

changes in the division of social and industrial labor, and more labor flexibility and mobility, the working class's generalized albeit implicit critique of capitalist production and consumption relations impaired the system's capacity for innovation, flexibility, and mobility. This contradiction and its implications for the production of surplus value and capital accumulation help to explain capital's twin obsession in the 1980s with restoring economic incentives *and* social motivations, and increasing labor productivity *and* reordering the chaotic conditions of social life. This obsession seemed to lie behind both the dramatic appearance of neo-liberal and neo-conservative ideologies in the late 1970s and early 1980s and also new ideas advanced by some politicians, businessmen, and policy planners to restructure production and reproduction processes along more explicitly social lines. These themes of crisis-induced neo-liberal/neo-conservative and corporatist/collectivist (as well as localist/populist) restructuring of work and social life are sketched out in Chapter 8. Beforehand, however, we need to investigate the ways in which government and state economic and social policy pertaining to economic and social reproduction reinforced US accumulation crisis tendencies and made them more intractable.

7

Economic and Social Reproduction and the Capitalist State

Introduction

The preceding chapters attempted to show that the processes of production, distribution, exchange, consumption, and competition in the model of US full capitalism were deeply inscribed by ideologies of individualism and their practices which, in turn, gave rise to different kinds of economic and social contradictions and crisis tendencies. This chapter discusses the ways in which the modern capitalist political system, parliament, and state in general and social democratic forms in particular, and their articulation with economic and social life, exacerbated these contradictions and crisis tendencies.

In Marxist theory, the "liberal democratic state" is still another capitalist weapon in the class struggle. This is so because the democratic form of the state conceals undemocratic contents. Democracy in the parliamentary shell hides its absence in the state bureaucratic kernel; parliamentary freedom is regarded as the political counterpart of freedom in the marketplace, and the hierarchical bureaucracy as the counterpart of the capitalist division of labor in the factory. In terms of the present argument, the important point is that the state bureaucracy and production process alike are emptied of traditional individuality/indivisibility, self-sufficiency, and autonomy, hence of the material and social basis of both Lockean natural rights individualism and authentic Romantic self-expressive individualism. The latter (it is argued) are replaced by modern ideologies of individualism and their material practices.

On the other hand, Marxism regards the liberal democratic state as another weak link in the chain of capitalist domination. This is so because in contradiction to the principle of bureaucracy is the "juridical ideal of the citizen." This ideal is the principle of self-determination, which is the "democratic subject" in capitalist society. Living individuals, i.e., social agents, are the "bearer[s] of [this] ideological structure which constitutes [them] as . . . subject[s]."[1] In the present work, social agents are identified not with capitalist and working-class fractions alone, but also with the working class as a whole. Civil society is in this sense not merely a fictitious community divided by the capital-labor relationship but also a juridical community united along ascriptive, industrial, and many other convergent and divergent lines.

Marx himself regarded liberal democracy as the "political form of revolution of bourgeois society," but not its "conservative form of life." Historically, propertied interests have, in fact, defined democracy as the political means whereby exploited classes may gain a measure of protection against exploitative classes, i.e., as a subversive doctrine and practice. Theoretically, "for Marx, universal suffrage *per se* stands for the end of the political state as previously known and introduces new conditions that do not preserve the alienation between state and civil society."[2] Real democracy, the triumph of working-class society over capital and the state, or the transcendence of bourgeois parliamentary forms via the "democratization" of the state, is thus a proletarian achievement. In sum, bourgeois liberal democracy negates itself if and when working-class content is poured into bourgeois political forms, which in this way are "sublated" in the specific sense that the distinction between law-making and law-implementation is abolished and popular representatives are made responsible for carrying out the laws which they make.

This theme of "democracy versus capitalism" was echoed by many writers during the late nineteenth and twentieth centuries,[3] albeit often in weakened and/or revised versions which obscured the distinction between parliament/law-making and the state/law-implementation. Most, if not all, orthodox Marxists today argue that during major "breakdowns" in social reproduction the result is either an openly repressive state or socialist revolution (or both, in that historical order). The moderate, official Marxist

---

[1] Ernesto Laclau, "Democratic Antagonisms and the Capitalist State," in M. Freeman and D. Robertson, eds, *The Frontiers of Political Theory* (Brighton, 1980), 109, 117.

[2] Shlomo Avineri, *The Social and Political Thought of Karl Marx* (London, 1968), 210. "Marx's hostility to the state bureaucracy stemmed from his deep and far-reaching commitment to democracy" (Arthur Lipown, "Karl Marx's Theory of Revolution," *Contemporary Sociology*, 7, 1, Jan. 1978, 96).

[3] More recently, Samuel Bowles and Herbert Gintis have argued that "capitalism structures practices through rights in *property* . . . while liberal democracy vests rights in *persons* formally independent from ownership." Given the coexistence of the "liberal democratic state and capitalist production . . . the dynamics of the whole cannot be reduced to the structure of either . . . [rather their] articulation may be described as a contradictory totality" ("The Crisis of Liberal Democratic Capitalism: The Case of the United States," *Politics and Society*, 11, 1, 1982, 52, 60).

theory is that "state monopoly capitalism," which combines the power of monopoly capital and the state, constitutes the normal political economic form of society. In this view, there is thought to be little or no stable middle ground between centralized control of the working class, on the one hand, and socialism, on the other. Marxist "capital logic" theory (which is more or less silent on the issue of capitalism versus democracy) offers a one-sided analysis of state *forms* while playing down contradictory social and economic *contents*. Orthodox Marxism in these senses has little or no tolerance for theories which express contingent and/or ambiguous social and economic realities.

In the post-fascist West there appeared various mixed forms – political capitalism, administered society, and (especially in the USA) the national security state. Political capitalism armed the parliament and state with Keynesian and neo-Keynesian economic theory and policy. Administered society equipped the elected and administrative branches with social programs and a vast apparatus of clientelism. "National security" programs and policies accumulated an obscene level of military might and a Kafkaesque security apparatus. All three forms emerged in the crucible of economic, social, and political crises. Political capitalism originated in capitalist concentration/centralization, the growth of science and technology as social productive forces, the interwar crisis, and the need for economic regulation or politically controlled economic system integration. Administered society appeared with the development of the working class/salariat and their organizations, the social crises of the 1930s and 1960s, and capital's need for social regulation or parliamentary and state-organized forms of social integration. National security state programs and policies arose in the context of the growth of the socialist world and Soviet power, and the development of revolutionary movements in the Third World, as well as in the context of domestic social and political struggles.

Parliamentary and state interventionism into processes of economic and social system domination/integration wre thus "overdetermined" by the development of large-scale capital and the labor movement defined in the broadest sense. This meant that political party programs, parliamentary law-making, and state/bureaucratic law-implementation in both the economic and social fields were potentially highly contradictory. The contradiction between "accumulation" (economic system domination/integration) and "legitimation" (social domination/integration) is, in fact, the focus of most neo-Marxist theories of the modern state. Neo-Marxist writers have argued that the modern "social democratic" state consisted of ambiguous political, economic, and social processes in which fateful choices between permanent repression and socialism were "postponed," but not without significant consequences for economic and social domination/ integration. Most of these writers have in one way or another stressed that parliament and state were part and parcel of the social and economic structures and processes of modern capitalism – material, ideological, and institutional embodiments of capitalist competition and/or class struggle. Increasingly, not only the parliament but also the state apparatus itself was seen as an arena of struggle to impose (and resist) capitalist forms of activity within the state agencies and between these agencies and society and economy.[4] In the present work, the most significant issue concerns the relationship between the contradictory character of the modern parliament and state and the problem of economic and social reproduction – in particular, the effects of economic and social policy infused with individualist ideologies and practices on capitalist accumulation and social integration/domination, respectively. The first step in attempting to address this issue is to develop a materialist concept of political legitimation as a conceptual frame of reference for the analysis of economic and social policy and economic and social reproduction.

Political Legitimation and Parliamentary and State Policy

In orthodox Marxist theory, "the function of the state [is] to secure the collective interest of capitalists, which would be unobtainable (and perhaps endangered) by the actions of individual capitalists, each maximizing profits and compelled by competition. This function is served . . . not through an uninterrupted process, but instead through a series of conflicts and confrontations, piecemeal changes and sudden spurts of action."[5] In other words, the parliament and state's function is to maintain the *conditions* of capitalist production and reproduction which individual capitals neither alone nor together can accomplish. More particularly, "it is . . . a matter of reproducing not labour-power, but the *conditions of existence of*

---

[4] Nicos Poulantzas, *State, Power, Socialism* (London, 1978). James O'Connor, "The Democratic Movement in the United States," *Kapitalistate*, 7, 1979; Gosta Epsing-Anderson, Roger Friedland, and Erik Olin Wright, "Modes of Class Struggle and the Capitalist State," *Kapitalistate*, 4–5, 1976; Francis Fox Piven and Richard A. Cloward, *The New Class War* (New York, 1982) ("A century and a half after the achievement of formal democratic rights, the state has finally become the main arena of class conflict" [124].

[5] Hugh Mosley, "Capital and the State: West German Neo-Orthodox State Theory," *Review of Radical Political Economics (RRPE)*, 14, 1, Spring 1982, 25.

labour-power."[6] In sum, the basic condition of capitalist production is the politically guaranteed existence and reproduction of labor-power in requisite quantities and qualities in particular times and places.

The political reproduction of the conditions of supply of labor-power is essential (the argument continues) because labor-power is not produced and reproduced as a commodity under capitalist conditions of production. Instead, it consists of the reproduction of the working class/salariat outside of the circuits of capital strictly defined. "It is the worker him or herself and not the labour-power that is reproduced on the basis of the consumption of commodities *and* of a labour process situated *outside* the process of production of commodities."[7]

Nineteenth-century Marxism did not have to confront the thorny question of what, if any, are the guarantees that sufficient capitalist labor-power qualified technically and socially in needed ways will actually appear on the labor market. In the epoch of industrial capitalist development, the process of capitalist concentration/centralization and proletarianization through economic crisis produced its own preconditions. The requisite quantity of labor-power materialized as the result of the crisis-induced decline of the old "moral economy," extensive recruitment of labor from the countryside, and population growth within landless and land-poor populations. The requisite technical quality of labor-power appeared because few, if any, qualifications were needed in early industrial employment, excepting traditional skills and crafts which capital adapted to its own uses. The requisite social qualities of labor-power were supplied, first, by the transfer of normative structures from the patriarchal household and village economy to the factory and mill, and, second, by poverty laws, the workhouse, prison, and other coercive state institutions. Doubtless for these reasons, classical Marxism neglected the relationship between capitalist production and the reproduction of labor-power (excepting the role of state repression).

Modern orthodox Marxism analyzes the problem of state policy and the conditions of reproduction of the working class in functionalist terms. It is typically not proven but assumed that since "at the heart of the capitalist

[6] Aboo T. Aumeeruddy, Bruno Lautier, and Roman G. Tortajada, "Labour-Power and the State," *Capital and Class*, 6, Autumn 1978, 50. Emile Altvater is favorably quoted thus: "The fundamental role of the bourgeois state is above all to 'guarantee the existence of the class of wage labourers as the object of exploitation ... Capital itself ... is not able to produce these foundations.'" Karl Polanyi first pointed out that wage labor required noncommodified social support systems.

[7] "In fact, wage-labour implies that the wage-worker must be a social subject who is partially autonomous ... But the capitalist cannot control the reproduction of the bearer of labour-power and of the conditions of the wage-exchange from within the field of value" (ibid., 47).

system is the buying and selling of labour power . . . inevitably . . . a central part of the activities of the state in capitalist society is directed towards ensuring the smooth and regular repetition of the exchange."[8] The need for state management of the working class is deduced from the premise that the reserve army of labor must be maintained to insure its availability for tours of industrial duty during economic booms as well as to keep up consumer demand.[9] In sum, Marxist orthodoxy argues that the state's main "function" lies in guaranteeing the availability of labor-power, work discipline, employment insecurity, reproduction of divisions within the work force, and so on.[10]

Neo-Marxists also stress the importance of state intervention in relation to the conditions of reproduction of the working class, including collective consumption, which in their hands leads to new and useful conceptualizations of class struggle.[11] It is agreed that the "factors of production" including labor-power are "developed, shaped, distributed, and allocated by specific state policies,"[12] which, however, are developed within the framework of liberal democratic or democratic corporatist state forms. Hence (as will be argued) to the degree that these policies are oriented to economic and social reproduction, democratic state forms may be appropriated by the working class and given democratic or semi-democratic contents. Parliamentary and state economic and social policies, therefore, may be regarded as at once "political" use values and exchange values (i.e., the basis of potential emancipation) and indirect valorization and social domination. State policies and services may be decoded to reveal elements of working-class resistance and/or social reconstruction as well as powerful elements of capitalist domination. In other words, precisely because the political system, parliament, and state are the main arenas of class struggle, and because working-class/salariat reproduction lies outside of the circuits

[8] David Purdy, "The State and Labour: A Brief Analysis," MS, University of Manchester, Sept. 1970.

[9] Suzanne de Brunhoff, *The State, Capital, and Economic Policy* (London, 1978), ch. 1. The author admits, however, that state reproduction of labor-power may loosen up the labor market.

[10] Aumeeruddy et al., "Labour-Power and the State," 44. De Brunhoff writes that "the need to maintain the continuous presence of the three elements – work discipline, insecurity of employment, and a permanent supply of proletarian laborpower costing as little as possible – *implies state intervention* which is *immanent* in the process of capitalist accumulation at the same time as it is fundamentally external to it. The exteriority of the state's management of laborpower is the actual precondition of its immanent quality" (*State, Capital, Economic Policy*, 11).

[11] A pioneer work in the area of collective consumption is Manuel Castells, *The Urban Question: A Marxist Approach* (Cambridge, Mass., 1977).

[12] Claus Offe, "The State, Ungovernability and the Search for the 'Non-Political,' " paper delivered to the Conference on The Individual and the State, Toronto, Feb. 3, 1979.

of capital, it is problematic whether strictly capitalist principles in fact govern economic regulation, socialization processes, labor market formation, and related processes in the fields of economic and social policy.

Two or three examples will make this clear. It is unarguably the case that concepts such as "social consumption" and "social wage" are inconceivable in the absence of some kind of working-class perspective on economic and social policy. The same thing may be said about the growth of welfarism in general, both the origins and functions of which are explicable to a lesser or greater degree in anti-functionalist terms, e.g., in terms of popular struggle.[13] Moreover, parliamentary and state structures and their "selection mechanisms" may or may not work in ways which make it possible to describe the parliament and state as effectively "capitalistic."[14] This is especially true within neo-Marxist perspectives which grasp parliamentary and state structures as the result of, as well as the terrain of, class struggle, which also inscribes particular programs and policies. Within these and related neo-Marxist theoretical approaches, there is a basic agreement that economic and social policies which "shape" the conditions of capitalist production and accumulation and reproduction of the working class cannot be understood without reference to social conflict and social destabilization, and also that state action may be "functional" or "dysfunctional" for capitalist accumulation and social domination.

The key difference between the approach of orthodox Marxism and neo-Marxism is that the former rejects the concept of "political legitimation" or defines it in functionalist terms. In Louis Althusser's work, for example, legitimation is the process whereby capital rationalizes its interests in ways which represent its domination as the general interest. Marxist structuralist writers concentrate "on state intervention to maintain social cohesion in the sense of maintaining a camouflage around an oppressive situation rather than maintaining the actuality of domination [perhaps because they] are more interested in relations between different fractions of the bourgeoisie than they are in the class struggle."[15] Some writers reject the concept of legitimation because it is said to depend on the "unwarranted rationalist assumption" that "people do not rebel because they believe their subordination justified."[16] It is said that legitimation

[13] Francis Fox Piven and Richard A. Cloward, *Regulating The Poor: The Functions of Public Welfare* (New York, 1971), and *The New Class War*.

[14] Claus Offe, "Structural Problems of the Capitalist State," in Klaus von Beyme, ed., *German Political Studies*, 1, 1975.

[15] Patrick Dunleavy, "Methodological Sectarianism in Urban Sociology," *International Journal of Urban and Regional Research (IJURR)*, 1, 1, 1977, 189.

[16] Göran Therborn, "What Does the Ruling Class Do When It Rules?" *Insurgent Sociologist*, 6, 3, Spring 1976, 171.

theory has no room for such issues as working-class ignorance of alternatives, apathy, and fear of coercion. In this sense, orthodox Marxism is not dissimilar to "left Weberian" theory, which uses an "ideological" concept of legitimation. In reply, neo-Marxism argues that the interpenetration of economy, society, and parliament and state subverts traditional exchange criteria and "normative structures of action" hence creates the need for new forms of consent and/or legitimation. In other words, the growth of political capitalism means that production and exchange processes lose their nature-like quality. The subsequent threat of over-politicization of the economy requires new forms of legitimation and social control.[17] Moreover, the need for consent and/or legitimation is reinforced when social democratic (and labor) parties transform themselves from political instruments of the working class into national ruling parties. Legitimation defined in narrow terms of mass consensus and also in broad terms of a historical "motive force" (rather than merely as the unintended byproduct of economic and social policy) thus becomes increasingly essential. Put another way, "accumulation policies" may not be "legitimate" in the context of working-class political majorities whose economic and social needs may not be consistent with the needs of the capitalist system as such. Certainly, it is difficult or impossible for any formally democratic government to retain working-class support, hence stable power, without attempting to prevent economic crises and/or moderating their effects. It is especially difficult when parliamentary and state policies themselves are "implicated" in crises, i.e., when capital politicizes not only the economy generally but also crises in particular, hence subverts the ideological separation of "economics" and "politics" in good times *and* bad, which in turn creates possiblities for workers to "make economic demands a political issue."[18] The growth of parliamentary and state regulation of the economy and society alike in this way legitimates economic and social movements seeking reform. "Government regulation makes it possible to exercise some leverage over private interests."[19] "Social costs" of capitalist accumulation as well as capitalist crises therefore may have to be dealt with not merely symbolically but also with material resources. Govern-

---

[17] Claus Offe, "The Abolition of Market Control and the Problem of Legitimacy," parts I and II, *Kapitalistate*, 1/1973, 2/1973. Offe has distinguished a sociological concept of legitimation (trust in the political system) from a philosophical one (ability to justify institutional arrangements and political outcomes via arguments validating the normative foundations of the system).

[18] Piven and Cloward, *New Class War*, 109, 114. This ideology was also overcome by workers themselves, whose struggles revealed time and again the limits of classical liberal doctrine.

[19] S. M. Miller, "Economic Crisis and Oppositional Movements in the USA," *International Journal of Urban and Regional Research*, 1, 1, 1977, 129.

ments may have to not only appear to, but also in fact devise economic and social policies which fulfill working-class/salariat needs whether or not these policies fulfill capitalist systemic economic and social needs. "It may reasonably be supposed that a basic, abiding, and eminently responsible concern of most politicians is that the legitimacy of government should be preserved, and hence they will have a fully rational aversion to policies that risk leading government into situations in which its authority would face a head-on powerful challenge."[20]

The issue of political legitimation may be posed in terms of bourgeois political theory itself. "Elite theory" ("power determines participation") rules out possibilities of popular power. Within its problematic, human labor-power assumes the status of social object, albeit an individual object. By contrast, "pluralist theory" elevates human beings into social subjects, albeit individual rather than collective subjects; its slogan, "participation determines power," exemplifies the working/class salariat as an active social agent in the political process.

In fact, pluralism or interest-group liberalism may be regarded as the main political vehicle of working-class/salariat economic struggle in post-war USA, i.e., as the form which social democracy (which was neither a mere ideology of "class harmony" nor "politics of the labor aristocracy") assumed. It may be construed as the field in which the working class moved on its own behalf, albeit in fragmented and individualistic ways.[21]

Interest-group liberalism was a "reliable" vehicle of class intervention into parliamentary and state processes because it did not appear to be such a vehicle at all. Class interests instead appeared in the form of interest-group demands. While coalitions of interest groups often varied from issue to issue, a common thread ran through the demands of the majority of groups – labor unions, consumer groups, welfare rights interests, organizations of the disabled, education associations, etc. – which helped to form these coalitions. All of them attempted to obtain the best terms of sale for the labor-power or labor services of their individual constituents, i.e., the concrete element in most interest-group organizations was precisely that the majority of constituents had only their labor-power or labor services to exchange. This was as true of corporatist-type associations whose members "existed for the sake of the organization" as it was for traditional voluntary

---

[20] John H. Goldthorpe, "The Current Inflation: Towards a Sociological Account," in Fred Hirsch and John H. Goldthorpe, eds, *The Political Economy of Inflation* (London, 1978), 210.

[21] "The principal combatants in virtually all post-War political battles have been one or more working class fractions arrayed against the business interests" (Richard Edwards, *Contested Terrain: The Transformation of the Workplace in the Twentieth Century*, New York, 1979, 205).

associations which "existed for the sake of their members." Individual workers/salariat employed both kinds of intermediate associations for individual ends; corporatist/pluralist forms thus concealed individualist as well as class contents. Intermediary associations were the way that individuals-as-class members as well as classes-as-individuals expressed themselves.[22]

Interest-group liberalism was a good vehicle for economic class struggle also because in the hall of mirrors of pluralistic politics particular capitalist and worker economic interests were often similar. Particular capitals often supported particular groups of workers and vice versa.[23] In other words, national, state, and local elected bodies did not represent working-class interests as such, but rather particular capitalist/worker interests defined in terms of specific firms, industries, and/or markets. Representative bodies in this way became "reelection machines" dominated by pork barrel, special interest, and individual casework which processed "legitimate" worker needs and demands by specific capitalist interests in fractionalized forms, especially demands by merchant capital, wage good industries, savings and loans associations, and other sectors dependent on working-class/salariat spending and consumer credit.

The long-run effect of these mechanisms was that particular forms of state underwriting of social reproduction (e.g., old-age benefits) which were originally confined to relatively small groups of workers tended to become generalized. This "nationalization" of conditions of reproduction of the working class/salariat created new terrains for economic struggle by partly transforming family relations in the home into state worker-client relations of various kinds, as well as relations within state worker and client populations. The effect was the partial socialization and particularization of gender and other family relations, which became less mediated by patriarchal familist norms and more by political democratic and state bureaucratic rational/legal principles.

At this point we can theorize the issue of political legitimation and social reproduction in explicitly Marxist terms. As we have seen, the living

---

[22] "Class increasingly creates a single social cleavage. Despite the disunity [i.e., individualism] of the working class, the central dialectic in the political arena remains the clash of class interests . . . the old class lines of cleavage continue to exert their force, only now they do so within the context of class fraction politics" (ibid., 208).

[23] For example, when the Nixon government attempted to reduce public housing expenditures, it was fought by a coalition which included not only welfare rights groups, public housing employees and bureaucrats, and construction workers, but also building contractors and mortgage bankers (James O'Connor, "Nixon's Other Watergate," *Kapitalistate*, 2, 1973). Food stamp programs have been supported by welfare populations and agribusiness alike. Both social security recipients and retail businesses which depended on consumer spending supported indexing of social security benefits, etc.

individual in the model of full capitalism is a nonidentical object/subject of production, distribution, exchange, and consumption. The individual may also be regarded as the object/subject of politics, parliamentary, and state processes. On the one hand, capitalist politics, parliament, and state reproduced the passive "voter" form of political life. The individual became a personification of the category "citizen," the object of politics and technocratic administration, the lonely and colonized state client.[24] On the other hand, the political system, elected bodies, and the state also reproduced the active "participant" form of political life and in this way politically subjectivized the individual. This legitimated the political order and the state to the working class/salariat (technocratic politics legitimated the same system to capital and propertied interests generally). Thus both economic and social policies, oriented to economic system and social domination/integration respectively, were inherently two-sided and antagonistic. *Both* capitalist systemic *and* societal needs *and* working-class material *and* social needs infused *both* economic and social policy, which explains in general terms the ambiguous and ineffective character of US state policy since World War Two and, in particular, since the social struggles of the 1960s and 1970s.

Two kinds of ideologies oriented policies which pertained to economic and social reproduction; both were based on a species of "national individualism" which may be called "utilitarian individualism," or "the greatest good for the greatest number." Put negatively, both rejected "natural rights individualism," which has no room for an activist state in the economy or society. These ideologies corresponded to the technological determinist and individualist humanist ideologies of control discussed earlier.

On the one side, technological deterministic ideologies consisted of the "autonomy of process," or the decline of individual political leadership and power, the concomitant rise of impersonal mechanisms of control, and the rule of experts lodged in the state bureaucracy who mastered "technique" (in the Arendtian sense) in relation to the identification of, and solution to, economic and social problems, including problems of politically and administratively organizing clients. Political parties, inter-

---

[24] In Nicos Poulantzas' words, the state "created modes of isolation" while "representing their unity" as a "people/nation" (*State, Power, Socialism*, 70). In other words, the administered society fragmented class relations into client relations and professionalized life forms, which recreated conditions of infant helplessness and omnipotence – the former because of the absence of traditional individuality/indivisibility, the latter because many if not all needs were assumed by professionalized state administrations. See also Marilyn Gittell, *Limits to Citizen Participation: The Decline of Community Organizations* (Beverley Hills, 1980); Adelaide H. Villmoare, "The Political Rhetoric of Law and Order: Ideological Modes of Legitimation," *Social Praxis*, 8, 1/2, 1981.

mediate associations, and the media developed a "technological politics" to organize the "passive consent" of abstract citizen-voters to the formulation of instrumental economic and social policy. The Congress and state administration "technologically" organized the compliance of reified "taxpayers," "clients," and others to these policies. The individual was regarded as a category which could be disaggregated and reaggregated in ways resembling the changing forms of capital and labor-power themselves. In sum, Congressional and state decisions were outcomes of economic and bureaucratic interests which objectified individuals and in this way protected the polity and state from popular power. This dimension of the capital-labor relationship was implicitly recognized by bourgeois elite theory which (as has been noted) studied wealth and power as sources of political participation, rather than vice versa.

On the other side, individualist humanist ideologies embedded in the juridical ideal of citizenship and principle of self-determination consisted of the "autonomy of the subject," or the rule of organized interest groups within the political system, parliament, and state bureaucracy. The political system was in this sense a means of responsibly channeling and resolving real conflicts between real people and economically and culturally diverse groups. Political parties, intermediate groups, and the media developed a "humanistic politics" to organize the "active participation" of living voter-citizens in formulating policy. Similarly, Congress and the state politically organized the compliance of living property owners, taxpayers, clients, etc. with implementing policy. The individual was regarded as a person with definite social needs and rights construed in part as the need for, and right to, political participation. The real individual was the subject of politically organized economic and social reproduction and administrative technique, i.e., a living person whose integration into the functions of capital and state forms was not so much problematic as absent from the agenda. This side of the capital-labor relationship was implicitly recognized by bourgeois pluralist theory which studied political participation as a source of power and wealth.

These two ideologies were organized by the political system and the state bureaucratic-salariat governed by rules of democratic procedure and rational-legal conditions of legitimate authority. The fragmented bureaucracy and its fetishism of the "role" attempted to organize the individual as both subject-object and object-subject of politics and state, or to combine the themes of manipulation and self-determination, symbolic and real politics. The general and ambiguous result was a politics and state structure organized around the contradictory principles of "active consent" and "passive participation."

More specifically, *capitalist* economic policy reproduced individuals as objects of exchange, labor, and consumption. The hegemonic capitalist concept of need was the "systemic needs of capitalist economy," or valorization and accumulation. At the level of individual capitals, the concept of need was "short-term profits," which was not necessarily consistent with capitalist systemic needs. On the other hand, *working-class* economic policy reproduced individuals as historical subjects in the quantitative sense of real people capable of fulfilling material needs independent of the systemic needs of capital as a whole. *Capitalist* social policy reproduced individuals as ideological subjects of exchange, labor, and consumption, or aimed to fit individuals into normative structures, roles, and positions. The guiding capitalist concept of need was the "social needs of capitalist society," i.e., the integration of individuals into the changing functions of the system of valorization. At the level of the individual capital unit, the concept of need was "short-term integration of workers into jobs," which was not necessarily consistent with the social needs of capitalist society as a whole. By contrast, *working-class* social policy reproduced living individuals as historical subjects in the qualitative sense of self-determination and the fulfillment of social needs for workers' work and workers' consumption independent of the societal needs of capital as a whole.

Both the concept and reality of "legitimate" programs and policies were therefore totally class-ridden and antagonistic. Policy in the economic and social fields exemplified bewildering contradictions between systemic capitalist needs, individual capitalist interests, and working-class needs. Both economic and social policy consisted of "conflicted compromises" which were at once the cause and effect of endless "compromised conflicts." The general result was the failure of both accumulation-system rationality and legitimation-social rationality from the standpoint of both capital and the working class, as evidenced by the mounting economic and social crises of the 1970s and early 1980s.

In sum, in a materialist concept of legitimation, the guiding definition from a working-class standpoint was material need and self-determination defined autonomously in relation to capitalist needs. Congress and the state, therefore, fulfilled needs as a result of popular struggles against and within elected bodies and the state – struggles which were encapsulated within the framework of "national individualism" in general and individualist ideologies of control and their material practice in particular. The struggle for security and stability by the working class was legitimated through roles of citizen, voter, taxpayer, etc., but these legitimations did not and could not replace struggles for self-determination and a "workers' state," or those waged with the goal of democratizing either the state apparatus, or the organization of social labor itself.

Economic Policy and Economic Reproduction

Economic policy historically developed within shifting theoretical guidelines which were shaped by changes in social class composition and class conflict. This was especially true of postwar US economic policy, which was doubly contradictory. First, Keynesian theoretical *premises* and *goals* which were structured into economic policy were stamped by class antagonisms.[25] Second, the actual *content* of economic policy was shaped by the political class struggle. These contradictions are important issues in relation to the elements which make up the model of full capitalist economic crisis, especially with regard to the way that individualism ideologies and practices function in the model, the ways in which these elements interact, and the possibilities of recombining or modifying these elements in a model of economic crisis resolution.

The development of "full capitalism" transformed not only economy, society, and the state, but also bourgeois economic thought. Keynes and his followers were, in effect, forced to abandon neo-classical economic theory and invent the modern theory of economic regulation which came to terms with contemporary constellations of class forces in two ways. First, Keynesianism presented itself as economic engineering. Second, it tried to legitimate this role by presenting itself as animated by the desire for "improvement" or economic reform.[26] Most if not all twentieth-century bourgeois economic and social thought reflected this "compromise" between natural rights individualism and utilitarianism, property rights and human rights, liberalism and welfarism, capital and labor – a compromise which became increasingly embedded in economic policy (which, in turn, created new economic contradictions which inspired the revival of monetarism and neo-liberal economics after 1979). Most important in the

[25] There have been two main pre-Keynesian paradigms in bourgeois economic theory which more or less corresponded with the two general stages of Western capitalist development and class struggles which preceded the model of full capitalism. The first was classical political economy, obsessed with the problem of economic growth and its social, economic, and political conditions – e.g., expropriation of the direct producers, dismantling of merchant monopolies, reductions in land rents, etc. – and in effect a part of the bourgeois struggle against the old order. The second was neo-classical economics, which neglected the subject of the conditions of economic growth and focused on the problem of economizing on workers' labor-time ("efficiency"), because by the last third of the nineteenth century capital had more or less freed itself from major social and political barriers to accumulation; i.e., capital's traditional enemies to the right and left (the old order) had been defeated or coopted and the new industrial working class remained socially undeveloped, politically oppressed, and economically weak.

[26] A discussion of this general issue is Reba N. Soffer, *Ethics and Society in England: The Revolution in the Social Sciences, 1870–1914* (Berkeley, 1978).

present context, while Keynesianism reintroduced the problem of the conditions of economic growth into economic theory, this was accomplished in ideological ways which helped to subvert the accumulation process.[27]

This claim may be illustrated with an account of the main premises and goals of Keynesianism and its applications in so far as these pertained to the modern class struggle. Keynesianism and traditional "underconsumption theory" both emphasized the problem of maintaining a growing level of aggregate demand. This is important because underconsumption theories were for a long time used by organized labor to "justify . . . the fight for higher wages."[28] "Underconsumption theories [therefore] have a long history. . . of influence in the working class movement."[29] The same is true of Keynesian theory; social democratic and labor governments have regarded Keynesianism as the "theory of working class economism."[30] More important, Keynesian theory was in part the unintentional *result* of the working-class struggle, not only a doctrine used to legitimate working-class demands.

This claim may be established by an examination of two or three of the main premises of Keynesian theory. One pertained to the movement of money wage rates. In neo-classical theory, it was assumed that big enough wage reductions would bring about full employment. In fact, wage cuts historically were increasingly resisted by the working class. This was reflected in the Keynesian premise that money wages were flexible only in the upward direction. In other words, working-class struggles against wage reductions in periods of economic crisis "forced" Keynes to abandon Say's Law and theorize the relationship between aggregate demand and the level of employment.[31] Theoretically, labor-power became "less

[27] This is not meant to deny that the "legacy of the Keynesian revolution was [that] the terrain of ideological conflict [was] conquered by technical economic theory" (nor that the same may be said of modern sociological theory) (Adam Przeworski and Michael Wallerstein, "Democratic Capitalism at the Crossroads," *Democracy*, 2, 3, July 1982, 53). It is true that "Keynesianism . . . provided the ideological and political foundations for the compromise of capitalist democracy" (ibid.). It is also true that the Durkheimian theory of the conditions of social integration was an important ingredient of this "compromise" (see below).

[28] Michael Bleaney, *Underconsumption Theories* (New York, 1976), 210–11.

[29] Ibid., 9.

[30] The theoretical point is that wage struggles for redistribution would raise the ratio of consumption to income, hence increase aggregate demand, and in this way help to increase economic growth (Bowles and Gintis, "Crisis of Liberal Democratic Capitalism," 68).

[31] There were, of course, many other premises of Keynesianism pertaining to relations between money, interest rates, and investment, which can be traced to changes in objective conditions such as the rise of finance capital. Disucssion of these would take us beyond the scope of this work. Yet it is interesting to note that Keynes theoretically dealt with these changes by using *individualistic* psychological categories, e.g., liquidity *preference, propensity* to save, etc.

variable" and the contradiction between wages as a cost of production, the basis of consumer demand, and income required to meet workers' material needs was intensified.

Another important premise in Keynesian theory concerned the relationship between worker consumption and income. In neo-classical theory, workers' income and consumption were explained in terms of the trade-off between leisure and income interpreted within the framework of marginalism and utility theory. Keynes' view was that consumption demand was determined by the level of disposable income (and, in later Keynesian theory, by the workers' stock of wealth). In the real world, worker income increasingly depended on the growth of unions, labor parties, welfarism, and the wage struggle, as well as increases in productivity. Hence, Keynes in effect assumed that the level of consumption was determined by worker struggles. Another premise pertained to the determinants of profits. Neo-classical theory assumed a so-called normal rate of profit (which concealed the fact that profits depended on the periodic "liquidation of labor"). By contrast, Keynesians assumed that (in the short run) profits depended on the rate of capacity utilization and level of aggregate demand, which in effect was an assumption that profits depended in part on the working-class movement generally and the wage struggle in particular.

The goals of Keynesianism – full employment, stable growth, and a stable level of prices – also largely owed their existence to working-class struggle. This was especially true in the regime of political capitalism in which "job rights" were normatively grounded and the state itself was held responsible for unemployment and (later) inflation. The workers' demand for employment has a long history. "The idea of a 'right to work' became an object of social policy" in England as early as the Industrial Revolution.[32] On one front, the struggle for employment was associated with political battles to reduce hours of work.[33] On a second front, the employment struggle went along with demands for state intervention in the economy, e.g., English trade union support for the postwar Labor Government's nationalization policies (which were seen as ways to maintain employment).[34] In the USA, key moments in the workers' struggle included mass agitation by unemployed workers during the crisis of 1893 and the Great Depression; the Employment Act of 1946; Great Society

[32] Alasdair Clayre, *Work and Play* (New York, 1974), 43.

[33] M. A. Bienefeld, *Working Hours in British Industry: An Economic History* (London, 1972), 226.

[34] Irving Richter, *Political Purposes of Trade Unions* (London, 1973), 221; Lewis Minkin, "The British Labour Party and the Trade Unions," *Industrial and Labor Relations Review* 28, 1, Oct. 1974, 13, 32.

public service job programs; and mounting demands for jobs in the early 1980s which forced the Reagan government to begin to rebuild the economic infrastructure and expand federally subsidized jobs. The editors of *Zerowork* concisely summed up the issue when they wrote that "the working class strategy for full employment provoked the Keynesian solution in the Thirties."[35]

This was true not only of state policies oriented to high employment but also of those directed toward stable economic growth and stable prices, hence stable employment and incomes. In Europe, the struggle for stable and secure income was exemplified by demands for monetary stability to protect real wages;[36] in the USA, by the development of "automatic stabilizers" such as unemployment compensation, social security, and progressive income tax structures which represented "the economic codification of some of the most important gains of labor and the left in the US in the 20th century,"[37] and which also moderated the capitalist cycle with the result that needed capital restructuring was for a long time "postponed."[38] The same demands were mirrored in indexing of wages under many union contracts, cost-of-living raises for many non-union workers, and indexing of social security and other state payments.

The premises and goals of Keynesianism, however, were no more than theoretical and political assumptions which provided the context in which political debate occurred and economic policy forged. Political opportunism, party competition, bureaucratic structures, and other features of modern politics and the capitalist state in various ways compromised working-class demands and capitalist economic needs.[39] The result was

[35] *Zerowork*, 1, 1975.

[36] Giovanni Arrighi, "The Class Struggle in Twentieth Century Europe," Paper prepared for the Ninth World Congress of Sociology, Uppsala, Sweden, Aug. 14–19, 1978.

[37] David Gold, "The Rise and Decline of the Keynesian Coalition," *Kapitalistate* 6, 1977, 136.

[38] See, for example, Bowles and Gintis, "Crisis of Liberal Democratic Capitalism." As David Gold has shown, the utilization of Keynesian policy pushed wages upward and reduced profits and raised prices, thus reducing the USA's capacity to compete internationally; hence, "the need for intervention into some of the conditions of supply became widely accepted" by the late 1960s. Gold concludes that "what started as a means of integrating labor and fostering aggregate demand ended up as one of the factors impeding accumulation and preventing the reorganization of the economy in the interests of capital" ("Limits and Contradictions of Macroeconomic Policy," paper delivered at Western Economics Association Conference, San Fransisco, June 26, 1976, 44). One may add that the "political business cycle" – the tendency for Federal spending to increase before national elections – had similar results.

[39] These contradictions were even embodied in the practical economic concepts employed by state policy-makers, e.g., changes in the official definition of unemployment and full employment targets which made it appear that economic conditions were better than they were.

state policies marked by deep contradictions which increasingly undermined capitalist accumulation.[40]

This claim requires a review of the recurring contradictions which
characterized political debates and which were "built into" economic
policy. In the early history of Keynesianism, during the Great Depression,
compensatory fiscal policy did not fail so much as it was never tried.
Perhaps the major explanation for relatively low levels of Federal spending
and deficits in the 1930s was that these were inextricably bound up with
the issue of economic and social reform in a milieu in which the industrial
working class was fighting for recognition and not yet politically organized.
During World War Two, loan finance was used to raise money for the
military effort; a policy of forced savings was politically more feasible than
tax increases. After 1947, the Cold War and growing world revolutionary
movements "legitimated" large military budgets; politically organized
labor helped to increase various kinds of social spending; large-scale
capital alone or allied with labor and small capital compelled Congress
and the state to underwrite social capital spending; and a *de facto* political
alliance between labor, wage good capitalists, merchants, finance capital
oriented to consumer credit, and professionals and salariat organizations,
among other class fractions, supported expansionary state budgets. Within
a relatively short period the Federal budget in relation to total spending
was large enough to make demand management practical in the form of
spending and tax policies. Theoretically, Keynesian theory shifted its focus
from problems of economic recovery to economic stabilization and
growth; practically, Congress and the state assumed increasing responsibility for economic regulation.

At levels both of formal employment policy and of practical spending
and tax policy, however, there was little if any political economic rationality excepting the contradiction-ridden Keynesian logic. Keynesian crisis
management evaluated the issue of aggregate demand in the system as a
whole without reference to the issue of the costs of social reproduction
generally and reproduction of the working class/salariat in particular.
Specifically, economic policy failed to control the development of wage
goods in relation to capital goods industries; the growth of consumer
credit and home mortgages in relation to business credit; and social
consumption and social expenses in relation to social investment.

The first Employment Act of 1946 "legislated" maximum employment,
but only in so far as high employment was consistent with maximum
production and price stability – a stipulation which promised to render the

---

[40] The state's "legitimation function" was also threatened to the degree that economic
policy had adverse social effects (see pp. 220–2).

Act ambiguous from the standpoint of both capital and labor.[41] The second Federal employment law – proposed in the mid-1970s under the name of Equal Opportunity and Full Employment Act – was also riddled with contradictions. In the present context, it is necessary merely to point to certain ambiguous clauses to illustrate the deep contradiction between "accumulation" and "legitimation." The former is exemplified in the "Subcommittee Print of H.R. 50 with Amendments" (referred to the Committee on Education and Welfare), which stated that the law would "establish and guarantee the rights of all adult Americans able and willing to work to *equal opportunities* for useful paid employment at fair rates of compensation."[42] The legitimation "function" is exemplified by the Committee's "Summary and Section-by-Section Analysis of the Act" (as amended by the Subcommittee Print cited above), which stated that the proposed legislation "guarantees the right for useful and meaningful employment to every adult American able and willing to work." The first statement exemplified not only the needs of minorities and women for "equal opportunity" but also capital's need to have the widest possible pool of labor-power at its disposal. The second statement expressed the working-class need for guaranteed employment, no ifs, ands, or buts.[43] In simplified terms, workers wanted laws to guarantee full employment because "people neded jobs"; capital's employment policy was, in effect, "jobs needed people." The first was the demand to transform labor surpluses into labor shortages; the second, to turn labor shortages into labor surpluses. In sum, working-class policy was to organize unemployment by means of job creation; capitalist policy was to organize unemployment by means of education, welfare, and related policies based on explanations of unemployment in terms of lack of skills and/or motivations, i.e., in ways which invidualized the whole problem.

The real, albeit hidden, employment policy in postwar USA was the chaotic expansion of Federal spending and Federal programs (and State and local spending) together with Federal Reserve policy, which until 1979 more or less consistently monetized increases in wages and other costs, prices, state spending, and aggregate demand generally. This policy

[41] Herbert Stein, statement included in the supplement to the Joint Economic Committee symposium, "Twentieth Anniversary of the Employment Act of 1946," cited by Hubert H. Humphrey, "A Strategy for Full Employment and Balanced Growth," National Conference on Full Employment and Balanced Growth," National Conference on Full Employment, March 19, 1976, 1.

[42] Italics added.

[43] When the present author pointed out this anomaly between the Subcommitee Print and the Summary and Section-by-Section Analysis, the response by Jerry Jasinowski, Senior Research Economist, Joint Economic Committee, was that it was a "misunderstanding" (letter, May 5, 1976).

originated in the late nineteenth and early twentieth centuries with the regime of industry-dominated state planning in which particular industries used state power to regulate themselves and advance their own interests.[44] In David Gold's words, "industry self-regulation was an attempt to solve the parallel crises of accumulation and legitimation by stabilizing production and by creating a new form of state activity, while maintaining the legitimating ideology and the actual fact of private action and initiative."[45] After the war, "the idea of sectoral rationalization was replaced by a notion of aggregate equilibrium";[46] however, the Keynesian "aggregative" strategy "was never able to displace the institutions and relationships left over from the previous attempts at stabilization."[47] The older "franchise state" policies in this way came to orient and underwrite the new Keynesian policy.

In this context, as noted above, three general sources of Federal spending may be identified. The first was military policy in the successive foreign policy environments of containment (1946–60); containment and "flexible response" (1960–72); detente and "flexible response" (1972–80); and nuclear defense and prevail (the Reagan policy). The second was social investment consumption policy in a milieu of increasing urban and regional competition for new capital and jobs. The third was social expense policy in the context of the political power and influence of various working-class fractions, wage goods industries, professional groups, etc.[48] The thread running through all three was the absence of any coherent plan for capital as a whole beyond Keynesian demand management. Instead, within the dominant ideology of American "national individualism," "Congress abrogated its responsibility to limit overall spending, preferring instead to smother interest groups with money. . . . Interest groups found it easy to treat subcommittees as forums for special pleading and favors. The arrangement encouraged the rise of 'iron triangles' between subcommittees, bureaucrats, and affected outsiders. . . . Congressional accommodation to all the liberal interest groups resulted in a relentless growth in spending [and] inflationary deficits. . . ."[49]

This political system was a kind of anarchic "micro-corporatism." Particular firms, industries, cities, and regions were nearly always politically supported by organized labor and/or workers and salariat employed

---

[44] Alan Wolfe, *The Limits of Legitimacy: Political Contradictions of Advanced Capitalism* (New York, 1977).

[45] Gold, "Limits and Contradictions," 5–6.

[46] Ibid., 7.

[47] Ibid., 13.

[48] James O'Connor, *The Fiscal Crisis of the State* (New York, 1973), passim.

[49] Andrew J. Polsky, "Political Parties and the New Corporatism," *Democracy*, 2, 3, July 1982, 47.

in the particular industries or areas involved. Military suppliers and arms workers alike clamored for more instruments of death and destruction, building contractors and construction workers lobbied for more public works, and so on. Moreover, this whole process was reinforced by the increasingly fragmented bureaucratic interests and state employee organizations.

From the standpoint of capital as a whole, the result was not only a rise in state spending, deficits, and inflation, but increased "frustration of coordinated policies."[50] State protection of individual capitals and industries (combined with the fact that short-term crises were not allowed to work themselves out in "normal" ways) had the unintended effect of reinforcing consumer and military capitalism. The failure to control and integrate the expansion of military production, investment and consumer goods industries, professional services, and the relevant state bureaucracies led to an increase in employment, wages, and credit beyond levels consistent with the needs of capital as a whole, and the relative neglect of capital goods production and technological change. The political system of interest-group liberalism or "special interests" created a *de facto* industrial policy oriented to preserving the traditional industrial base, i.e., to more individual speculation, on the one side, and more inflexibilities in the utilization and allocation of productive capital, on the other.[51] (By contrast, in countries such as France and Japan, which lack powerful traditions of individualism, state spending was the vehicle for more coherent planning of the relationship between capital and wage good production, profits and wages, etc.) The cultural hegemony of "national individualism" in the form of militarism and the protection of individual capitals at the expense of the requirements of capital as a whole was an important source of federal spending, employment, and industrial policy and their economic effects.

From the workers' point of view, class struggle organized in fragmented and pluralistic forms was ultimately politically self-defeating. It was impossible to articulate a general working-class interest so long as worker struggles remained enveloped within the dominant ideologies of individualism – as Reagan's victory in 1980 made abundantly clear. It was in

[50] Ibid., 47.

[51] Lester Thurow has pointed to tariffs, quotas, marketing agreements, tax breaks, bailouts, and other sources of inflexibility. Robert Reich summed up the issue thus: "Put simply, American political and economic institutions [based on the national ideology of individualism] have been relatively incapable of adapting to a new world economy" (Robert B. Reich, "Industrial Evolution," *Democracy*, 3, 3, Summer 1983, 11). Thurow and Reich are in the forefront of the movement to develop a "democratic corporatism" which would permit American capitalism to compete effectively in the new world economy (see Chapter 8).

part this self-inflicted failure by labor as well as capital which created new economic, social, and political terrains in the late 1970s and 1980s.

Until the 1960s, Keynesian policymakers were confident that demand expansion, economic growth, and political legitimation and/or consensus were linked in a tight bond. On the one side, "the program of government intervention for full employment [was] embraced by the dominant stratum of labor as well as by the new middle class, by most farmers, intellectuals, and the like."[52] On the other side, demand expansion meant that "the cost of fulfilling people's aspirations can be met out of a growing horn of plenty – instead of robbing Peter to pay Paul – hence ideological roadblocks fade away, and consensus replaces conflict."[53] Political consensus was seen as both the condition and result of the expansion of federal spending and aggregate demand;[54] economic growth as the way to "solve" the problem of economic inequality without threatening capitalist interests and/or democratic institutions.[55]

The basic contradiction of this model of economic expansion and political consensus was that it neglected conditions of economic supply (excepting local economic infrastructure at the micro-economic level). "The Keynesian emphasis on demand management and demand stimulation . . . meant a relative deemphasis on the need to discipline labor."[56] Keynesian theory in this way failed to come to terms in a realistic way with the working class as a potential limit to accumulation; specifically, traditional demand-led expansion failed to distinguish between consumption and investment and wages and profits. By 1960, neo-Keynesian economics thus began to replace "depression Keynesianism." The Kennedy government tilted economic policy towards an expansion of profits and investment spending, meanwhile cutting taxes to stimulate aggregate demand and in particular the demand for and supply of capital goods.[57]

The basic tenets of Keynesianism, however, were retained through the 1960s and most of the 1970s. The 1975 individual income tax cut may be

[52] Paul Baran, *The Political Economy of Growth* (New York, 1957), 100.

[53] Walter Heller, *New Dimensions of Political Economy* (Cambridge, Mass., 1967), 12.

[54] Gold, "Rise and Decline of Keynesian Coalition."

[55] Fred Hirsch, *Social Limits to Growth* (Cambridge, Mass., 1977). Alan Wolfe's book, *America's Impasse: The Rise and Fall of the Politics of Growth* (New York, 1981), documents both US growth policy and also the ways in which growth not only permitted US policymakers to postpone difficult political choices but also tended to create more inequalities.

[56] Gold, "Rise and Decline of Keynesian Coalition," 18.

[57] The Revenue Acts of 1962 and 1964 in effect reduced corporate income tax rates from 52 to 34 or 29 per cent (depending on the ratio of equity to total capital) ("Review of the Month," *Monthly Review*, Feb. 1965). The investment tax credit has a lineage which goes back to a 1954 bill which permitted accelerated depreciation allowances (after many years of "straight-line" depreciation).

used as an example of the conflict between accumulation and legitimation principles as well as of the way that accumulation policies based on Keynesian demand theory were legitimated.[58] Two opposing positions emerged in the political debate over the tax reduction. Secretary of the Treasury William Simon argued that anti-recession policy required that the market for consumer durable goods be sharply stimulated. He observed that about three-quarters of consumer good purchases were made by roughly one-half of American households in the middle and upper-middle income brackets. He thus favored relatively large tax cuts in incomes in the middle and upper range. His view in effect was that "the system needed people to spend more money." (Underlying this view was what many politicians regarded as the "big social issue . . . the preservation of the middle class [which] has defended the system and gotten no thanks").[59] The Democrat-controlled House Ways and Means Committee and Congress opposed Simon on the grounds that tax cuts should favor low-income families. Their view was in effect that taxes should be cut "because people needed more money to spend." Simon's view was grounded in his perception of the systemic needs of capital as a whole. The Democrats' view was oriented to working-class material needs. The result of the House-Senate compromise bill was "to throw more of the reduction to the middle class."[60] Subsequently, there was an outcry in the Congress that low-income workers had been sold out; meanwhile President Ford announced that "the Congress passed tax reductions that are unfairly concentrated in the very lowest income bracket," adding that "low-income people should indeed be helped, but not to the exclusion of the rest of the population."[61] In ordinary discourse, "fair" pertains to equity and ability to pay. In effect, therefore, Ford turned the language upside-down and used the word to mean "unfair to the system."

While no empirical method exists whereby it is possible to disentangle the effects of these (and other) tax changes on aggregate demand, living standards, "middle-class loyalty," and so on, the signs are that this and other compromises in the tax field resulted in economic and political "deficits" all around. A similar conclusion may be drawn with regard to Jimmy Carter's early budgetary policies. By 1977–78, the contradiction

[58] In the USA, more than any other country, tax policy was based on individual income (as opposed to "class taxes" on value added, retail sales, and the like). This reflected the ideological domination of "national individualism."

[59] George Wallace, quoted in *Newsweek*, April 21, 1975, 44.

[60] "How the Tax Pie was Sliced," *Business Week*, April 7, 1975, 30.

[61] *Wall Street Journal*, April 8, 1975. Ford meant that the tax cut "places an increasing burden on the middle-class taxpayers" because it "took some six million Americans off the tax rolls."

between capital and labor (hence between accumulation and legitimation) was deepening, which was reflected in the increasing vacuity of economic policy. Organized labor defined the economic issue as "unemployment." Capital defined the problem in terms of "growing inflation" and "insufficient investment." Proposals for the 1977 budget were divided along these lines. In the middle, Carter abstracted all content from proposals advanced by both capital and labor and defined the problem as "the general economy." Labor's theory of unemployment was the traditional theory of "insufficient demand." Capital's theory of insufficient investment and excessive inflation was that government spending and Federal deficits were too high. Labor sought government job programs; capital wanted more encouragement to new investment including tax cuts on capital income; Carter believed in a "balanced" stimulus. The Republicans demanded a halt to new government spending; labor Democrats demanded an additional $30 billion in Federal spending; Carter proposed a dead-center compromise of $15.5 billion.[62] In the following year, Carter (who embodied the contradiction between capital and labor in the most politically compromised way in modern American history) argued that taxes should be cut on low-income families with the aim of stimulating aggregate demand. Such was the tortured logic of political leaders who persisted in trying to "regulate the relations between contending classes" in a climate of deepening crisis.

In sum, the class struggle and "political factors" compelled most national governments most of the time to persist in spending and tax policies which were governed in part by "legitimation" requirements, and which, therefore, enlarged working-class and salariat income, credit, and spending.[63] Only in the last two years of the Carter government did economic planners abandon the traditional Keynesian policy of expanding consumption, and also begin to change the neo-Keynesian policy of expanding investment more rapidly than consumption. Instead, first Carter, then Reagan, tried to adopt a neo-liberal policy of attempting to expand profits and investment *at the expense of* wages, salaries, welfare, and consumption; business credit at the expense of consumer credit; loans for new plant and equipment at the expense of money for home mortgages and consumer durables; and so on – an attempt which was, in part, defeated in the 1980s by structural mechanisms of consumer capitalism beyond government control.

[62] House Budget Committee, "The Economy and Economic Stimulus Proposals," Washington, DC, Jan. 1977.

[63] For variations on this and related themes in this section, see Bob Rowthorn, "Review of *Late Capitalism*," *New Left Review*, 98, July–Aug. 1976; Thomas Weiskopf, "Marxian Crisis Theory and the Rate of Profit in the Post-War U.S. Economy," *Cambridge Journal of Economics*, 3, 4, Dec. 1979; Bowles and Gintis, "Crisis of Liberal Democratic Capitalism."

Social Policy and Social Reproduction

Social policy (like economic policy) historically developed within shifting theoretical guidelines which were shaped by changes in class composition and class conflict. This was particularly true of postwar US social policy, which was thus doubly contradictory. First, Durkheimian theoretical premises and goals which were structured into social policy were inscribed by class antagonisms.[64] Second, the content of social policy was shaped by the political class struggle. These contradictions are central issues (as in the case of economic policy) in relation to the elements making up the model of full capitalist social crisis, especially with regard to the way that individualist ideologies and practices function in the model, the way these elements interact, and the possibilities of recombining these elements in a model of social crisis resolution.

The development of "full capitalism" transformed not only bourgeois economic thought but also sociological theory. Durkheim and his followers were forced by circumstances to develop the modern theory of social regulation which culminated in Parsonian structural-functionalism.[65] Like economic thought, modern sociology attempted to come to terms with contemporary class relations by presenting itself as social engineering and also as inspired by the idea of social reform. Also like economic thought, sociology reflected the "compromise" between property rights and human rights, capital and labor, etc. – a compromise which became embedded in social policy (which, in turn, created new social contradictions which inspired more theoretical and applied social science).[66] In addition, social

[64] There have been two main pre-Durkheimian/Parsonian paradigms in bourgeois sociological theory which more or less corresponded with the two general stages of Western capitalist development and class struggles which preceded the model of full capitalism. The first was Enlightenment sociology, best exemplified by Comte; the second, liberal sociology, best illustrated by the works of Spencer. Just as Adam Smith's work was a blow against traces of the old order, Comte's work was part of the struggle against religious mystification and dogma. Just as neo-classical economics was obsessed with economizing on workers' labor-time, Spencer was obsessed with social efficiency.

[65] It was Durkheimian, not Weberian, theory which became the main basis for the theory of social regulation because the former had the good sense to identify deep dysfunctional as well as functional elements in modern capitalism. The reason was doubtless the tradition of French anarchism and socialism and class struggle generally. Weber's "iron cage" fit better with German economic, social, and political history. Durkheim's "self-destruct machine" (my term) fits better with French experience – with the single and crucial exception of the conservative role of the French rural and small-town classes after the French Revolution.

[66] For example, Merton's "middle range" theory, unlike Parsons' version of Durkheimian theory, focused on institutions, hence offered powers of social prognosis absent in Parson's original model.

policy was also underwritten by pluralistic forms of working-class struggle as well as by capital's desire for social regulation. In other words, policy in the social field was similar to that in the economic field in that it may be regarded as the unintentional result of the struggle between and with capital and labor fractions. Most important, while Durkheimianism re-introduced the problem of the conditions of social integration and solidarity into sociological theory, this was accomplished in ideological ways which, in the last analysis, subverted the process of capitalist social domination/integration.

These claims may be illustrated by a brief account of the main premise and goal of sociological theory and its policy applications in so far as these pertain to social reproduction and class conflict in the USA. The most important premise of Durkheimian theory was that the collective mind of society was the main source of morality, i.e., that the cohesive bonds of social solidarity were common values or what would be later called "normative structures of action." In precapitalist societies, common values ("mechanical solidarity") were the result of a primitive division of social labor which afforded little opportunity for individual separateness and differentiation; "individuality" meant, in effect, "indivisibility" alone. By contrast, Durkheim regarded capitalist society as characterized by an extensive division of social labor and functional specialization and differentiation of individuals. Durkheim and his followers argued that the only lasting source of social solidarity in "modern" society was the integration of individuals into specialized, functional tasks in accordance with their interests and capabilites. Both overt coercion, and the assignment of tasks according to ascriptive characteristics of individuals, were forms of a "forced" division of labor which were bound to result in social disintegration and/or disorder. Later sociologists argued that an "unforced" division of labor was especially important when traditional collective "meanings" in "social subsystems" (e.g., the family) vanished with the rise of the bureaucratic administration of society, which was itself incapable of producing meaning.

The main goal of sociological theory was loosely based on Durkheim's basic premise. Social barriers which prevented individuals from distributing themselves between functional tasks in accordance with their interests and abilities threatened social solidarity, hence should be lowered or removed. The condition of social integration was that every individual have an "equal opportunity" to compete with every other individual to fulfill particular, functional tasks. (Some sociologists even considered "equal opportunity" to be important in relation not only to social solidarity but also to economic rationality, which presupposed social solidarity as a cultural productive force, e.g., Mayoism.)

However, in the context of the capitalist monopoly of ownership of the means of production (i.e., the class division of labor), the concept of "equal opportunity" was ideological to the core. First, Durkheim's theory of the conditions of social integration in fact presupposed a socialist society in which there existed some kind of democratic division of social labor.[67] The premise and goal of sociological theory in this sense may be regarded therefore as a "working-class premise" which owed its existence to the workers' struggle. A second and closely related point is that sociological theory failed to distinguish between the division of labor and specialization of work, on the one hand, and the division of laborers and specialization of workers, on the other. In capitalist production, in so far as capital can be regarded as social domination (although not system domination), the former presupposes the latter; in socialism, the former presupposes the abolition of the latter. The significance of this is that "functional specialization" meant that individuals were required to tailor themselves to fit specialized capitalist functions, or ideologically defined roles and positions. In the model of full capitalism, real functions were not tailored to fit individual interests and capabilities; rather, it was attempted to tailor real individuals to fit particular ideological functions (in this sense, Durkheim's theory may be regarded as a theory of "ideological organic solidarity").

The basic Durkheimian premise and goal were modified in various ways by later sociologists (including Durkheim himself). However, they remained at the heart of sociological theory in so far as theory was seen as relevant for practical social policy. The absence of "equal opportunity" between capital and labor was dealt with by replacing class analysis with theories of status and occupational stratification. This ideological feat, however, could not exorcize the class-ridden character of the concept of "equal opportunity," which was thus split into two separate and opposing theoretical concepts. The most general capitalist version of Durkheim's thesis (which Durkheim himself rejected) was that individuals should have equal opportunities to compete with other individuals for all scarce values. In the purely capitalist version, individuals should have equal chances to compete not only for employment but also education, housing, and other values. This version was based on the ideology of individual advancement and success, i.e., that job, income, social position, etc. depend on individual effort, persistence, and talent. A softened capitalist version required the additional premise that individuals should have the right to equal opportunity for education, professional training, and the like as a pre-

---

[67] James O'Connor, "Emile Durkheim's *Division of Labor*," *Insurgent Sociologist*, 9, 3, Winter 1979.

condition for meaningful rights to equal opportunities to compete for employment (e.g., policies favoring school desegregation, affirmative action, etc.). This exemplified natural rights individualism marginally reformed by utilitarian doctrine. At the other extreme, the purely working-class version was that individuals should have the right to equal opportunity not only in education, etc., but also in income and employment itself (i.e., not the right to compete equally for the means of survival but equal rights to employment and material and social well-being). This version (like its counterpart in the field of economic policy) was the theoretical result of practical working-class struggles for equality.[68]

The premise and goal of sociological theory were theoretical assumptions which provided the ideological frame of reference within which political struggles determined the actual content of social policy. The proximate determinants of US social policy included the ebb and flow of social struggles and the changing configurations of political power, as well as other conjunctural factors.[69] The determinants of social policy also included the ways in which the political system, elected bodies, and structural features of the state filtered social demands and reform proposals in ways which compromised the implementation of either capitalist or working-class conceptions of equal opportunity (which, in their pure forms, would have resulted in "runaway" anomie or mass role refusal, respectively). The result was three decades of social policy marked by deep contradictions which threatened the capacity of Congress and the state to fulfill the legitimation "function."[70] For example, the education system could not reward competition and enforce affirmative action at the same time; social security could not encourage self-help and also alleviate poverty; in social services, individual need and "freedom" were mutually contradictory. In sum, it proved impossible to effectively blend the oil and water of working-class concepts of social justice and capitalist concepts of equal opportunity, which, in any case, originated in different (albeit

[68] "What is now being demanded is *equality of result* – an *equal outcome for all*" (Daniel Bell, "The Revolution of Rising Entitlements," *Fortune*, April 1975.

[69] "No government can afford to expand welfare services beyond a certain limit without being punished by inflation, unemployment, or both . . . the welfare state is developing step-by-step reluctantly and involuntarily. It is not kept in motion by the 'pull' of a consensus political will, but rather by a 'push' of emergent risks, dangers, or bottlenecks and . . . insecurities or potential conflicts which demand immediate measures that avoid the socially destabilizing problem of the moment" (Claus Offe, "Political Authority and Class Structure: An Analysis of Late Capitalist Societies," *International Journal of Sociology*, 2, 7, Spring 1972, 94).

[70] The state's accumulation "function" was also threatened to the degree that social policy had adverse economic effects (see next section, 222–4).

related) traditions, the latter in classical liberalism softened by utilitarianism, the former in working-class life struggles.

To the degree that the working-class concept of social justice combined with liberal-utilitarian concepts of equal opportunity, hence became an ingredient in the making of social policy, the result was the "modern liberal theory of citizenship."[71] This "theory" views the state (as did traditional liberalism) as the result of individual wills and actions with the new and potentially radical perspective that individual subjectivity and dignity can develop if, and only if, the government and the state safeguard not only political rights but also "social rights" (according to T. H. Marshall, the "project" of citizenship is inherently egalitarian because its realization depends on the universal establishment of social rights). In other words, this perspective recognizes the rights of individuals as social as well as political subjects – a view which could only emerge when the working class began to make itself into a social subject using political means. There is a strong lineage between this line and that of Jürgen Habermas and others to the effect that modern democracy is a process of the democratization of equity claims, or the formation of social welfare and security. There is also a lineage between these ideas and the development of Democratic Party "utilitarian-corporatist" views which have ideologically underwritten the welfare state, or, put negatively, the decline of Republican Party "natural rights" individualism which presupposes self-sufficient individuals, hence which makes little sense in the modern epoch of abstract social labor.[72] More specifically, the Great Depression practically revealed the basic theoretical flaw in "natural rights" individualism – namely, its indifference to the unequal outcomes of economic activity. In subsequent years, New Deal-Democratic Party utilitarianism increasingly transformed Congress and the state into "referees" (the classical utilitarian concept of the state) which regulated the relationship between capital and labor, and also which became themselves arenas of class struggle, albeit in individualist-pluralist forms.

[71] T. H. Marshall's views are in "Citizenship and Social Class," *Sociology At the Crossroads* (London, 1963). A good summary of various theories of social welfare and policy is R. Mishra, *Society and Social Welfare: Theoretical Perspectives on Welfare* (London, 1977). A social democratic classic is Richard Titmuss, *Essays on the Welfare State* (London, 1963). Titmuss distinguishes between a "residual welfare model" in which the state intervenes only when a person's private resources break down; an "industrial achievement-performance model" in which welfare policies are designed to reinforce capitalist discipline; and an "institutional redistributive model" in which the state deliberately and in non-stigmatizing ways redistributes values.

[72] Frederick Jackson Turner, for example, saw through the "natural rights" equation of economic liberalism and democracy once the frontier shifted from the West to the new industrial economy.

As we have noted, the welfare state defined as a utilitarian-corporatist middle ground between capitalist repression of labor and socialism is regarded by most neo-Marxist writers to be shot through with ambiguity and conflict. "Social rights" doctrines ideologically underwrote welfare transfers and income maintenance programs. By contrast, "equal opportunity" to compete for jobs was associated with education, job training, and other programs, whose ostensible purpose was to prepare individuals to engage one another in the competitive struggle more or less equally. Especially those sociologists who theorized the "poor" in terms of individual psychological disabilities (hence who rejected income maintenance programs) stressed the importance of educational and job opportunities for social integration. "Equal opportunity" for employment per se was associated with government job programs and "full employment" policies. "Equality of result" was exemplified by income transfers. The result was a messy potpourri of contradictory ideologies, policies and programs, and their effects.

This line of analysis may be pushed one step further when the concepts of social rights and equal opportunity are examined in light of the dominant ideology of American individualism. In the USA (as in other advanced capitalist countries), there appeared historically "a range of vital needs [which] are institutionally and politically determined and distributed, for example, education, social security, physical safety, health, transportation, housing, and the use of leisure time. . . ."[73] Political and state intervention in social reproduction, however, also redefined needs in ideological terms; social policy was politically constructed within the problematic of US "national individualism." Hence "politically determined" needs were normatively structured as individually defined needs, individually defined and delivered services, and individual transfer payments. Social policy was thus oriented to the problem of integrating individuals not into corporatist groups (Durkheim's solution, which many European countries have attempted to apply), but rather into social functions defined in individualistic and nationalist ways. More specifically, the fact that "individualism" was a "national" ideology meant that individuals regarded themselves as "American citizens" or "Americans." This meant that people construed their needs as social entitlement within the problematic of the destiny of the "world's first democracy." In this sense, they raised themselves to the status of political subjects. This process was closely linked to the orientation of welfare and social services in ways which were inspired by values and struggles in the bottom layers of

[73] Goldthorpe, "The Current Inflation," 210.

society.[74] Hence social services became means of survival and development within "new social movements" and local cultures. In sum, "universally applicable rights" assumed the form of the demand for social rights, i.e., to be treated in ways consistent with the individual's rights as a citizen. At the same time, the fact that the national ideology was "individualism" meant that needs for security, good health, equal life chances, and so on were construed as individual needs. The combination of these ideological cross-currents meant that needs were construed as individual demands for entitlement to individualized services and income.

The individualization of needs was further overdetermined by state mechanisms of social control which *supplied* individual services and incomes. Structural pressures from state contractors engaged in product competition tended to replace traditional services (e.g., private physicians) with capital-intensive commodities and services (e.g., hospital equipment). Also state mechanisms of social control were based on the ideological principle that social problems were, in fact, individual problems. "Individualization is the process of narrowing structural issues into single ones, or fragmenting class relationships into atomized segments of the social order. Bureaucratization offers a method whereby 'individuals' can be removed from their class relations in production . . . and reconstituted as a 'mass of individuals'. Professionalization further insures that these individuals are kept from recognizing their own class position and needs."[75] For example, in the health field, "the first and easiest [path] is to put the blame for bad health on the individual . . . [health] policies focus on individual at-risk behaviors and all have in common the imputation of responsibility on the individual."[76] In the area of alcohol problems, policy originally emphasized "overall prevention." More or less rapidly, however, it was reoriented to "individualized treatment" and the "onus of the problem" changed from the "substance" itself to the "individual's pathology."[77] These and other social policies defined in this way thus tended to infantilize

[74] "There is another reform tradition that lies buried deep in the anonymity of neighborhood and shop. . . . In this world, people do good for themselves . . . a different dynamic is encountered: the establishment of universally applicable rights to have common needs satisfied" (John Grady, Review of William Gaylin et al., *Doing Good: The Limits of Benevolence* (New York, 1978), in *Telos*, 38, Winter 1978–79, 218.

[75] Pat Morgan, "From Battered Wife to Program Client," *Kapitalistate*, 9, 1982, 19, citing John Holloway et al., "The Crisis of the State and the Struggle Against Bourgeois Forms," Paper presented to the CSE State Expenditure and Cuts Groups, London, 1978.

[76] Marc Renaud, "On the Structural Constraints to State Intervention in Health," *International Journal of Health Services*, 5, 4, 1975, 568.

[77] Pat Morgan, "The State as Mediator: Alcohol Problem Management in the Post-War Period," unpublished MS. This change was rooted in the liquor industry's campaign in favor of a "disease concept of alcoholism" (31). It was associated with the rise of professionalism and a system governed by professionals who define their job as "treating" individuals.

the individual.[78] The result was an epidemic of self-blame and scapegoating and widespread personality disintegration (hence the rise of the mental health establishment) and social disintegration (hence the expansion of law and order mechanisms). It appeared that social policy undermined social domination/integration from *both* capital *and* labor's standpoint.

Social "dysfunctions" took place within the context of a physical and social infrastructure which in various ways reproduced fragmented social policies and a privatized existence. These included urban renewal, highway programs, recreation programs, and land use policies which reinforced an individualistic way of life, hence stimulated the commodity form of need satisfaction. They also included State government legislation facilitating suburban "home rule." "Working class suburbanization has contributed to public sector fragmentation of local government, often militantly defending it, and thus to the construction of a complicated network of class stratified public service units surrounding the metropolitan area."[79] Related to this was state underwriting of individual home mortgages (average mortgage amortization increased from less than 10 years in the 1920s to over 20 years by the 1960s). In these and other ways society was fragmented in ways which thoroughly concealed the class basis of political rule. "The integrity of people's lives and the connections between their problems are split up in fractional aspects of their administration."[80]

On the other hand, social policy based on the ideology of national individualism had two counter-effects: first, the construction of social problems as individual problems and social needs as individual needs frustrated social solutions to social problems which, in turn, set the stage for "bottom-up" social solutions. Second, social policy had the effect of making individuals more autonomous, not in relation to control of capitalist means of production, but in relation to access to and control of means of subsistence. Social policy thus had similar effects to the accumulation of housing, consumer durables, and so on (Chapter 6).

Social policy increased the survival and resistance capacities of large numbers of people independent of traditional family bonds and ethnic ties (and also, as we will see, the capital-labor relationship). On the one side, social programs replaced community and ethnic brokers who constituted at one time a single point of access to social services and resources of various kinds. At one level, therefore, personal life became more dis-

---

[78] Gaylin et al., *Doing Good.*

[79] Ann Markusen, "Class and Urban Social Expenditure: A Local Theory of the State," *Kapitalistate*, 4–5, 1976, 60–1.

[80] Norman Ginsberg, *Class, Capital, and Social Policy* (London, 1979), 6. One economic effect, of course, was to multiply indirect social capital costs and social expenses (O'Connor, *Fiscal Crisis of the State*).

oriented and fragmented. On the other side, social security helped the elderly to become more independent of their children; home ownership subsidies and rent underwrites helped to free tenants from landlord control; student loans tended more or less to free young people from dependence on their parents; school lunch programs and services within the high schools had similar effects; welfare made poor people more independent of their families, neighbors, and community volunteers; health services liberated countless individuals from dependence on their relatives and/or volunteers in times of sickness. And so on. In this way, social policy and social programs constituted a significant material basis for the development of "new social movements" and community activities, the immediate adversary of which necessarily became the state bureaucracy itself. This was perhaps the main origin of the politicization of social struggles and the fight to democratize the state bureaucracy, i.e., the struggle for a "workers' state" and a new, democratic administration of the division of social labor.

Economic Policy and Social Reproduction, and Social Policy and Economic Reproduction

The last two sections discussed the ways in which bourgeois economic and social theory contaminated economic and social policy. They also analyzed the self-paralyzing nature of economic and social policy and the ways in which they reproduced the model of economic and social reproduction based on ideologies of individualism. What has not yet been dealt with is the fact that economic policy had qualitative social as well as quantitative economic effects, and that social policy had quantitative economic as well as qualitative social effects. Accordingly, this section discusses the contributions of economic policy to social crisis tendencies and of social policy to economic crisis tendencies (hence ultimately to the need for new social and economic policies).

The first thesis is that economic policy undermined traditional values and norms of social integration such as patriarchy and respect for formal authority. Keynesianism had both direct and indirect effects on social integration. Its direct effect was to subvert traditional values by resocializing youth and others into the culture of consumption. Its indirect effect was to expand noncommodified social services, hence depersonalize and politicize social issues and social struggles. The first effect is self-explanatory. Keynesianism's indirect effect requires a brief elaboration of the political economics of Keynesian policy. This policy spliced additional credit money and effective demand into the money and commodity circuits of capital with the effect of activating wage goods production, consumer product innovation, and wage struggles. Also, demand management in the context of interest-group liberalism and the "franchise state" increased social consumption and social expense spending, which were partly financed by the growth of the Federal debt.[81] Increases in social spending and the public debt combined with interest payments on the debt to people who consumed most or all of their interest income (e.g., the salariat, professional classes, etc.) expanded working-class/salariat claims on the social product, which tilted the economy further in the direction of consumer capitalism. As we have seen, this reinforced the tendency of the rate and mass of surplus value to decline, hence stagflation tendencies, which created political pressures to expand public credit and effective demand still more. The result was a treadmill effect; Keynesianism was a cause *and* effect of the growth of consumer capitalism.

Keynesian's aggravation of stagflation, high interest rates, fiscal crisis, and urban poverty (among other problems) further bifurcated the working class and society generally into "core" and "peripheral" sectors. Keynesian policy thus exacerbated social problems associated with the marginalization of a growing fraction of the working class — problems of illiteracy, bad health, crime, family distress, and so on. Put another way, politically uncontrolled economic growth and capitalist concentration and centralization had adverse social effects which created new forms of "insecurity and structurally induced needs."[82] These needs were defined in noncommodified forms and organized by professionalized social service bureaucracies. In this way, the social residues of economic policy "provoke[d] interpretations of needs which negate[d] the form of social reproduction as a capitalist one."[83] Keynesianism thus not only reproduced the model of consumer capitalism but also paradoxically resulted in the expansion of

[81] Federal deficits in recent years absorbed about 40–45 per cent of total private and business savings (or about 5 per cent of the 12–13 per cent savings rate). If Federal deficits increase at rates prevailing in the early 1980s, it is expected that all private savings will be absorbed by Federal borrowing by the late 1980s or early 1990s.

Federal credit is divided between repayment, social consumption and social expenses, and military spending. Social expenses (subsidies to the poor) absorb less than 10 per cent of the Federal budget. The remainder consists of social consumption (mainly retirement payments) and military spending. Social investment spending at the Federal level is relatively small.

[82] Offe, "The State, Ungovernability . . .", 6. This "structuralist" approach to the expansion of welfare and other social policies is developed in *The Political Economy of the Welfare State*; a different but closely related approach is O'Connor, *Fiscal Crisis of the State*. A more "action theory" oriented approach is Larry Hirschorn, "The Theory of Social Services in Disaccumulationist Capitalism," *International Journal of Health Services*, 9, 2, 1979.

[83] Claus Offe, "Crisis of Crisis Management: Elements of a Political Crisis Theory," *International Journal of Politics*, 1977, 56.

noncommodified social services, which tended to politicize social issues and social struggles.

The second thesis is that social policy undermined traditional values and norms of economic integration such as carrot-and-stick economic incentives and labor mobility. First, welfare spending together with social consumption and private and public credit broke the link between wages and salaries advanced by private capital and the amount of the social product appropriated by the working class and salariat, which weakened the economy's capacity to produce surplus value.[84] Moreover, not only the size of the average "social service consumption basket" but also its "value content" increased, which further impaired the system's productive capacity. This was so because of the individuation of social services; rising popular demand for high-quality services in the health, environmental, and other fields; the interests of individual capitals and industries in supplying high-value commodities to public and quasi-public agencies; and the interests of state workers and planners in expanding public employment and administrative and social infrastructures.

Last, social programs and social welfare impaired workers' economic incentives to compete with one another within the reserve army of labor. This indirectly reduced competition between the reserve army and the productive work force, which, in turn, reduced competition within the latter in external and internal labor markets. Social programs and welfare also impaired workers' economic incentives to adjust themselves to changes in economic system functions, i.e., to dispose of their labor-power as variable capital.[85] The conditions of social welfare were thus not tied to conditions in the labor market as a result of the tendency for social consumption and social expenses (including social services) to become more generalized and also for income and access to resources to be redistributed within the working class and salariat.[86] While individualist worker struggles in the labor, commodity, and consumer credit markets set older against younger workers, whites against blacks, etc. (Chapter 4),

---

[84] "The distributional power afforded labor has proven to be the central impediment to continued accumulation in the present situation," i.e., the expansion of the "citizen wage" led to a redistribution of the social product away from capital (Bowles and Gintis, "Crisis of Liberal Democratic Capitalism," 53; 71–8, especially Tables 3–6). This otherwise illuminating account of the issue misses, however, the issue of the expansion of wage goods relative to capital goods industries and the implications for relative surplus value production.

[85] As Claus Offe and others have shown, citizenship and social rights posed threats to capital's control of production through the creation of values which undermined the achievement principle (e.g., Goldthorpe, "The Current Inflation," 203).

[86] Within expanded education, welfare, and other systems *new* inequalities were constantly produced and reproduced (see, for example, Norton Grubb and Marvin Lazerson, *Broken Promises: How Americans Fail Their Children*, New York, 1982).

there occurred a political redistribution of income and services from the employed to the unemployed, healthy to sick workers, employed to retired workers, and so on. The effect was that both unemployed and employed (and old and young, etc.) had fewer economic incentives to make their labor-power into variable capital. This was so because the former received what the latter regarded as "too much" while the latter received what they themselves perceived as "too little" income. In this way, also, the welfare state reduced competition between the reserve army of labor and the employed work force, hence undermined the former's function as a "level of accumulation."[87] It should be stressed that this was not the result of generous welfare payments or the benevolence of the state administration and capital, nor of the autonomous workers' struggle alone, but rather the unintended effect of the scope and diversity of "life support systems" rooted in interest-group liberal policies. Last but not least, the "welfare expenditure became part of the subsistence wage,"[88] with the effect of increasing average and total wages advanced and the capacity of the working class/salariat to expand consumer borrowing. The expansion of social consumption and expenses raised the floor on private wages; the struggle for real wages in labor and product markets exerted upward pressure on "social wages"; increased private wages intensified pressures on large-scale capital to socialize variable capital outlays (i.e., expand social consumption); and wage demands by state employees independently effected private wage demands and "social wage" claims (see below).

Economic and social policy had deep and lasting effects on social class composition generally and working class/salariat composition in particular, hence indirectly on economic and social integration. Specifically, state policy was accompanied by the growth of a state work force and technical-administrative salariat which was, in effect, the consequence of working-class economic and social demands and capital's plan to regulate the economy and society. In similar ways that the private salariat mediated the relationship between capital and labor within the production process, the state salariat mediated capital and labor at the level of economic and social reproduction as a whole. The increased numbers and organizational capacity of the state work force and salariat exacerbated the economic and

[87] Many writers have pointed to the "failure of the reserve army of labor to restore profitability by minimizing wage increases" (Bowles and Gintis, "Crisis of Liberal Democratic Capitalism," 53). The authors present much data to the effect that the reserve army no longer regulates either the money or real wage (80–1, Table 7).

[88] Mariolina Graziosi, "Notes for a Research Project on Social Welfare and the Labor Market," unpublished MS, undated. One Rand Corporation study indicated that California welfare mothers leave welfare only for significantly better-paying jobs than they had before they went on welfare, i.e., welfare payments mean that individuals can extend their search for a better job.

social crisis tendencies discussed above. First, state employees were paid a premium to insure their loyalty and responsiblity to the social order, hence were expensive to maintain (e.g., relatively high pensions). Second, economic struggles by state employees who sought to close gaps which did exist between wages and salaries in large-scale capital and the state sector (together with client struggles to close gaps between small-scale capital wages and welfare income) undermined capitalist valorization as a whole.[89] Third, the state sector prevented competition between employed and unemployed workers by absorbing and clientizing surplus labor. Also, state employees fighting for their own economic interests helped to raise average wages and further reduced competition between the reserve army and the employed work force. Last, but not least, state employees exchanged their labor services (but not labor-power) for public salaries and wages; worked within public bureaucracies (not private capitalist firms); and were charged with performing "public services" (not maximizing production per unit of labor-time). These special conditions of exchange, labor, and product of labor exacerbated in various ways economic and social crisis tendencies. This was so because economic and social reproduction organized by the state was inflexible and unresponsive to changing needs and demands. Cost inefficiencies inherent in bureaucratic production relationships raised the "value content" of state programs in the economic and social fields. There was little if any effective public control of (and self-control within) state agencies because hegemonic ideologies of natural rights individualism and "Romantic individualism" were antithetical to bureaucratic regulation and formal rationality – the first because "economic man" constantly defeated middle- and long-range state planning, the second because self-centred, hedonistic individuals were incapable of organizing their lives within the narrow boundaries of bureaucratic formal rationality. In these ways, the state sector indirectly reproduced the general tendency for labor-power to become less variable and to be defined more in concrete than abstract terms. It thus became increasingly difficult to rationalize the state administration, retrain and reorient state employees technically and normatively, reorganize the division of labor within state agencies, modify or replace ideologies of control which outlived their usefulness, and inspire capitalist economic incentives and social motivations. The bureaucracy became "too big" and "too bureaucratic." State employees functioned less as "civil servants" and more as "state workers."

To sum up, economic and social policy was the result of the develop-

---

[89] "When equity becomes a reality – which it in fact has – then there is a limit to the self-expansion of capital and there develops an accumulation crisis" (Stanley Aronowitz, "Notes and Commentary: Symposium on Class," *Telos*, 28, Summer 1976, 166).

ment of large-scale capital, the modern working class/salariat, and social democratic forms of the capitalist state – all of which were forged in the cauldron of historical economic and social crises. The appearance of the modern working class/salariat in the USA and "New Deal" forms of social democracy in this sense may be regarded as two sides of the same historical process. To apply the formula used throughout the present work, historical crises created large-scale capital and the working class/salariat, which created social democratic state forms and contents – all of which were at the root of the modern accumulation crisis. On the one hand, the working class/salariat forced the state to protect and enhance the value of its labor-power and labor services, increase stability in labor markets, compensate for losses to the value of labor-power, and so on. In this way, the state followed policies which intensified the tendency for the rate of exploitation and profit to decline. On the other hand, the state also needed to compensate for previous policies which adversely affected exploitation and profits. Precisely because state intervention into the determination of the conditions of economic and social reproduction (including the value of labor-power) increased, the need for further intervention to offset unfavorable effects on the rates of exploitation and profit also increased. State intervention on behalf of workers subverted conditions of capitalist economic and social integration. State intervention on behalf of capital was determined by the need to control the rate of exploitation or to compensate for the damage to capitalist valorization arising from policies which strengthened the working class and/or raised the value of labor-power. The state was constantly trying to undo with one hand what it had done with the other.

This contradictory model of capital, working-class, and state relations profoundly undermined the crucial role of economic crisis in capital restructuring and accumulation. Crisis prevention, management, and compensation policies postponed the day of reckoning. From the mid-1950s through the late 1970s, state policies increasingly frustrated strong and growing pressures to restructure capital and society generally. These pressures were suppressed not only because of monopoly pricing, wage floors, and economic and social rigidities of various kinds, but also because the working class, in effect, refused to permit the normal cycle of economic boom and bust. Political decisions required to engineer effective recessions, lay off masses of state workers, and effectively control wage and salary income, consumer credit, Federal deficits, and so on, were conspicuous by their absence. Hence, while political decisions favoring capital became increasingly necessary, they became less and less possible. The greater the degree and kind of state intervention in economy and society, the longer was capital restructuring in all its forms postponed, and the stronger were the pressures in favor of state accumulation policies pure and simple. The key to capital restructuring thus became the restructuring of the political system and the state itself. From the standpoint of large-scale capital, the concept of "crisis" was therefore increasingly used as an ideological ploy to legitimate changes in the political system and the reorganization of state structures and policies.[90]

Meanwhile, the cycle of breakdowns in economic and social integration and economic and social policymaking increased in duration and magnitude. Economic policy weakened economic incentives directly and social motivations indirectly; social policy weakened social motivations directly and economic incentives indirectly. Economic and social distress and the crisis of Keynesian and Durkheimian theory and policy were mutually reinforcing. Faith waned not only in the model of political capitalism and administered society, but also in the theories of economic and social steering and regulation, as well as the policies which were based on these theories. Economic policy failed to regulate the economy; social policy failed to control social movements. Instead, there emerged an informal economy and new social movements hostile respectively to capitalist valorization and to bureaucratic-administrative politics.

These tendencies were reinforced by the strident ideology of "national individualism" which equated the values and purposes of the individual with those of the imperial nation-state. Threats to the dominance of the USA in world politics were regarded by millions as threats to their "individualism." Social solidarity thus was organized around national solidarity as well as individual opportunities and social rights. The Cold War and foreign economic and cultural expansion were perceived as widening the field of individual opportunity; economic and social policy based on the spread of individual opportunity and social rights consolidated support for American world hegemony. "National security" equated the security of the American empire with the economic and social security of the individual; economic and social policy and foreign and defense policy became inextricably bound up with one another. It was the combination of the failure of the empire in the 1960s and 1970s and that of economic and social policy which threatened both national and individual identities and values and which, finally, cleared the path for both new popular movements and new right politics.

As we have seen, economic and social policy and the rise of the state salariat/work force politicized social and economic struggles and issues. Moreover, political forms of economic and social struggles resulted in a considerable degree of democratization of economic and social policy

[90] Related views have been expressed by Mandel, Poulantzas, and others (see Bob Jessup, "Recent Theories of the Capitalist State," *Cambridge Journal of Economics*, 1, 1977, 365).

formation and legislation. However, there was little or no democratization of the actual work of carrying out economic and social policy.[91] The state agencies responsible for implementing and enforcing policy were too bureaucratized and wedded to administrative determinations, or too immunized against popular pressures and needs. It was, therefore, more or less inevitable that the center of political gravity would shift from the legislative arena to the state bureaucracy, i.e., that pressure from below would built up to democratize the actual work of the state. This new struggle within and against the capitalist "state form" became most active at local levels of government where bureaucracies were accessible, hence where the development of participation, power, and responsibility were more feasible. This struggle within and against political capitalism and administered society was, in effect, a struggle for the popular administration of the division of social labor. In this sense, the accumulation crisis constituted a crisis not only of the wage and commodity forms but also of the state form of politics – a political crisis in which administered society and political capitalism and the hegemonic ideology of individualism themselves were at stake. In other words, it was precisely the struggle for a "workers' state," or the use of collective means for collective (not individualist) ends which was the main vehicle for the development of a new "social individuality."

It is in this context of the struggle for a "workers' state," as well as in that of economic and social crisis trends and the failures of economic and social policy, that we must evaluate possibilities for crisis resolution. Traditional capitalist restructuring, especially in the form of the new international division of labor, which maintains the wage and commodity forms of social existence, is not likely to resolve the crisis at home. On the contrary, it has and may continue to deepen it. Not only does the productive circuit of capital and money, credit, and commodity markets need to be restructured; so does political-social life itself. Either this will occur through austerity which selectively reduces the size and value content of the consumption basket, lowers social consumption and social expense spending, cuts social services and their "value content," and is legitimated by neo-liberalism and neo-conservatism. Or it will occur through restructuring the conditions of economic and social reproduction through planning – statism or democratic or undemocratic forms of corporatism, or popular power and responsiblity. It is to these issues that we now turn.

[91] "American politics . . . is far too bureaucratized on the output side and, while there have been major improvements on the input side, e.g., the Democratic Party is far more of a democratic arena . . . than ever in its history, it turns out that grass roots participation in the era of bureaucratic politics does not produce visible results" (Bogdan Denitch, "Social Movements in the Reagan Era," *Telos*, 53, Fall 1982). Denitch, however, ignores or plays down grass roots participation in the work of the state itself.

Part Three

Conclusion

8

Neo-Individualism and Beyond

Introduction

Natural rights individualism was powerfully revived by Reagan government ideology and policy in the early 1980s. So was the specter of the New Leviathan. The former was reinforced by new immigrants from Asia and Latin America running away from war, poverty, and communism; the backlash to anti-racist and anti-sexist struggles and the economic and social programs of the 1960s and 1970s; and the growth of individual self-help and survivalism. The latter was attested by the purge of democratic practices in EPA, OSHA, and other agencies (those which were not simply dismantled or left to die on the vine), and above all by beefed-up "national security" and the spread of the surveillance state.

However, the dominant reality in American economic life remained corporate collectivism, monopoly capitalism (independent property in the forces of production lay in the past; corporatism or state capitalism perhaps in the future). Industrial and financial restructuring and integration reinforced the power of the giant conglomerates and the self-regulation of large-scale capital. New trends in monopoly capitalist planning in the financial and raw material sectors in particular reproduced in exaggerated forms the unbalanced "partnership" between big business and Federal agencies charged with regulating business.

The contradiction between forms and contents of economic and social life thus was not resolved but deepened in the 1980s.[1] Problems of economic and social integration became more intractable from the standpoint

---

[1] The classic study of these contradictions earlier in the century is James Gilbert, *Designing the Industrial State: The Intellectual Pursuit of Collectivism in America, 1880–1940* (Chicago, 1972).

of capital and labor. The Republican Party remained the party of capital and the ideology of natural rights individualism. However, the Democratic Party became less the vehicles of "special interests" and more swayed by and divided between statist/corporatist and localist/populist forces – both of which began to perceive that individualism was more and more a luxury which the economy, society, and polity could less and less afford. Yet (in the absence of an alternative political economy, cultural values, and social relations) without the hegemonic idea of national individualism, American economic, social and political structures would come tumbling down.

Individualism and its "special interest" variants did not come under attack only by home-grown corporatist and populist ideas. It was also being modified or replaced in the minds of some politicians, planners, and others by statist, corporatist, and collectivist ideologies of economic and social reproduction in continental Europe and Asia, as well as by socialist theories and practices in Africa, Central America, and elsewhere.

The American establishment's search for new legitimating ideologies of labor and life which might replace expensive and chaotic New Deal-Great Society policies began in the 1960s and 1970s. The democratic corporatist countries in Europe were regarded by politicians like John F. Kennedy and many policy-oriented political scientists as the best hope for maintaining an adequate social budget and social justice with minimum problems of inflation and fiscal strain. In policy planning circles, the argument was more often heard that corporatist ideologies and practices were indispensable for economic planning, industrial policy, and economic recovery, and that the vicarious democracy which corporatism afforded was the best hope for social peace.

In the 1970s, concepts of "team work," "quality circles," and "corporate culture" were imported by businessmen and managers from East Asia and developed at home in the business schools and high-tech industries. Meanwhile, workers at the community level and in local counter-institutions recreated in new forms American traditions of communalism and populism, which were also influenced by revolutionary experiences in the Third World. Community organizations and "new social movements" were often sites of democratic forms of collective decision-making and social action. These ideologies, theories, and practices and their significance for economic and social reconstruction will be briefly discussed below. Meanwhle, the next section will review the emergence of neo-liberal and neo-conservative ideas and policies – and the ideological cement which bound them together, neo-individualism and neo-imperialism – in the early 1980s.

Neo-Liberalism and Neo-Conservatism

In the late 1970s, the model of economic and social reproduction based on modern individualism, pluralism, and "special interest" became less viable. Signs of economic and social crisis multiplied. The second "oil shock" and rising costs of wages, salaries, and social welfare, inflation and high interest rates, among other factors, intimated that economic regulatory mechanisms had begun to break down. Confusion and conflict over form and substance among those who governed health, education, law and order, and other systems signified an overload on social control mechanisms. Politically, the system of interest-group liberalism became less tenable. Signs were the inability of Congress to control the Federal budget; the breakdown of the 1930s Democratic Party coalition; ominous warnings amongst some Western leaders and their academic apologists that democracy in America was "excessive"; and, at the other end of the political spectrum, the independent growth of alternative media, rank and file worker groups, and community, feminist, "right to know," and other movements outside the framework of the traditional party system.

Beginning in the early 1970s, the right wing began to launch a co-ordinated offensive against New Deal-Great Society economic policy. Their arguments were based on classical liberal theories of the economy and its proper relation to the state – theories here called neo-liberalism. Their first claim was that political capitalism had damaged capitalist accumulation, hence was itself the source of economic crisis.[2] It was said that the politicization of economic issues depersonalized economic dependency and materially and ideologically supported new economic movements and economic subjects. The neo-liberal consensus which emerged from discussions and debates in the 1970s held that the economic crisis was a crisis of individual incentives, savings, and work discipline attributable to excessive government intervention in the economy.

The Reagan government accepted this analysis more or less without qualification. Its strategy was to redistribute income from labor to capital to start up investment spending, and also from the "lower class" to the "middle class" to retain the latter's loyalty and enhance incentives in both groups. Along with this it had to try to reestablish the family as a cushion

[2] Even Walter Dean Burnham spoke of "political capitalism reaching a conspicuously degenerate condition during the Carter administration . . ." ("The Eclipse of the Democratic Party," *Democracy*, 2, 3, July 1982, 16). See also Adam Przeworski and Michael Wallerstein, "Democratic Capitalism at the Crossroads," in the same issue of *Democracy*.

to absorb the social effects of economic hard times.[3] The Reagan policies sought to depoliticize economic issues and return them to the "private sector" by removing social and political constraints on investment decisions, realigning carrot-and-stick economic incentives, increasing capital and labor mobility, and repersonalizing economic dependency.

Also in the 1970s, the right-wing and conservative intellectuals, echoing the warnings of Herbert Hoover half a century earlier, launched an attack on New Deal-Great Society social policy. Their arguments were based on classical conservative theories of society and its proper relation to the state – theories here called neo-conservatism. They charged that the administered society had damaged capitalist social integration, hence was itself the source of social crisis. It was said that the politicization of social issues depersonalized social dependency and thereby materially and ideologically supported new social movements and social subjects. The neo-conservative consensus developed by writers such as Irving Kristol and Norman Podhoretz held that the social crisis was a crisis of morals: the family, religious and patriotic sentiment, and traditional authority needed refurbishing. The cause was said to be excessive government intervention in society and public "subsidization" of social permissiveness.

The Reagan government also accepted this analysis. Its strategy called for the depoliticization of social issues and their return to the "family" and other traditional institutions. By cutting back welfare, reviving familist, patriotic, and other older social motivations, and repersonalizing social dependency via charity, the state would be withdrawn from social welfare obligations. In turn, this would reduce the social base of Democratic Party political strength, break down institutions that had been built from the 1930s on, and reduce the need to mobilize consent politically.

"Deregulation" became the code word for depoliticizing the economy and society. It was a central issue for two reasons: first, because much government regulation in the 1960s and 1970s was the result of popular economic and social struggles; second, because regulatory bodies such as EPA, OSHA, and many bureaus within the old Department of Housing and Urban Development and Department of Health, Education, and Welfare, among others, promoted the development of economic and social

---

[3] The informal economy was also regarded by some as a crisis cushion for workers as well as a way to lower the costs of reproducing labor-power. As Enzo Mingione has pointed out, however, informal activities entering into capital accumulation do not lower product prices; also, informal services lower the costs of reproduction of marginal, not mainstream, workers ("Informationalization and Restructuring: The Problem of Social Reproduction of the Labour Force," University of Messina, Italy. Paper prepared for the Xth World Congress of Sociology).

movements.[4] Deregulation involved a shift in economic and social power from these regulatory bodies within the Federal government to large-scale capital and the sunbelt accumulation centers, and to the patriarchal family and Church, respectively. The aim was to purge utilitarian-social democratic ideology and personnel from the Federal bureaucracy and to restore the variability of labor-power and the invariability of traditional authority.[5]

The contradictions within and between neo-liberal and neo-conservative ideology and practice were manifold and deep-rooted. Neo-liberalism presupposed economic conditions – autonomous property in the forces of production and/or free competition between independent capitals – which had long since disappeared. Similarly, neo-conservatism presupposed social conditions – a confident capitalist class with few social barriers to its development and power and a moral basis of society anchored in older values of deference, moderation, respect for authority, and unquestioning patriotism – which had also vanished.

In the event, neo-liberal ideology and Reagan government economic practice came into conflict. Reagan's capitalist constituency was big business and the anti-union primary and tertiary sectors of the economy centered in the South and West. Reagan government policy was to defend the private capitalist bureaucracies and "national security" state bureaucracies, while opposing the bureaucratized economy and society in principle. It actively sought to increase the flow of Federal moneys from the Northeast and Midwest to the South and West and redistribute natural resources to the "quasi-renter bloc with great objective interests in the maintenance of boom conditions in the Sunbelt and the preservation of inflated land values and resource inequities."[6]

Contradictions also arose between neo-conservative ideology and Reagan government social practice. Reagan's working-class voting constituency was the socially conservative Anglo and white ethnic proletariat. Reagan government policy aimed to defend conservative social values in ethnic and fundamentalist districts while opposing government interference in society in principle. It actively tried to pound the round peg of

---

[4] S. M. Miller, "Economic Crisis and Oppositional Movements in the USA," *International Journal of Urban and Regional Research (IJURR)*, 1, 1, 1977, 129.

[5] The Federal bureaucracy promulgated 30 to 40 times more regulations every year than the Congress passed laws.

"The objectives of capital may be summarized as the depoliticization of the accumulation process and the commodification of the state " (Herbert Gintis and Samuel Bowles, "The Crisis of Liberal Democratic Capitalism: The Case of the United States," *Politics and Society*, 11, 1, 1982, 92).

[6] Mike Davis, "The New Right's Road to Power," *New Left Review*, 128, July–Aug. 1981, 74.

the "modern" individual into the square hole of nineteenth-century values by promoting Federal intervention in support of traditionalist struggles against women's rights, especially the right to have abortions, affirmative action, gay rights, bussing, and even secular education and voting rights.

Most significantly, neo-liberal ideology and economic policy and neo-conservative ideology and social policy when put together became a potentially unstable mixture. The former was implicitly as anti-family, anti-Church, and anti-tradition as the latter was explicitly pro-family and pro-Church.[7] Unrestrained neo-liberal policy would increase the proletarianization of women and feminization of poverty, the transformation of adolescents into a consumer class, and the institutionalization of the sick and elderly in profit-based hospitals and nursing homes, leading to the isolation of the latter deprived of meaningful social roles. Unrestrained neo-conservative policy would push women back into the home, de-institutionalize the elderly and sick, inculcate youth with old ideas of obedience and deference, and in other ways undermine sources of cheap labor-power and/or new capitalist market opportunities. While economic liberalism (and economic individualism) and traditional morality (and the patriarchal family) at first presupposed one another in the nineteenth century, they proved to be totally inconsistent in the course of capitalist development in the twentieth. Nothing that the Reagan government might do could actually turn the clock back to early capitalist economic and social life. The relationship between neo-liberalism and neo-conservatism is therefore a highly unstable one which is not likely to bring about lasting political legitimation or a solid political consensus.

Neo-Individualism and Neo-Imperialism

The ideological magic cement which was intended to bind the oil and water of the new liberal and conservative thought and practice was neo-individualism and neo-imperialism. Neo-individualism was a revival of ideas of traditional individuality which had deep roots in early American life: self-help based on economic and social autonomy; voluntary association of property owners; and anti-statism. It was illusory, a wish. Nevertheless, Reagan's ideologues and the new right hoped to deploy these traditions as part of a general economic and social crisis management

[7] Michael Walzer ("Nervous Liberals," *New York Review of Books*, Oct. 11, 1979, 5) describes Irving Kristol as standing "with one foot firmly planted in the market, while with the other he salutes the fading values of an organic society. It is an awkward position" (6). See also Alan Wolfe, "Sociology, Liberalism, and the Radical Right," *New Left Review*, July–Aug. 1981.

strategy.[8] The President himself appealed to individuals to assume econ-omic initiative and increase productivity, and cited the responsibility of individuals to traditional family roles. How ideas of traditional individual autonomy and self-help could be reconciled with corporate and state bureaucratic collectivism he left unanswered. How the tradition of volun-tary association could be reconciled with direct-mail Republicanism in which party "members" existed for the sake of the party rather than vice versa was answered by the promise of a big tax cut for all. How both the giant corporation and the autonomous family could be restored to their "rightful place" in American life also remained a matter of faith and patriotism.[9] Neo-individualism would therefore likely fail; to the degree that neo-liberal economic policy worked, neo-conservative social policy would not. And vice versa.

The Reagan government also used the imperatives of "national security" against the "communist threat" – or the ideology of neo-imperialism – as a rhetorical bridge over the gap between neo-liberal and conservative illu-sions and modern reality. Neo-imperialism was a revival of ideas of traditional national power which also had deep roots in American history: continental and overseas expansionism, racism, and the idea that Americans were God's chosen people. It was also illusory, a daydream. Yet Reagan's ideologues also hoped to deploy these traditions as part of an economic and social crisis management strategy. The President himself appealed to the responsibility of individuals to support a strong "national defense" and "country." How the strong pro-statism of American expan-sionist traditions could be reconciled with the equally strong anti-statism and anti-imperialism of the American liberal, individualist tradition was another puzzle (the only solution was the argument that a strong state was needed to stop godless, anti-individualist communism; international rela-tions became a good versus evil issue, thereby turning US citizens into God's unquestioning agents). So were the questions of how the new

---

[8] "Capital itself must today begin to reconstitute that individuality which it so success-fully destroyed during the transition period to accommodate the requirements of monopoly capitalism" (Tim Luke and Paul Piccone, "Debrizzi's Undimensionality," *Telos*, 37, Fall 1978, 152).

[9] Perhaps the solution was the attempt to restore long-dead English traditions of con-tractual family life and family capitalism, e.g., Individual Retirement Accounts for house-wives and "corporate culture," respectively. However, the American family remained in a state of flux and more or less immunized against rationalist, contractual relations and the corporation remained devoted to profits and power and immunized against a resurgence of family capitalism (especially given the number of small business bankruptcies), despite the fact that new right capital consisted in large part of companies controlled by single families which enjoyed a significant degree of financial and managerial independence (Davis, "New Right's Road to Power," 40).

imperialism could be reconciled with growing nationalist aspirations and national struggles in the Third World, and how increased military budgets could be brought into line with lower Federal deficits and more money for capital investment. It was, therefore, likely that neo-imperialism would also fail. The deep contradiction between neo-liberal and neo-conservative ideologies and practices – the former looking ahead to future profits, the latter looking backwards to traditional America – appeared to be in the long run unbridgeable.

By the second half of Reagan's term, neo-liberalism had proven that inflation could be controlled at the expense of higher unemployment, Federal deficits, and permanently high real interest rates (which exported some of the harmful effects of huge deficits to Europe at the cost of choking off American exports).[10] Deregulation helped to increase speculative investment, enhance a boom-or-bust mentality in South and West, and cause a depression in the Northeast and Midwest. Quasi-secret financial planning by the Federal Reserve Bank and Federal financial bureaucracies, as well as natural resource planning by the Department of the Interior, tarnished the neo-liberal image. Poverty became more widespread. The "Reagan recession" of 1980–82 posed so many dangers that the monetarists and supply siders altered course in late 1982.

However, the "Reagan recovery" in 1983 did not significantly lower unemployment, the Federal deficit, or real interest rates. In fact, the "recovery" resembled past experience. Not only was it likely to be moderate and relatively short-lived; also, it was led by the expansion of consumer credit and consumption spending, not investment. Neo-liberalism and monetarism were being dashed on the shoals of the structural realities of consumer capitalism. Only the rising military budget and the growth of high-tech industries and natural resource exploitation promised a more long-lived expansion.

Meanwhile, right-wing groups such as the Moral Majority and anti-ERA forces learned that it was easier to talk about than to legislate a return to the good old days. Particularly when Reagan was forced by events to move closer to the political center, conservative social policies consisted more of rhetoric than substance.

In the foreign policy arena, Reagan moved ahead with neo-imperialist policies. "Nationalism" was increasingly linked by all conservatives to the "fight against communism" and the defense of "individualism." By 1983, the center of gravity had shifted away from a positive policy to bring the American way of life and democracy to the rest of the world to a negative

[10] Normally, high Federal deficits cause inflation, not unemployment; however, tight money policy had the effect of turning inflation into unemployment.

policy of prevention and subversion of socialism and communism. The American White God had slowed down; however, there remained to defeat the Red Devil.

Even in foreign policy, however, the Reagan government faced growing opposition. Even so, it pushed aggressively for its domestic and foreign policy agenda. And because of its ability to intimidate, Reaganism did succeed in setting back many past economic and social gains and social movements and in altering the context of political debate. The effects of Reagan government policy were to reduce selectively money wages, hence the size of the average consumption basket for workers in older industries; encourage the production of more small cars, condos, mobile homes, etc., and in this way lower the quality of the average consumption basket; cut the social budget, eliminate some welfare functions and shift others to State governments where financial constraints were tighter, and reduce Federal taxes, hence lower social consumption and social expenses and their "value content"; reduce taxes on capital and redistribute mortgage money from labor to capital; threaten the labor movement; and undermine environmental, feminist, and other gains. Yet Reaganism did generate opposition (albeit disorganized) in the trade unions, community organizations, and Congress. Also, his government's policies (however devastating for the poor) had failed by mid-1983 to restore favorable conditions of broad-scale capitalist accumulation and social order.[11]

A renewal of capitalist accumulation today especially depends on sharp reductions of the costs of economic and social reproduction and increases in the rate of exploitation. The reason is that the restructuring of production itself consisted in large part of the internationalization and interregionalization of industrial capital which in the long term may indirectly benefit capital in "sunset" regions because of a reduction of the costs of reproduction of labor in the system as a whole.[12] In the short term, however, the new international and interregional divisions of labor threatened capital in the old industrial zones. This means that capital needed to find ways to lower the costs of reproduction not only through traditional methods of increased capitalist efficiency in the production process, but also through more cooperative forms of cooperation, "team

[11] It is, in fact, difficult to imagine any successful neo-liberal, neo-conservative consensus which could support or legitimate policies designed to restructure not only the production process but also the geography of social life itself. As we have argued, this is the crucial problem today precisely because capital has become "social capital" and capitalist society a "social factory."

[12] See, for example, Maurice Felton, "Industry's Viewpoint of Rural Areas," *Rural Industrialization: Prospects, Problems, Impacts, and Methods*, Subcommittee on Rural Development, Committee on Agriculture and Forestry, US Senate, April 19, 1974, Washington, DC, 1974.

work," and so on, which might be expected to increase productivity and at the same time reduce working-class/salariat demands for "more." Other ways which might raise the rate of exploitation included increased and more flexible collective reproduction; controls on consumer credit and unrestrained production competition; and restructured state programs and policies which remained inscribed with individualist forms and contents.

Moreover, control of social reproduction today means control of the mountain of symbols and ideologies which have accumulated in the USA since World War Two alongside the accumulation of capital. An attack on the value of labor-power, and on economic and social reproduction costs and expenses in general, especially requires that corporate and state reformers confront ideologies of "national individualism." Temporary reductions in the size of the average private and social consumption basket and deterioration of work and environmental conditions and public physical and social infrastructures may be politically acceptable if Americans believe in illusory threats to "national security" and retain their deep fear of socialism. However, a new and less expensive way of life based on new living and working conditions emptied of omnipotent fantasies of American individualism presupposes a shift of hegemonic cultural values in more cooperative or communitarian directions.

Beyond Neo-Individualism

Such a cultural sea change – first registered in the 1960s and complicated by new cross-currents in the 1980s – was clearly visible. Conservatives reacted against the "me-firstism" of the 1970s, albeit in self-righteous ways. Patriots celebrated national unity – defined largely in chauvinistic terms. Religious revivalists promised collective salvation in the hereafter and "me first" success in the here and now. These ambiguities doubtless were related not only to the contradiction betwen neo-liberal and neo-conservative ideologies, but also to the decentralization of industrial capital which tried to cash in on revived collective representations of the "rural," "home," and "family."

However, right-wing ideas and symbols of patriarchal family, bourgeois morality, and hierarchical community did not go uncontested. While Reagan's budget cuts ended most social programs which helped to empower community organizations in the 1960s and 1970s, social struggles within and against the wage, commodity, and state forms of labor and life remained charged with humanistic impulses inherent in Anglo-American culture and a strong belief in the legitimacy of government intervention on behalf of the poor, aged, sick, and economically insecure. Further, the new power of industrial capital in "sunrise" regions often unintentionally animated new definitions of community loyalty and local labor struggles rooted in workplace conditions and also redefined community, ethnic, racial, and other values. The same can be said of much popular reaction to the growing hegemony of finance and administrative capital in the racially diverse new "world cities." New groups in "sunset" industrial zones to save industry and jobs raised demands for community and worker participation in economic decision-making. The peace movement and international solidarity groups organized against Reagan government neo-imperialism also developed new ways of "working together" drawn from new and old left cultural practices and political action. One catalogue of the cultural elements making up these struggles included communitarian values and close attention to community needs; participatory democracy and the rights of members of organizations; holistic approaches to environmental, health, education, and other issues; and support for democratic government planning and coordination.[13] There is a good fit between these elements and persistent values in American culture such as voluntarism, self-help, a "can do" mentality, innovativeness, optimism about the results of action, anti-authoritarianism, and equality (as listed by Alex Inkeles).

The cultural stage was thus partly set for less individualistic and more cooperative solutions to the economic and social crisis. The gap between values and economic realities created a vacuum in theory and policy which diverse intellectuals and technicians from the right, center, and left, who recognized that an accumulation crisis had set in and that new ways of organizing production and social relations had to be devised, tried to fill with alternative programs for economic and social reconstruction. Two alternatives emerged. The first was statism and/or corporatism, a kind of "capitalist collectivism" which emphasized "reindustrialization." The second was localism and populism, a kind of "workers' collectivism" which stressed the theme of "democracy." Both were based on new and revived cultural concepts (distorted and real) of the individual as a social entity.

Statism-corporatism is a catch-all term which includes a multitude of political economic ideas and practices. Statist programs which called for TVA-like state planning by a powerful executive were conspicuously absent from public debate. Labor leaders, a few visible business leaders,

[13] George C. Lodge, *The New American Ideology* (New York, 1976), 16.

and many "liberal" Democrats and intellectuals, however, proposed various local, regional, and national corporatist forms of interest mediation and aggregation which (like their European counterparts) blurred the distinction between "private" and "public" in ways reminiscent of the short-lived 1930s National Recovery Administration. Corporatist ideas focused especially on economic issues, production groups, and (in contrast to "incomes policy corporatism" in the 1960s) reindustrialization. Some versions called for top-down control by finance capital with merely symbolic representation by other groups; others for the restoration of a strong party system within which "peak associations" could flourish; still others for a kind of "functional democracy" of productive groups. More "democratic" versions growing out of New Deal/Great Society politics were advanced by those concerned with equity and a degree of popular participation as well as with economic efficiency.[14]

In practice, corporatist ideas and policies developed at three levels: first, "micro-corporatism" in the capitalist workplace; second, "middle-level corporatism" or local and/or regional planning of collective economic and social reproduction; third, "macro-corporatism" or the national regulation of production and reproduction as a whole by "peak associations" allied with a strong centralized executive. The implicit or explicit goal at all three levels was to lower the value content of the average consumption basket and increase the rate of exploitation.

The most novel was micro-corporatism. Examples ranged from union-management agreements to restructure work and pay systems to more

[14] The distinction between "democratic" and "undemocratic" corporatism is made in J. T. Winkler, "Corporatism," *European Journal of Sociology*, XVII, 1, 1976. State corporatism and "societal bargaining" are contrasted in W. Korpi, *The Democratic Class Struggle* (London, 1982). Corporatism defined as an alternative to pluralism and interest representation is discussed in Philippe Schmitter, "Still the Century of Corporatism?" *Review of Politics*, 36, 1974, and "Modes of Interest Mediation and Models of Societal Change in Western Europe," *Comparative Political Studies*, 10, 1, 1977. Corporatism interpreted as a political system of class collaboration is analyzed in Leon Panitch, "The Developmet of Corporatism in Liberal Democracies," *Comparative Political Studies*, 10, 1, 1977, and "Recent Theories of Corporatism: Reflections on a Growth Industry," *British Journal of Sociology*, 30, 1, June 1980.

One argument for economic planning and industrial policy based on politically "undemocratic" corporatism is made in Felix Rohatyn, "Reconstructing America," *New York Review of Books*, March 5, 1981.

More "democratic" corporatist approaches to industrial policy include Lester Thurow, *The Zero Sum Society* (New York, 1980); Ira C. Magaziner and Robert B. Reich, *Minding America's Business* (New York, 1982); Robert B. Reich, *The Next American Frontier* (New York, 1983). Democratic Party reindustrialization legislation in the 1980s which straddled the fence between "democratic" and "undemocratic" corporatism is reviewed in Val Burris, "Beyond Reaganomics: Corporatist and Neo-Liberal Strategies for Economic Recovery," Paper prepared for American Sociological Association meeting, Aug. 30, 1983.

innovative social devices such as "work teams" and "quality circles."[15] More than any other experiment, "corporate culture" exemplified the new capitalist concept of social production and cooperation. The aim of "corporate culture" was to mobilize worker cooperation as a productive force and to cash in on post-material, post-acquisitive values. It therefore appealed more to workers' emotions and sentiments than to traditional rationalistic methods of operation. It used rituals and ceremonies to promote shared values with the purpose of subordinating individual interests to those of the corporation as a whole. The uniqueness of "corporate culture" lay in its "attempts to get workers to devote themselves to the firm regardless of incentives or lack thereof and regardless of whether or not the worker's present task, home life, or work group relations are 'fulfilling' or 'rewarding.' "[16] In this way, labor-management conflict which "wasted" economic resources,[17] and expensive individualist ideologies of control which no longer paid dividends, would be replaced by "groupist" ideas and more cooperative forms of social labor. The particular conceit of those who promoted "corporate culture" was that it was possible to turn back the clock of work relations to the organicism of "primitive" societies – a possibility which was ridiculous on its face. Moreover, micro-corporatism mediated and aggregated individual interests within single corporations only. Also, it provided no control of conditions of economic and social reproduction outside the workplace.

Better established as an idea and practice was middle-level corporatism, or locally and/or regionally planned systems of collective reproduction. Examples include regional health maintenance organizations, land use and transportation planning, and industrial/residential/recreational planning.[18] The latter included the "satellite city," or the new "companies' town," which was an updated social version of traditional "company towns." These and related programs and policies may be regarded as rationalized versions of traditional city planning. They stemmed from

---

[15] Work teams "increase productivity as well as job satisfaction [and] are replacing the old, narrow production jobs. . . Increasingly, the experiments with teamwork and worker participation demonstrate that this is not only possible, but imperative if the U.S. is to compete in the world market" ("A Work Revolution in U.S. Industry," *Business Week*, May 16, 1983, 100, 110).

[16] Carol Ray, "Corporate Culture: Its Features, Uses, and Potential as a Form of Control," University of California, Santa Cruz, unpublished MS, March 6, 1983.

[17] William J. Abernathy, Kim Clark, and Alan Kantrow, *Industrial Renaissance* (New York, 1983).

[18] The literature on regional planning of various aspects of economic and social reproduction is vast. A sample proposal by a corporatist politician was Hubert Humphrey's scheme to bring work and residential districts into line with the aim of reducing transportation costs, which are "too high" because factory workers tend to live in the city and commute to the

political pressures to socialize the costs of physical and social infra-structure.[19] They were also inspired by experiments in other capitalist countries designed to control the cost of wages, salaries, and welfare. The explicit or implicit function of regional planning was to modify expensive ideologies of individualism and their practice which had outlived their usefulness in the sphere of consumption, i.e. to lower the costs of fixed and circulating capital, especially variable capital and social expenses,[20] by replacing individual with collective reproduction.

The limits to middle-level corporatist planning were threefold. First, it mediated and aggregated individual interests in one region and/or sphere of reproduction alone. Second, middle-level corporatism nevertheless required a relatively high degree of interest aggregation, hence political barriers absent at the level of micro-corporatist planning posed difficult problems for policy makers. Regional transport planning, for example, depended on corporatist-like agreements between competing corpora-tions and builders, unions, landowners, and local, County, and other government agencies. Finally, collective reproduction within corporatist political forms ran up against the wall of neo-liberal "reprivatization" policy. For example, in the 1980s there was a proliferation of profit-oriented health services which developed at the expense of regional health maintenance organizations – themselves designed as models of cost con-tainment.[21]

Reprivatization in the health, transport, housing, and education fields was also the result of the absence of module systems of collective reproduc-tion, i.e. inflexibilities which created "surpluses" and "shortages" of particular kinds of social and physical infrastructure.[22] Yet reprivatized

---

industrial suburbs while office workers live in the residential suburbs and commute to the city (*Challenge*, March–April 1975, 231). See also Sid McClausland, Deputy Secretary of California's Business and Transportation Agency in the mid-1970s ("Getting Better Public Transportation," American Public Transit Association, Western Regional Conference, San Fransisco, California, May 5, 1975).

[19] James O'Connor, *The Fiscal Crisis of the State* (New York, 1973), chs 4 and 5.

[20] Jean Lojkine, "Contributions to a Marxist Theory of Capitalist Urbanization," in C. G. Pickvance, ed., *Urban Society: Critical Essays* (New York, 1976). The most comprehensive work on the city as collective consumption and the way the latter creates urban struggles which cut across class lines is that of Manuel Castells (for example, "Collective Consump-tion," in *City, Class, and Power*, New York, 1978).

[21] Only 4 per cent of the US population is enrolled in HMOs. Almost one-third of nearly one million community hospital beds belong to private corporations (Paul Starr, *The Social Transformation of American Medicine*, New York, 1982).

[22] Edmund Preteceille, "Collective Consumption, the State, and the Crisis in American Society," in M. Harloe and E. Lebas, eds *City, Class and Capital* (New York, 1981). The works of David Harvey are central in the discussion of this whole issue.

health, education, and other services were proving to be very costly from the standpoint of capital as a whole; capitalist firms were beginning to market module systems which could be used in public, collective reproduction in the education and health fields; and neo-liberal ideologies which inscribed the reprivatization process were weakening. This means that collective reproduction (like new social forms of social production) probably may be regarded as an irreversible albeit uneven historical process.

Despite its roots in late nineteenth-century "collectivist" thinking, the model of national corporatism is least well established in theory and practice. In the 1890s, many businessmen, intellectuals, and labor leaders associated economic crises and bitter labor struggles with the rise of the trusts and large corporations and the rapid growth of the industrial working class. In various guises – Industrial Democracy, Cooperation, Socialism – "collectivist" thinkers held that both economic crises and capital-labor conflicts were the result of unregulated, competitive capitalism. Cooperation within the ranks of big business and between labor and management, it was thought, would solve both problems.[23] The post-World War Two capital-labor compromise and Keynesian regulation may be regarded as one fruit of earlier "collectivist" ideology. Today, as noted above, many intellectuals, economists and others have argued that the resolution of the accumulation crisis hinges on economic planning organized within a corporatist and/or statist political model. The reasons given include the need to reduce investment risks and encourage modernization and expansion of capital spending; mobilize state funds to help companies prepared to radically restructure their operations; determine the rate of investment and its allocation without creating unmanageable inequalities in the distribution of income; and coordinate research and development.[24] The basic rationale for economic planning appears to be capital's need to increase dramatically the rate of exploitation by expanding the production of relative surplus value.

The political and ideological barriers to national corporatism are many and varied. Most business leaders oppose both a corporatist policy and national economic planning. In the ideological climate of national individualism, corporations and special interests are used to getting their own way (as exemplified by the chaotic administration of such politicized industries as defense contracting, communications, and aerospace). If planning is too sensitive to the interests of individual capitals, it defeats its own purpose; if too insensitive to these interests, it is likely to be defeated

[23] Gilbert, *Designing the Industrial State.*
[24] For example, Wassily Leontieff, "What Hope for the Economy?" *New York Review of Books*, Aug. 12, 1982; Przeworski and Wallerstein, "Democratic Capitalism."

by the non-compliance of key corporations and industries. Moreover, although organized labor supports corporatist planning, in the absence of worker radicalization or mass mobilization, labor leaders have little political clout. Labor leaders and intellectuals who propose corporatist solutions also tend to favor "democratic" corporatism, which is anathema to business leaders. Furthermore, corporatism presupposes an efficient Federal bureaucracy which minimally requires tightening up "porous" state structures (David Harvey's apt phrase). The Federal bureaucracy, however, is demoralized and increasingly corrupt since the Nixon years; its performance rating is low also as a result of Carter's civil service reforms and Reagan's attitude of benign neglect and deregulation policies.

More, national corporatism requires the highest possible degree of individual interest aggregation – not merely into "corporate cultures" or even "regional identities" but into national peak associations, which are weak compared with those in corporatist European states and also (like individual capitals) used to getting their own way. Finally, the question of how it is possible to integrate individuals into corporatist groups in a country with a powerful heritage of natural rights individualism appears to be a real dilemma (for example, individualism divides the corporatist-oriented professions and education establishment in too many ways to count). This is the most important issue because in a corporatist order, " 'individualism' is a label for stigmatizing recalcitrance, not eulogizing freedom."[25]

An American corporatist polity at the national level, however necessary in the long run, does not seem to be politically feasible in the short term. More likely is the "self aggregation" of individual capitalist interests at increasingly higher levels through "normal" processes of capital concentration, centralization, and agglomeration. The integration of energy, chemical, and agribusiness capital; forward and backward integration and "product extension" mergers in many industries; the growth of the new financial conglomerates; and the nuclear energy complex, which combines themes of monopoly production and regulation, centralized economic and political power, and secrecy and "national security," all point in this direction. Also more likely in the short term is the continuing use of national chauvinism and blind patriotism (and, if necessary, political repression) to regulate the relations between capital and labor as a whole.

The "alternative" political economic scenario which emerged in the 1970s and 1980s may be called localism/populism.[26] This is a catch-all

[25] Winker, "Corporatism," 107.

[26] The most comprehensive albeit mixed populist/social democratic/democratic corporatist program put forth so far is: Samuel Bowles, David M. Gordon, and Thomas Weiskopf, *Beyond the Waste Land: A Democratic Alternative to Economic Decline* (New

term which includes diverse local social, economic, and political initiatives taken as a result of the weakening of systems of interest representation associated with the welfare state, the appearance of "new social movements," the high costs of individualistic ways of life, and the accumulation crisis itself, among other reasons. Localism/populism included territorially organized, decentralized, non-party-based urban movements; ascriptive and single-issue organizations; State-wide coalitions of community and other groups in search of a common program; and organizations striving to establish a national presence. At the level of material life, it included communal self-help of many kinds; small businesses producing "ecologically sound," "non-sexist," etc. products; an active underground economy of personal and business services; alternative energy distribution systems; rank and file worker groups organized around "right to know" issues; and so on. In "sunset" regions, localism/populism was oriented mainly to economic issues and production politics; in "sunrise" regions to social, community, and enviromental issues; in the "world cities" to a rich and contradictory mixture of economic, social and political concerns. In all three regions, demands for political self-administration and economic self-management were widespread, albeit in highly fragmented and contradictory forms.

The weak development of corporatist and/or state capitalist modes of life and labor (hence the persistence of the hegemonic ideology of individualism) was arguably the main barrier to the evolution of local populist struggles into a national movement for democratic political administration and economic self-management. The ability of "social individuality" to legitimately compete with "individualism" in the ideological marketplace perversely depended on the development of the vicarious democracy characteristic of corporatism and/or authoritarian versions of social individuality manifest in monopoly state capitalist regimes.

In general terms, political power within the corporatist politics of group accommodation has a social character.[27] The same may be said of the dominant cultural sense of "individual" defined as a political subject. Specifically, in micro-corporatism, "if the unions give up the kind of rule-setting that limits flexibility, management will have to let them in on

---

York, 1983). A program for "reindustrialization from below" may be found in Staughton Lynd, "The View from Steel Country," *Democracy*, 3, 3, Summer 1983. Closely related ideas are developed in Dan Luria and Jack Russell, *Rational Reindustrialization* (Detroit, 1982).

The most comprehensive account of the new populist movement itself is Harry Boyte, *The Backyard Revolution: Understanding the New Citizen Movement* (Philadelphia, 1981).

[27] Claus Offe, "The Future of European Socialism and the Role of the State," III International Colloquium, Interuniversity Center for European Studies, Montreal, March 30, 1978.

decision-making."[28] In middle-level corporatism, processes of collective reproduction tend to subvert ideologies of individualism while creating possibilities for autonomous spheres of life oriented to concepts of equity and production based on need. In macro-corporatism, the political regulation of production and reproduction as a whole tends to create a milieu in which unions, single-issue groups, and other organizations may have more of a say about the allocation of investment and distribution of benefits, among other national economic issues.[29] A shift to corporatist and/or statist *practices* thus may be expected to undermine hegemonic ideologies of individualism. The same conclusion may be drawn in relation to the shift to corporatist/statist authoritarian *concepts* of democracy and social individuality. Local populist struggles and political practices based on more democratic forms of social individuality may continue to subvert individualist ideologies from below. It is likely, therefore, that "individualism" as the hegemonic national ideology will be caught in a squeeze between ideological concepts and practices of democracy and social individuality, on the one side, and real, democratic theories and practices of social individuality, on the other.

The competition between ideological and real concepts and practices of democracy and social individuality is also likely to occur in the course of social and political struggles within the state bureaucracy. This is so because corporatist/statist models presuppose a more active and undemocratic state administration, top-down decision-making by individual elites, and collective responsibility by the masses to carry out these decisions in ways which blur the distinction between state and society. Populist models *transposed to the level of national politics* presuppose an active, democratic state administration, bottom-up collective decision-making, and individual responsibility to carry out these decisions in ways which sharpen the distinction between civil society and the state. This means that there are likely to be more intense struggles around the issue of the meaning and structure of the state itself, or the process of planning and plan implementation, the public work process, and the division of administrative labor.[30]

In conclusion, the two models of economic, social, and political reconstruction may be regarded as ideological and practical opposites. The corporatist/statist model makes the division of social labor more opaque; the populist model makes the division of labor more transparent. The

[28] Michael Piore, quoted in "A Work Revolution in U.S. Industry," *Business Week*, May 16, 1983.

[29] Przeworski and Wallerstein, "Democratic Capitalism".

[30] James O'Connor, "The Democratic Movement in the United States," *Kapitalistate*, 7, 1978.

corporatist/statist model separates still more sharply the mind and manual labor of conceiving and doing; the populist model unites the mind and manual labor of administering the division of social labor. The former model reifies individuals at higher levels of social mystification; the latter dereifies individuals. The former creates more nightmares that individuals are merely roles and categories; the latter frees individuals for the dream that we are what we socially, morally, and imaginatively conceive and do. The former increases dangers that local movements will play into the hands of those who propose authoritarian solutions; the latter increases chances that local movements will transcend their condition of "urban reservations" and "counter-culture ghettos" (in Manuel Castells' words). The former keeps alive time-worn arguments between state socialists and anarchists; the latter sublates this argument, while bridging anti-bureaucratic, anti-national chauvinist, and communal popular concerns. The former creates illusory prospects for individual self-development; the latter creates chances for real prospects of individual self-development through and with rather than over and against society. The former increases dangers that communal self-help will remain an end alone – a crisis cushion and ideology of austerity; the latter enhances hopes that communal self-help becomes a means or process of developing social individuality.

Index